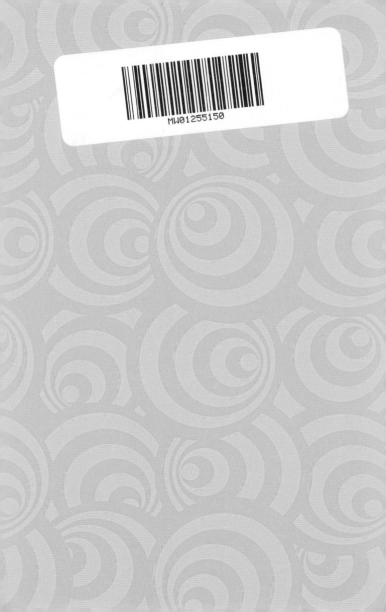

STORIES OF
PEOPLE & CIVILIZATION
GREEK
ANCIENT ORIGINS

FLAME TREE PUBLISHING
6 Melbray Mews, Fulham,
London SW6 3NS, United Kingdom
www.flametreepublishing.com

First published and copyright © 2023
Flame Tree Publishing Ltd

23 25 27 26 24
1 3 5 7 9 10 8 6 4 2

ISBN: 978-1-80417-577-4

Cover and pattern art was created by Flame Tree Studio, with elements courtesy
of Shutterstock.com/svekloid/Dalhazz. Additional interior decoration courtesy of
Shutterstock.com/paseven.

Special thanks to Liz Wyse.

Judith John (lists of Ancient Kings & Leaders) is a writer and editor specializing in
literature and history. A former secondary school English Language and Literature
teacher, she has subsequently worked as an editor on major educational projects, including
English A: Literature for the Pearson International Baccalaureate series. Judith's major
research interests include Romantic and Gothic literature, and Renaissance drama.

The text in this book is compiled and edited, with a new introduction, from elements of
the following: *The Book of the Ancient Greeks* by Dorothy Mills, published by G. P. Putnam's
Sons, 1925; interwoven with extracts from: *A Manual of Ancient History* by M.E. Thalheimer,
published by Van Antwerp, Bragg & Co., 1872; *The Geography of Strabo*, translated by H.C.
Hamilton and W. Falconer, published by Henry G. Bohn, 1854; *Pausanias' Description of
Greece*, translated by Arthur Richard Shilleto, George Bell and Sons, 1886; *The History of
Herodotus*, translated by G.C. Macaulay, published by Macmillan, 1890; and *The History of
the Peloponnesian War*, by Thucydides, translated by Richard Crawley, 1874.

A copy of the CIP data for this book is available
from the British Library.

Designed and created in the UK | Printed and bound in China

COLLECTOR'S EDITIONS

STORIES OF
PEOPLE & CIVILIZATION
GREEK
ANCIENT ORIGINS

With a New Introduction by
LINDSAY POWELL
Further Reading and
Lists of Ancient Kings & Leaders

FLAME TREE PUBLISHING

CONTENTS

CONTENTS

CONTENTS

STORIES OF
PEOPLE & CIVILIZATION
GREEK
ANCIENT ORIGINS

@@@@

SERIES FOREWORD

Stretching back to the oral traditions of thousands of years ago, tales of heroes and disaster, creation and conquest have been told by many different civilizations, in ways unique to their landscape and language. Their impact sits deep within our own culture even though the detail in the stories themselves are a loose mix of historical record, the latest archaeological evidence, transformed narrative and the unwitting distortions of generations of storytellers.

Today the language of mythology lives around us: our mood is jovial, our countenance is saturnine, we are narcissistic and our modern life is hermetically sealed from others. The nuances of the ancient world form part of our daily routines and help us navigate the information overload of our interconnected lives.

The nature of a myth is that its stories are already known by most of those who hear or read them. Every era brings a new emphasis, but the fundamentals remain the same: a desire to understand and describe the events and relationships of the world. Many of the great stories are archetypes that help us find our own place, equipping us with tools for self-understanding, both individually and as part of a broader culture.

For Western societies it is Greek mythology that speaks to us most clearly. It greatly influenced the mythological heritage of the ancient Roman civilization and is the lens through which we still see the Celts, the Norse and many of the other great peoples and religions. The Greeks themselves inherited much from their neighbours, the Egyptians, an older culture that became weary with the mantle of civilization.

Of course, what we perceive now as mythology had its own origins in perceptions of the divine and the rituals of the sacred. The earliest civilizations, in the crucible of the Middle East, in the Sumer of the third millennium BCE, are the source to which many of the mythic archetypes can be traced. Over five thousand years ago, as humankind collected together in cities for the first time, developed writing and industrial scale agriculture, started to irrigate the rivers and attempted to control rather than be at the mercy of its environment, humanity began to write down its tentative explanations of natural events, of floods and plagues, of disease.

Early stories tell of gods or god-like animals who are crafty and use their wits to survive, and it is not unreasonable to suggest that these were the first rulers of the gathering peoples of the earth, later elevated to god-like status with the distance of time. Such tales became more political as cities vied with each other for supremacy, creating new gods, new hierarchies for their pantheons. The older gods took on primordial roles and became the preserve of creation and destruction, leaving the new gods to deal with more current, everyday affairs. Empires rose and fell, with Babylon assuming the mantle from Sumeria in the 1800s BCE, in turn to be swept away by the Assyrians of the 1200s BCE; then the Assyrians and the Egyptians were subjugated by the Greeks, the Greeks by the Romans and so on, leading to the spread and assimilation of common themes, ideas and stories throughout the world.

The survival of history is dependent on the telling of good tales, but each one must have the 'feeling' of truth, otherwise it will be ignored. Around the firesides, or embedded in a book or a computer, the myths and legends of the past are still the living materials of retold myth, not restricted to an exploration of historical origins. Now we have devices and global communications that give us unparalleled access to a diversity of traditions. We can find out about Indigenous American, Indian, Chinese and tribal African mythology in a way that was denied to our ancestors, we can find connections, plot the archaeology, religion and the mythologies of the world to build a comprehensive image of the human experience that is both humbling and fascinating.

The books in this series introduce the many cultures of ancient humankind to the modern reader. From the earliest migrations across the globe to settlements along rivers, from the landscapes of mountains to the vast Steppes, from woodlands to deserts, humanity has adapted to its environments, nurturing languages and observations and expressing itself through records, mythmaking stories and living traditions. There is still so much to explore, but this is a great place to start.

Jake Jackson
General Editor

STORIES OF
PEOPLE & CIVILIZATION
GREEK
ANCIENT ORIGINS

INTRODUCTION
& FURTHER READING

INTRODUCTION TO
GREEK ANCIENT ORIGINS

THE ENDURING APPEAL OF ANCIENT GREECE

Agony, **drama, economy**, enthusiasm, gymnasium, metropolis, music, phenomenon, philosophy, symmetry – these are among an estimated 150,000 words of Greek origin which have been imported into the English language. Our cities are filled with architecture and art that echo styles first developed in ancient Greece. For two centuries, beginning around 480 BCE, it enjoyed a 'golden age', the impact of which reverberates down to our own times. What can account for the influence of a civilization which thrived 2,500 years ago on our modern world? What explains the extraordinary burst of creativity from such a small cultural group in a single region of the world? How did the ancient Greeks understand their own origins?

Like us, the Greeks pondered deeply about who they were, where they came from and how they got to the land they called home. This volume begins with Dorothy Mills' *The Book of the Ancient Greeks: An Introduction to the History and Civilization of Greece from the Coming of the Greeks to the Conquest of Corinth by Rome in 146 B.C.*, published in 1925. Augmenting it, there are extracts from translations of texts representative of ancient Greek writings, which bring the authentic voices of these ancient people to this survey. Their peculiar landscape, history and culture shaped their responses to life, revealing deeper universal truths that still resonate with us. Indeed, the Greeks often had a word for them.

FROM LEGEND AND TRADITION TO
ARCHAEOLOGY AND HISTORY

According to the Greek poet Hesiodos (Hesiod, c. 750–c. 650 BCE) and others, mankind was created by Prometheus the Titan (from *titanos*, meaning 'white earth', 'chalk', 'clay' or 'gypsum'), son of Uranus (primordial god of the Sky) and Gaia (goddess of the Earth). After the Titanomachy, a decade-long war, the Titans were overthrown by the Olympians. Prometheus formed a human being (*anthropos*) from a lump of clay and the goddess Athene breathed life into it. Man overran the world, then populated with giants and monsters, but the Olympian gods were ever present, influencing the affairs of men for the better – or the worse.

In modern times, we understand the past very differently. Archaeology (from the Greek words *archaios*, 'ancient' or 'primal', and *logos*, 'study', 'discourse' or 'reason') uses scientific methods to examine and explain the origins of the peoples and their civilizations in the land we now call Greece. Combining analysis of material finds from the excavations of cities and shipwrecks with a careful study of surviving records, written by the Greeks themselves and their rivals, a robust chronology (*chronos*, 'time') of ancient Greece can be assembled.

Historians divide the timeline of ancient Greece into seven ages (*aeones*, the origin of 'eon'):

1. **Stone Age (9000–3300 BCE):** during the Neolithic (*neo* 'new' + *lithos* 'stone') era, humans establish a farming economy based on cultivating plants, raising animals, fishing, developing tools of obsidian, making pots of clay and fashioning items for personal adornment.

2. **Bronze Age (3300–1200 BCE) aka the 'Homeric Age':** Greeks gain mastery of smelting, melting and casting copper alloy; the Minoan culture (based at Knossos in Crete) and the Mycenean culture (based at Mycenae on the Greek mainland) both flourish; they develop the Linear A and B writing systems for stock keeping; seafaring Greeks trade with the Egyptian and Hittite empires; if a real historical event, the Trojan War occurs during this period; the Minoan and Mycenean civilizations fall, possibly the result of an eruption of Thera around 1450 BCE or its aftermath.

3. **'Dark Ages' (1200–776 BCE):** following the fall of the Minoan and Mycenaean civilizations, Greek communities resettle in Attica and Ionia; production of iron becomes widespread; Greeks establish trading links with the Levant coastal region.

4. **Archaic Age (776–479 BCE):** historical Greece begins; the first Olympian Games (776 BCE) take place; Greeks adopt the alphabet based on the Phoenician model; city-states (*poleis*) form, some adopting *demokratia*; the first Greek colonies are founded overseas; Athens builds up its naval capabilities under Themistokles (c. 524–459 BCE); Athens and Sparta collaborate to repel invasions of the Persian Empire under Darius (492–486 BCE) and Xerxes (480–479 BCE); Athens leads the Delian League (from 487 BCE).

5. **Classical Age (479–323 BCE):** under Perikles (c. 495–429 BCE) Athens flourishes, but abuses its leadership of the Delian League; in the ensuing Peloponnesian War (431–404 BCE) Athens is defeated by Sparta; Philip II of Macedon (382–336 BCE) defeats Athens and Thebes at Chaeronea (338 BCE), then annexes southern Greece; Alexander III (Alexander the Great, 356–323 BCE) founds Alexandria in Egypt (331 BCE).

6. **Hellenistic Age (323–146 BCE):** after the death of Alexander the Great, his generals divide up his conquests among themselves; Hellenic culture and the Greek language spread through Egypt, the Near and Middle East; the first frictions occur with Rome emerging in the West; Roman legions overwhelm Greek *phalanges* at Cynoscephalae (197 BCE), the Macedonians at Pydna (168 BCE) and the Athenian Confederacy at Corinth (146 BCE).

7. **Roman Age (146 BCE–582 CE):** Greek *poleis* are organized into provinces of Rome; Roman tourists travel to Greece to see the sights, learn Greek and the art of public speaking, trade in its art or aggrandize their own cities with new buildings; even as the provinces of the Western Empire fade away, Greek cities prosper under Roman administration.

PEOPLE AND POLITICS

The ancient Greeks identified themselves by what they shared in common (*koine*): language, gods (*theoi*) and culture (*politismos*). They called themselves *Hellenes*. There was no unified country of Greece; rather, the Greek world was a loose network of a few hundred *poleis*. Each *polis* was an independent, self-governing city-state. Most were poor, although there were wealthy exceptions (notably Athens, Corinth, Sparta and Thebes). A few were monarchies (*monos*, 'only' + *arche*, 'power' or 'authority') – notably Epirus under Pyrrhus (r. 297–272 BCE) and Sparta, which had two kings (*archagetai*). Some were tyrannies, ruled by men (*turannoi*) who had seized and wielded absolute power; both Athens and Corinth had periods during which tyrants ruled. Others were oligarchies (*oligoi*, 'few') ruled by a small number of wealthy individuals; Athens briefly became an oligarchy when the 'Council of the 400' assumed power in 411 BCE.

Several *poleis* adopted *demokratia* (*demos*, 'common people' + *kratos*, 'rule' or 'strength') for their elected representative government, notably Athens (from 508/7–322/1 BCE). The model of Athens was a limited democracy, however. Any male citizens of the *poleis* aged 20 or older could speak and vote in the People's Assembly (*ekklesia*), but only those over 30 years of age could take part in the selection of jury members by casting or drawing of lots. A citizen was expected to participate in the public affairs (*politiki*) of his community; an *idiotis* ('idiot') was a citizen indifferent to doing so. Women, resident aliens (*metics*) and slaves had no political voice.

Geopolitics in ancient Greece was local and independent. In a region devoid of well-made roads (which did not come until the Romans), rough pathways meandering though the rugged Balkan landscape made physical communications between urban communities difficult. Going by sea was often the most convenient – sometimes the only – way to travel over long distances. Several islands were home to rich and influential communities, such as Crete and Thera in the Bronze Age and Delos, Lesbos and Rhodes in the Classical, Hellenistic and Roman Ages.

In times of crisis, *poleis* could form alliances and confederacies. Created after the invasion by Persia, the Delian League brought together some 150–300 Greek-speaking communities. From 487 BCE Athens led the League, but wielded its power clumsily over the membership, leading to conflict with Sparta in the Peloponnesian War.

LAND AND SEA

Where Greece was the centre of the world, Delphi was the centre (*omphalos*, 'navel') of Greece. The oracle of Apollo was located there, and the high priestess or Pythia gave prophecies while possessed by the god (*enthusiasmos*).

Approximately 80 per cent of the land (*gi*, 'earth') of Greece is mountainous, with rocky valleys or coastal plains making up the rest. Apart from Thessaly, there are few prairies to provide fertile ground for harvesting cereal crops. Smallholdings are the norm, where sheep and goat herds, vines and olive trees cling to rugged hillsides. Just one per cent of the landscape is lake or marsh, and no rivers are wide or deep enough to be navigable by ship. Sea (*thalassa*) surrounds the land except on the landlocked north side. The coastline is twice the length of Italy's and no single place in Greece is more than 97 km (60 miles) from the sea. Some 6,000 islands peak through the azure Aegean, Ionia, Libyan, Mediterranean and Myronean Seas. With limited natural resources, the Greeks looked overseas for prosperity as early as the Archaic Age.

Greek-speaking communities began setting up their own remote centres of commerce. Satellites of *poleis* in the Greek Peninsula were initially established as trading posts (*emporion*), settlements (*apoikia*, 'away from home') or cleruchies (*klirouchia*, literally 'lot-holder'). The free cities of Chalcis and Eretria in Euboea founded colonies in Chalcidice, notably Olynthos in Central Macedonia. The first colony they founded in Italy was Pithecusae on the island of Ischia. Subsequently the Greeks built colonies at Cumae, Naxos, Rhegium and Zancle.

Other *poleis* followed, in particular Athens, Corinth and Sparta. Between them they established colonies around the Ionian and Black Seas, in Anatolia, Macedonia, Thrace, southern Italy and Sicily. Settlers from Miletos founded Odessa, Ukraine; others from Rhodes established a settlement at Neapolis (*nea*, 'new' + *polis*, modern Naples); colonizers from Phokis founded Massalia (Marseille) on the coast of Gaul. Greeks also established an *emporion* in the city of Herakleion (Thonis) in Egypt: located at the Canopic mouth of the Nile, it was the largest port in Egypt on the Mediterranean Basin before the founding of Alexandria.

Recent study of pollen samples from cored sediments in southern Greece, carried out by researchers at the Jagiellonian University in Krakow, Poland and the Max Planck Institute for the Science of Human History in Jena, Germany, suggest that a market-driven export economy may have been established there much earlier than previously thought. Archaic-period Greek farmers began to specialize by growing fewer cereal crops and purposely cultivating olive oil and wine expressly for export. These agribusiness entrepreneurs shipped their high-value processed food and drink overseas in return for cash crops imported from Greek colonies on the Black Sea.

Normally colonists in an *apoikia* enjoyed the full rights and privileges of the mother city (*metropolis*). However, sometimes by policy, sometimes by mismanagement, this was not always the case. Colonists at Corcyra on Corfu had to sail to Corinth to find justice, which made them resentful. Ties to the mother city might also embroil daughter colonies in conflicts not of their own making. In the Classical Age, for example, the Peloponnesian War (431–404 BCE), fought between the Delian and Peloponnesian Leagues, spread to Sicily. A military taskforce was dispatched from Athens to the island to protect its colonies against Sirakousai (Syracuse), which was backed by Corinth (its founder and patron) and Sparta (its ally). The campaign (415–413 BCE) ended in a defeat for the Athenian forces; Sirakousai remained free.

As it developed, a colony could become independent of its *metropolis* or spawn colonies of its own. Colonizers from Sirakousai in Sicily founded the city of Kamarina in the south of the island. So many Greek-speakers settled in southern Italy that later writers, such as P. Ovidius Naso (Ovid, 43 BCE–17 CE) and Polybios of Megalopolis (Polybius, *c.* 200–*c.* 118 BCE), nicknamed the region *Magna Graecia* ('Great Greece').

GLORY AND EXCELLENCE

Seeking *kleos* ('glory' or 'renown') was an obsession of ancient Greek men. Achieving *kleos aphthiton* ('deathless fame') or dying a *kalos thanatos* ('beautiful death') or an *euklees thanatos* ('glorious death') in war (*polemos*), like Patroklos or Hektor at Troy or the 300 Spartans at Thermopylae (480 BCE), was the ultimate desire of every Greek warfighter (*polemisti*). Through his deeds, such as *mache* ('combat', 'battle'), a man could demonstrate *arete* ('excellence', 'goodness' or 'moral aesthetic'). In pursuit of *arete*, Greeks studied the arts of war as exemplified by its best practitioners. Homer's *Iliad* – an epic (*epikos*, from *epos* 'word' or 'song') poem composed sometime in the eighth century BCE – told the story of the Trojan War. Treatises distilled best practice by experts, such as Xenophon (*c.* 430–350 BCE), on topics ranging from generalship (*strategia*) to commanding cavalry (*hipparchikos*).

There were plenty of opportunities for combat. Military conflicts were both frequent – often annual – *and* local, since the geography of Greece meant that battles were fought in the same choke points in the landscape. Sparta was unusual in training its men from childhood to fight; by adulthood they had become professional soldiers. In Athens and other *poleis* citizens donned military panoply and went to war in defence of their community only when called up.

In the Homeric Age battles were fought between armed men. Each was equipped with a boar-tusk helmet, a shield, either rectangular or shaped like a figure-of-eight, a spear and sometimes a sword of cast bronze. Some warriors drove into battle in chariots.

In the Classical and Hellenistic Ages battles were clashes between opposing *phalanges*. The *phalanx* was a rectangular mass formation in which soldiers stood side by side in ranks. Equipped with a bronze helmet and body armour (*linothorax*), each hoplite (from *hoplon*, 'stuff' or 'kit') stood overlapping his round, concave shield (*aspis*) with his brother's to his right; each also held a long spear (*dory*), 2.4m (7.9 ft) in length, in the space between, forming a dense 'hedgehog' of deadly points. Ancient texts refer to the *othismos* ('push'), which may be literal or figurative. At the Battle of Coronea (394 BCE) the opposing Theban and Spartan forces were 'shield against shield'; at the so-called 'Tearless Battle' (368 BCE) Spartan troops meted their first casualties upon the men of Argos the moment they were within range of their spear tips.

Athens also boasted a navy. The richest men in Athens paid a public service tax or liturgy (*leitourgia*) which required each to provision a trireme (a three-banked warship) for a whole year. They took great pride in doing so. The less affluent men of the city provided the navy's crews of oarsmen and marines (*epibati*). At Salamis (480 BCE) the amateur Athenians proved how effective they could be when they defeated the fleet of the Persian king Xerxes.

However, *kleos* could also be won by competing (*agon*, 'contest', 'struggle' or 'fight') in athletic sports. From the sixth century BCE the Panhellenic Games brought athletes together from all over the Greek-speaking world. They started at Olympia (dedicated to Zeus every four years). Competitions were also held at Delphi (for Apollo every four years), at the Isthmus of Corinth (for Poseidon every two years) and at Nemea (for Zeus every two years). The four-year cycle was called an Olympiad. The first began in 776 BCE; the last was held in 393 CE. The first modern version of the Olympic Games was held in Athens in 1896.

Men – and only men – competed naked (*gumnos*) in distance racing, long jumping, discus and javelin throwing, as well as boxing and wrestling. Fines were issued to anyone found cheating and there were no prizes for coming second or third. The winner was awarded a crown made of a branch of leafy wild olive (Olympia), laurel (Delphi), pine (Corinth) or wild celery (Nemea). The associated prestige and bragging rights from victory (*nike*) led to fame and fortune for the lucky few – men such as Milon of Kroton, who lived in the sixth century BCE. A wrestler, he came first six times at Olympia, seven times at Delphi, ten times at Isthmus of Corinth and nine times at Nemea. Milon was the most successful athlete of ancient Greece, for which he received the honorary title *Periodonikes* ('Circuit Victor').

GODS AND MYTH

Ancient Greek religion was about ritual, prayer and offering sacrifices or votive objects, not about belief or doctrine. Citizens took part in public ceremonies to maintain good relations with the gods or hoping to influence them in ways that were favourable to the *polis*.

The Greek *pantheon* (*pan*, 'all' + *theoi*, 'gods') comprised 12 anthropomorphic (*anthropos* + *morphe*, 'form') deities: Zeus, Athene, Apollo, Ares, Aphrodite, Artemis, Demeter, Dionysos (or Hestia), Hephaestos, Hera, Hermes and Poseidon. Mount Olympos – Greece's highest mountain – was their home. The Greeks told stories (*mythos*) of the struggles of gods, spirits (*daimones*), creatures (*theres*), heroes (*iroes*) and ordinary mortals. Many myths dealt with life issues such as love (*eros*), family (*oikos*), hospitality (*xenia*) or the abuse of it, reverence or shame (*aidos*) and death (*thanatos*). Others explained the origin of places or natural phenomena.

As for those giants and monsters, there may be a historical/ scientific explanation for them. According to Adrienne Mayor, research scholar at Stanford University, they were actually the bones of dinosaurs and prehistoric mammals. Seeking to explain the fossils they retrieved from the ground, the Greeks created elaborate tales about powerful giant humanoids and terrifying wild creatures – such as Centaurs, Cyclopes, Gigantes and the Minotaur – who lived alongside humans in the past.

INQUIRY AND KNOWLEDGE

The Greeks were constantly reflecting and asking questions. The disciplines of logic (*logos*, 'study', 'word', 'discourse', 'reason') and philosophy (*philo*, 'love' + *sophia*, 'wisdom') were developed by teachers and students who gathered in the covered market halls (*stoai*) of ancient Greek cities. Sokrates (c. 470–399 BCE) discussed questions of rationalism and ethics, famously remarking that 'the unexamined life is not worth living'. His words were preserved in the various dialogues of Platon (Plato, 428/427 or 424/423–348/347 BCE), which led to the establishment of the school of philosophy called Platonism. Epikouros (Epicurus, 341–270 BCE) rejected Platonism, arguing that the purpose of philosophy was to attain a happy, tranquil life.

Greek philosophers and natural scientists closely studied the natural world and the universe (*cosmos*). Herakleitos of Ephesos (Heraclitus, c. 535–475 BCE) observed the *cosmos* as everchanging, remarking that 'No man ever steps in the same river twice'. Pythagoras (c. 570–490 BCE) worked on mathematical problems. Demokritos (c. 460/57–c. 370 BCE) developed his theory of atoms. Hippokrates (c. 460–c. 370 BCE) studied medicine, writing more than 70 books. Aristoteles (Aristotle, 384–322 BCE) studied logic, metaphysics, philosophy, ethics and political theory; he wrote hundreds of books and was also tutor to Alexandros Megalos (Alexander the Great). Eukleides (Euclid, *c.* 300–240 BCE) worked on mathematical problems and wrote his famous *Elements*, still studied today. Archimedes (*c.* 287–212/11 BCE) worked on mechanical inventions. Hero of Alexandria (fl. 60 CE) designed pneumatic machines.

Others applied their insights in practical ways. Several Greek scientists investigated how to improve existing technologies. *Episteme* referred to 'scientific knowledge' or 'system of understanding'; it was distinct from *techne*, meaning 'craft' or 'skill'. Dionysios of Syracuse assembled a team of engineers to build weapons able to overcome the limitations of human power. His engineers constructed the *gastraphetes* ('belly bow'), which used twisted skeins of animal gut or horsehair to shoot heavier arrows further than was possible with a regular bow; the weapon saw service in the Siege of Motya in 397 BCE. The treatises of Aristotle, Athenaeus of Seleucia (200–150 BCE), Biton of Pergamon (third or second century BCE) and Hero of Alexandria demonstrate their ongoing fascination with applying science to firing projectiles. Archimedes developed an array of war machines to impede the Romans who were besieging Sirakousai in 213–212 BCE.

The 'Antikythera Mechanism' seems to have been an analogue computer for predicting astronomical positions (*astronomos*, 'star-arranging') and eclipses (*ekleipsis*, from *ekleipein* 'fail to appear'). The enigmatic device, recovered from a shipwreck in 1901, may date from between 205 to 60 BCE. It features several high-precision gearwheels, one measuring 13cm (5 in) in diameter with 223 teeth, revealing knowledge of a technology that the Greeks were presumed not to have mastered.

The first history books were also written by Greeks. When Herodotus of Halicarnassos (*c.* 484–*c.* 420 BCE) wrote his *Histories*, he was doing more than chronicling: he was engaging in inquiry (*istoria*). In attempting to understand the causes and course of the great war between the Greeks and Persians, he considered the different civilizations relatively equally. He sought to understand the geographical and cultural context in which events took place. To gather material for his book, Herodotus interviewed witnesses and realized that people often remembered things differently. In contrast the Athenian general Thoukudides (Thucydides, *c.* 460–*c.* 500 BCE), when writing his *History of the Peloponnesian War*, gave primacy to politics, statecraft, power and war. Quoting King Archidamnos of Sparta, he observed, 'war is a matter not so much of arms as of money, which makes arms of use'.

ART AND CULTURE

Having created man, the most important gifts the mythical Prometheus gave the Greeks was fire (*aitho*) and the arts. From the earliest times Greek artists depicted life around them in their works of clay, stone or paint. Using their know-how (*techne*), artisans aspired to reach the perfection of the gods in their work.

In the Bronze Age, the palaces of Akrotiri, Knossos and Phaistos were decorated with colourful murals in two dimensions. They showed people engaged in performing rituals, swimming, boxing and leaping over bulls. In the Archaic Age Greek sculptors were the first to fashion free-standing statues in three dimensions of a naked boy (*kouros*) or a clothed girl (*kore*); their movement was controlled, their faces expressionless.

By the Classical Age sculptors sought to represent the ideal body. Polykleitos (*c.* 460–410 BCE) articulated his *kanon* ('rule') of *symmetria* ('balance', 'equilibrium' or 'perfection'). Pheidias (c. 465–425 BCE) erected the iconic, colossal bronze statue of Athena Promachos on the Acropolis in Athens. Myron (c. 470–440 BCE) carved his emblematic *Diskobolos* ('Discus Thrower') from a single block of marble. We have become used to seeing ancient sculptures as white. However, studies by Prof. Dr. Vinzenz Brinkmann, Head of the Department of Antiquity at the Liebieghaus Skulpturensammlung, Dr. Ulrike Koch-Brinkmann and others prove unequivocally that statues were often painted to make them as lifelike as possible.

In the Hellenistic Age bronze became the preferred medium for statuary, enabling fine detailing of facial expressions. Hypernaturalistic sculpture was the result. Sculptors explored emotion and physicality – *pathos* ('lived experience'), *dunamis* ('power' or 'potential') and *kratos* ('bodily strength'). Multiple copies of the same model could also now be produced from a single mould. When new and polished, the skin and hair glowed in coppery and golden splendour; eyes made of coloured stone, paste or glass sparkled in natural or artificial light. In the fourth century BCE, Praxiteles (c. 375–330 BCE) produced his masterpiece *Knidia* (allegedly modelled after his mistress Phyrne). Lysippos (c. 370–315 BCE) – some of whose acclaimed works are known by name, such as the *Apoxyomenos*, 'Scraper', but have not survived – found favour with Alexander the Great. Skopas (c. 370–330 BCE) was famous for his architectural sculptures.

Greek engineers sought perfection in architecture too. Pheidias (c. 465–425 BCE) oversaw the design and construction of the Parthenon – notably the Parthenon Marbles – on Perikles' renovated Acropolis in Athens. Using geometry (*gi* + *metron*, 'measure'), architects such as Iktinos and Kallikrates angled or bevelled the blocks of Pentelic marble of the steps of the

Parthenon and tilted, widened or narrowed the Doric columns to create the optical illusion of perfect verticality and symmetry. In Egypt the architect Dinokrates of Rhodes used geometry and surveying to lay down the rational grid street pattern and harbour of Alexandria.

The Greeks also developed innovative ways to tell stories. Pindar (c. 518–c. 438 BCE) wrote widely admired victory odes (*paianon*), lauding the achievements of victorious athletes. Multi-act tragic (*tragoidia*) and comic (*komoidia*) plays – featuring poetry, prose, music and dance – were performed by competing troupes of playwrights, amateur actors and choruses in purpose-built theatres in Athens and Epidaurus. Theatre (*theatron*, from *theasthai* 'behold') evolved through the Archaic Age, honed by the skill of great dramatists: Aiskylos (Aeschylus, ?525/4–456/5 BCE) developed the format; Aristophanes (c. 450–c. 388 BCE), Euripides (c. 484–407 BCE) and Sophokles (c. 496–406 BCE) perfected it in the Classical Age. In the Hellenistic Age Menandros (Menander, ?344/3–292/1 BCE) further refined stage plays in 108 comedies, taking first prize at the Lenaia festival eight times. We still quote his lines 'I call a fig a fig, a spade a spade' and 'whom the gods love dies young'.

THE LEGACY OF ANCIENT GREECE

Our idolization (from *eidolon*, 'apparition' or 'phantom') of the ancient Greeks is partly down to the Romans. Having subjugated the region, they treated Athens, Sparta and Corinth as tourist destinations and went on to adopt their cults, adapt their myths and purchase their art. In doing so they preserved and propagated these aspects of Greek civilization for future generations. One Roman poet remarked:

Captive Greece took captive her savage conquerer and the arts
It brought to rustic Latium.
Horace: *Epistles* 2.1.156, 65–8 BCE

So thorough was the Romans' assimilation that we even use a derivative of the Latin word *Graecus*, rather than *Hellene*, for these ancient people.

The literature and poetry of Greece directly influenced those of Rome. Homer's epics were studied by Roman children not only for the fine verses and mythological stories, but also for the astronomical, geographical and military information they contained. The *Aeneid* of P. Vergilius Maro (Virgil, 70–19 BCE) was a Roman take on the Trojan War and the survivors' journey to Italy, modelled on the work of Homer. C. Julius Caesar (101/100–44 BCE) and M. Tullius Cicero (106–43 BCE) learned public speaking techniques from Apollonius, a Greek rhetorician from Rhodes. Cicero regarded Herodotus as 'the Father of History'. The historians of Imperial Rome followed the model of Thucydides and they, in turn, informed the chroniclers and historians of late antiquity and medieval times. Roman architects mimicked and adapted Greek styles of architecture and its orders in the buildings they erected, both in Rome and across the cities of its sprawling empire, reaching lands the Greeks had never seen. The great builder emperor Hadrian (r. 117–138 CE) promoted Hellenic culture in the Roman Empire, but was derided as a *Graeculus* ('Greekling') for it. Menander's work informed the Latin comic plays of T. Maccius Plautus (c. 205–184 BCE), which in turn inspired William Shakespeare (1564–1616) to write his comedies in sixteenth-century England.

After the demise of the Roman Empire in the West, many books in Greek only became available following the fall of Constantinople in 1453. Reproduced in printed copies, Greek texts circulated among scholars and the intelligentsia. Shakespeare found inspiration for his tragedies in reading Thomas North's 1519 translation of *Parallel Lives of the Noble Greeks and Romans* by L. Mestrius Plutarchus (Plutarch, before 50–after 120 CE). Scholars of the Age of Enlightenment also read the works of Aristotle, Plato, Thucydides and others. The Founding Fathers studied these books at school and used their insights from them to draft, in 1787, the constitution for a new, democratic nation: the United States of America.

The typical Grand Tour undertaken by young English gentlemen did not usually include Greece, then a subject nation of the Ottoman Empire. However, the poet George Gordon Byron (1788–1824) did travel in Greece and present-day Albania, becoming enamoured with all things Greek as a result. He devoted his talents to supporting the Greek War of Independence (1821–29), himself dying at Missolonghi in the struggle. Byron captured in words the enduring romance of this ancient people and place:

> *Fair Greece! sad relic of departed worth!*
> *Immortal, though no more! though fallen, great!*

Lord Byron: *Childe Harold's Pilgrimage* **10–11, 1812–18**

Ancient Greece beguiled Lord Byron in the nineteenth century and it continues to fascinate us now in the twenty-first. As Dorothy Mills rightly concluded, 'The Greek spirit was never to die.'

Lindsay Powell

FURTHER READING

ANCIENT TEXTS

Aeschylus (trans. Robert Fagles), *The Oresteia* (Penguin Classics, reprint edition, 1977)

Apollodorus (trans. Robin Hard), *The Library of Greek Mythology* (Oxford University Press, 2008)

Aristophanes (trans. Alan H. Sommerstein), *Lysistrata and Other Plays* (Penguin Classics, revised edition, 2003)

Aristotle (ed. Richard McKeon), *Basic Works of Aristotle* (Modern Library, new edition, 2001)

Euripides (trans. Philip Vellacott), *Medea and Other Plays* (Penguin Classics, reprint edition, 1963)

Herodotus (trans. Anrdea L. Purvis), *The Landmark Herodotus: The Histories* (Anchor Books, annotated edition, 2009)

Homer (trans. Robert Fagles), *The Iliad* (Penguin Classics, revised edition, 1999)

Homer (trans. Emily Watson), *The Odyssey* (W. W. Norton & Co., 2018)

Menander (trans. Norma Miller), *Plays and Fragments* (Penguin Classics, reissue edition, 1987)

Pausanias (trans. Peter Levi), *Guide to Greece* (two volumes) (Penguin Classics, illustrated edition, 1979)

Plato (trans. Harold Tarrant), *The Last Days of Socrates* (Penguin Classics, revised edition, 2003)

Sophocles (trans. Robert Bagg and James Scully), *The Complete Plays of Sophocles: A New Translation* (HarpPeren, 2011)

Thucydides (trans. Richard Crawley), *The Landmark Thucydides: A Comprehensive Guide to the Peloponnesian War* (Simon & Schuster, Touchstone edition 1998)

MODERN TEXTS

Barca, Natale, *Knossos, Mycenae, Troy: The Enchanting Bronze Age and its Tumultuous Climax* (Oxbow Books, 2023)

Cole, Myke, *The Bronze Lie: Shattering the Myth of Spartan Warrior Supremacy* (Osprey, 2023)

Davidson, James, *Courtesans and Fishcakes: The Consuming Passions of Classical Athens* (Fontana Press, revised edition, 1998)

Dover, K.J., *Greek Homosexuality* (Bloomsbury Academic, illustrated edition, 2016)

Fox, Robert Lane, *Alexander the Great* (Penguin, UK edition, 2004)

Kitto, H.D.F., *The Greeks* (Penguin Books, revised edition, 1991)

Martin, Thomas R., *Ancient Greece: From Prehistoric to Hellenistic Times* (Yale University Press, 2nd revised edition, 2013)

Neer, Richard T., *Art & Archaeology of the Greek World* (Thames and Hudson Ltd, 2nd edition, 2019)

Rhodes, P.J., *A History of the Classical Greek World: 478–323 BC* (Wiley-Blackwell, 2nd edition, 2010)

Scott, Michael, *From Democrats to Kings: The Brutal Dawn of a New World from the Downfall of Athens to the Rise of Alexander the Great* (Abrams Press, 2010)

Smith, Jeffrey, *Themistocles: The Powerbroker of Athens* (Pen and Sword Military, 2023)

Strauss, Barry, *The Battle of Salamis: The Naval Encounter that Saved Greece – and Western Civilization* (Simon & Schuster, reprint edition, 2005)

Taub, Liba, *The Cambridge Companion to Ancient Greek and Roman Science* (Cambridge University Press, 2020)

Tomlinson, R.A., *Greek Architecture* (Bristol Classical Press, illustrated edition, 1991)

Waterfield, Robin, *Creators, Conquerors, and Citizens: A History of Ancient Greece* (Oxford University Press, USA, illustrated edition, 2020)

Lindsay Powell (Introduction) is a historian and author who writes about the conflicts, commanders and campaigns of the Ancient World. He edited, and wrote the introductions for, the volumes *Hannibal* and *Julius Caesar* for Flame Tree Publishing. His critically acclaimed books include the biographies *Marcus Agrippa*, *Eager for Glory*, *Germanicus* and *Bar Kokhba*, as well as the military histories *Augustus at War*, *Roman Soldier versus Germanic Warrior*, *1st Century* AD and *The Bar Kokhba War*, AD *132–136*. Lindsay is news editor of *Ancient History* and *Ancient Warfare* magazines and his articles have also appeared in *Military History*, *Strategy and Tactics* and *Desperta Ferro* magazines. A regular guest on the *Ancient Warfare* and *History Hit* podcasts, he is also a ten-year veteran of the Ermine Street Guard, the world's leading Roman army re-enactment society. Lindsay has a BSc (Hons) in managerial and administrative studies from Aston University, England, and divides his time between Austin, Texas and Wokingham, England.

LAND OF SEA & MOUNTAINS

To the people of the ancient world the Mediterranean was "The Sea"; they knew almost nothing of the great ocean that lay beyond the Pillars of Hercules. A few of the more daring of the Phoenician navigators had sailed out into the Atlantic, but to the ordinary sailor from the Mediterranean lands the Ocean was an unknown region, believed to be a sea of darkness, the abode of terrible monsters and a place to be avoided. And then, as they believed the world to be flat, to sail too far would be to risk falling over the edge.

The land to which people belong always helps to form their character and to influence their history, and the mainland of Greece, its rugged mountains and fertile plains, its sea and sky, was of great importance in making the Greeks what they were. One striking feature of the whole country is the nearness of every part of it to the sea. The coast is deeply indented with gulfs and bays, and the neighbouring sea is dotted with islands. It is a land of sea and mountains.

THE MEDITERRANEAN SEA

But the Mediterranean was familiar to the men of the ancient world, it was their best known highway. In those ancient times, the Ocean meant separation, it cut off the known world from the mysterious unknown, but the Mediterranean did not divide; it was, on the contrary, the chief means of communication between the countries of the ancient world. First the Phoenicians and later the Greeks sailed backwards and forwards, North and South, East and West, trading, often fighting, but always in contact with the islands and coasts. Egypt, Carthage, Athens and Rome were empires of the Mediterranean world; and the very name Mediterranean indicates its position; it was the sea in the "middle of the world."

In the summer, the Mediterranean is almost like a lake, with its calm waters and its blue and sunny sky; but it is not always friendly and gentle. The Greeks said of it that it was "a lake when the gods are kind, and an ocean when they are spiteful," and the sailors who crossed it had many tales of danger to tell. The coast of the Mediterranean, especially in the North, is broken by capes and great headlands, by deep gulfs and bays, and the sea, more especially that eastern part known as the Aegean Sea, is dotted with islands, and these give rise to strong currents. These currents made serious difficulties for ancient navigators, and Strabo, one of the earliest writers of Geography, in describing their troubles says that "currents have more than one way of running through a strait." The early navigators had no maps or compass, and if they once got out of their regular course, they ran the danger of being swept along by some unknown current, or of being wrecked on some hidden rock. The result was that they preferred to sail as near the coast as was safe. This was easier, as the Mediterranean has almost no tides, and as the early ships were small and light, landing was generally a simple matter. The ships were run ashore and pulled a few feet out of the water, and then they were pushed out to sea again whenever the sailors were ready.

The early Mediterranean civilization is sometimes given the general name of Aegean, because its great centres were in the Aegean Sea and on the adjoining mainland. The largest island in the Aegean is Crete, and the form of civilization developed there is called Cretan or Minoan, from the name of one of the legendary sea-kings of Crete, whilst that which spread on the mainland is called Mycenaean from the great stronghold where dwelt the lords of Mycenae.

THE GREEK MAINLAND

Mainland Greece can be divided into three broad parts: Northern Greece, a rugged mountainous land; then Central Greece with a fertile plain running down to more mountains; and then, across a narrow sea, the peninsula known as the Peloponnese.

About one-third of the country is mountainous and unproductive and consists of rock. The land used by the Greeks for pasture was that which was not rich enough for cultivation. Goats and sheep and pigs roamed over this land, and the bees made honey there. The cultivated land lay in the plains, and it was here that the Greeks cultivated their corn and wine and oil, and that their cities grew up separated from each other by the mountains. Corn, wine and oil were absolutely necessary for life in the Mediterranean world. Every Greek city tried to produce enough corn, chiefly wheat and barley, for its inhabitants, for the difficulties and sometimes dangers were great when a city was not self-sufficient. Oil was even more important, for it was used for cleansing purposes, for food and for lighting. The olive is cultivated all over Greece, but especially in Attica, where it was regarded as the gift of Athena herself. It was looking across the sea to Attica that:

> In Salamis, filled with the foaming
>   Of billows and murmur of bees,
> Old Telamon stayed from his roaming,
>   Long ago, on a throne of the seas;
> Looking out on the hills olive-laden,
>   Enchanted, where first from the earth
> The grey-gleaming fruit of the Maiden
>   Athena had birth.

Euripides: *The Trojan Women*, translated by Gilbert Murray

BRONZE AGE GREECE

The southern Mediterranean island of Crete is the home of one of Europe's oldest civilizations, and the peaceful palace-based societies that developed there in the second millennium BCE would spread their influence throughout the eastern Mediterraean. Called 'Minoan' after the mythical King Minos, Cretan civilization was built around a series of local administrative and trading centres that centred on palaces and controlled a local hinterland.

Minoan culture declined because of the rise of the more dominant Mycenaen culture that arose on the Greek mainland, which flourished in the late Bronze Age (c. 1600–1100 BCE) and spread its influence throughout the Peloponnese, and across the Aegean Sea to the Cyclades and Crete. More militaristic and austere than Minoan Crete, Mycenean civilization made a lasting impression on later Greeks, especially in their myths of the Trojan War and Bronze Age heroes such as Achilles and Odysseus.

THE ISLAND OF CRETE

The long narrow island of Crete lies at what might be called the entrance to the Aegean Sea. This sea is dotted with islands which form stepping stones from the mainland of Europe to the coast of Asia Minor.

The Aegean world is rich in myth and legend. It was said to be the land where Zeus was born, and that a nymph fed him in a cave with honey and goat's milk. Here, too, in the same cave was he wedded and from this marriage came Minos, the legendary Hero-King of Crete. The name Minos is probably a title, like Pharaoh or Caesar, and this Minos, descendant of Zeus, is said to have become a great Sea-King and Tyrant. He ruled over the whole of the Aegean, and even demanded tribute from cities like Athens. But Theseus, helped by the King's daughter Ariadne, slew the Minotaur, the monster who devoured the Athenian youths and maidens, and so defeated the vengeance of the King. This Minos fully realized the importance of sea-power in the Aegean. Thucydides, the Greek historian, tells us that he was the first ruler who possessed a navy, and that in order to protect his increasing wealth, he did all that was in his power to clear the sea of pirates. Minos himself may have been a great pirate who subdued all the others and made them subject to him, but whether this were so or not, he was evidently not only a great sea-king; legend and tradition speak of him as a great Cretan lawgiver. Every year he was supposed to retire for a space to the Cave of Zeus, where the Father of Gods and Men gave him laws for his land. It is because of the great mark left by Minos on the Aegean world, that the civilization developed there is so often called Minoan, thus keeping alive for ever the name of its traditional founder.

The Labyrinth in which the Minotaur was slain was built by Daedalus, an Athenian. He was a very skilful artificer, and legend says that it was he who first thought of putting masts into ships and attaching sails to them. But he was jealous of the skill of his nephew and killed him, and so was forced to flee from Athens, and he came to Knossos where was the palace of Minos. There he made the Labyrinth with its mysterious thousand paths.

But Daedalus lost the favour of Minos, who imprisoned him with his son Icarus. The cunning of the craftsman, however, did not desert him, and Daedalus skilfully made wings for them both and fastened them to their shoulders with wax, so that they flew away from their prison out of reach of the King's wrath. Icarus flew too near the sun, and the wax melted, and he fell into the sea and was drowned; but Daedalus, we are told, reached Sicily in safety.

The Athenians believed that Theseus and Minos had really existed, for the ship in which, according to tradition, Theseus made his voyage was preserved in Athens with great care until at least the beginning of the third century BCE. This ship went from Athens to Delos every year with special sacrifices, and one of these voyages became celebrated. Socrates, the philosopher, had been condemned to death, but the execution of the sentence was delayed for thirty days, because this ship was away, and so great was the reverence in which this voyage was held that no condemned man could be put to death during its absence. It was held that such an act would bring impurity on the city.

THE PALACES OF CRETE

The first traces of history on Crete take us back to about 2500 BCE, but it was not until about a thousand years later that Crete reached the height of its prosperity. The Cretans built their cities without towers or fortifications; they were a mighty sea power, but they lived more for peace and work than for military or naval adventures, and having attained the overlordship of the Aegean, they devoted themselves to trade, industries and art.

The Cretans learnt a great deal from Egypt, but they never became dependent upon that great civilization. They dwelt secure in their island kingdom, taking what they wanted from the civilization they saw in the Nile Valley; but instead of copying this, they developed and transformed it in accordance with their own spirit and independence.

The great palaces of Crete were build at Knossos, Phaistos, Mallia and Khania. The chief city in Crete was Knossos, and the great palace there is almost like a town. It is built round a large central court, out of which open chambers, halls and corridors. This court was evidently the centre of the life of the palace. The west wing was probably devoted to business and it was here that strangers were received. In the audience chamber was found a simple and austere seat, yet one which seizes upon the imagination, for it was said to be the seat of Minos, and is the oldest known royal throne in the world.

The furniture has all perished, but many household utensils have been found which show that life was by no means primitive, and the palaces were evidently built and lived in by people who understood comfort. In some ways they are quite modern, especially in the excellent drainage system they possessed.

In the east wing lived the artisans who were employed in decorating and working on the building. The walls of all the rooms were finished with smooth plaster and then painted; frescoes evoked the world of nature in which the Cretans took such a keen delight. The frescoes are now faded, but traces of river-scenes and water, of reeds and rushes and of waving grasses, of lilies and the crocus, of birds with brilliant plumage, of flying fish and the foaming sea can still be distinguished.

The frescoes on the walls, as well as small porcelain statuettes that have been found, give us a very clear idea of how the people dressed. The dress of the Cretan women was surprisingly modern. The women wore dresses with short sleeves, with the bodice laced in front, and wide flounced skirts often richly embroidered. Yellow, purple and blue seem to have been the favourite colours. They wore shoes with heels and sometimes sandals. Their hair was elaborately arranged in knots, side-curls and braids.

The men's only garment was a short kilt, which was often ornamented with designs in colours, and like the women, they had an elaborate method of hair-dressing. In general appearance the men were bronzed, slender and agile-looking.

CRETAN RELIGION AND CULTURE

We know almost nothing of the Cretan religion. There were no idols or images for worship and no temples. The people worshipped in their houses, and every house seems to have had a room set apart for this purpose with its shrine and altar; pillars were one of the distinguishing marks of these shrines. The chief goddess was the Mother Earth, the Source of Life. Bulls were sacrificed in her honour – scenes representing such sacrifices are to be found on engraved gems – and the horns of the bull are frequently found set up on altars and shrines. This Earth Goddess was Goddess both of the Air and of the Underworld: when she appears as the Goddess of the Air, she has doves as her symbol; when she appears as the Goddess of the Underworld, she has snakes.

Another sacred symbol found in connection with shrines and altars is the Axe and often a Double Axe. This seems to have been looked upon as a divine symbol representing power, for it is the axe which transforms all kinds of material into useful articles and supplies human needs. Ships could not be built without an axe, and as it was the ship which gave Crete power in the Aegean, the axe came to be looked upon as symbolizing this spirit.

These early Aegean people did not feel the need of any temples. When they worshipped in what they thought was the dwelling place of the gods, they chose lonely places, remote hill-tops or caverns or the depths of a great forest. They selected for this worship some place that was apart from daily human life and one that had never been touched by human hand, for they felt that it was such places that the god would choose for his dwelling. From such spots developed the idea of a temple; it was to be a building enclosed and shut out from the world, just as the forest grove had been surrounded by trees, a place apart from the life of man.

It was the custom in these early times for people to bring to the god or goddess offerings of that which was most valuable to them. The best of the flock, the finest fruit, the largest fish, the most beautiful vase, were all looked upon as suitable offerings. But many people could not afford to part with the best of the first fruits of their toil, and so it became the custom to have little images made of the animal or other offering they wished to make, and these were placed in the shrine. Such images are called *votive offerings*, and they are a source of rich material out of which the archaeologist has been able to rebuild parts of ancient life.

One reason why it has been so difficult to know much about the Cretan religion is because the Minoan writing system, known as Linear A, has not yet been deciphered. Over sixty different signs have been recognized, but no key has yet been found by means of which the writing can be read. In the palace at Knossos a great library was found, consisting of about two thousand clay tablets. At Knossos, uniquely, a Linear B script was also used, which appeared in the later Mycenaean palaces on the mainland and encodes the earliest form of Greek. The Knossos tablets were devoted to lists and records and were used primarily as an economic and administrative tool, recording the palace's assets, including sheep, wool, orchards, figs, olives and grapes. It seems strange that people dwelling in a land so rich in legend and story, and possessed of the art of writing, should not have left a literature. But in those days the minstrel gathered his tales together and handed them down to his successor by word of mouth. This was actually considered a safer way of preserving the tales and poems than trusting them to the written form.

THE DESTROYERS

After the **glory** of the Golden Age of Crete came destruction. Some tremendous disaster broke for ever the power of the Sea-Kings. There may have been some terrible sea fight, in which the fleet was worsted and driven back upon the shore. The city of Knossos was besieged and utterly destroyed by fire. Egyptian records of this time say that "the isles were restless, disturbed among themselves". It is also speculated that civilization on Crete was devastated by natural events, such as earthquakes or a volcanic eruption on the neighbouring island of Thera (Santorini) in the sixteenth century BCE, and the consequent tsunami.

And so Knossos fell, tasting "the woes that come on men whose city is taken: the warriors are slain, and the city is wasted of fire, and the children and women are led captive of strangers." (Homer, *Iliad*, IX)

The old Knossos was never rebuilt, though another city grew up in the neighbourhood. The site of the old palace became more and more desolate, until at length the ruins were completely hidden under a covering of earth, and the ancient power and glory of Crete became only a tradition. And so it remained for long centuries, until archaeologists, discovering what lay beneath those dreary-looking mounds, recalled for us that spring-time of the world.

THE MYCENAEAN AGE

When Knossos was destroyed around the sixteenth century BCE, the centres of civilization on the mainland, such as Mycenae and Tiryns, became of greater importance, and Mycenaean civilization flourished in mainland Greece in the Late Bronze Age (*c.* 1600–1100 BCE). All this was the Greece of the Heroic Age, the Greece to which the Greeks of the later historical times looked back as to something that lay far behind them.

An ancient tradition told the story of how Helen, the beautiful wife of Menelaus King of Sparta, had been carried off by Paris, son of the King of Troy, and of how the Greeks collected a mighty army under Agamemnon, King of Argos and his brother

Menelaus and sailed to Troy to bring back the lost Helen. For ten years they besieged Troy, during which time they had many adventures and many hero-deeds were performed. Glorious Hector of the glancing helm was slain by Achilles fleet of foot, and the gods and goddesses themselves came down from high Olympus and took sides, some helping the Trojans and some the Greeks. At length Troy was taken and the Greek heroes returned home, but their homeward journey was fraught with danger and they experienced many hardships. The wise Odysseus, especially, went through many strange adventures before he reached Greece again. All these tales were put together by the Greek poet Homer, and may be read in the *Iliad* and the *Odyssey*.

Until the beginning of the nineteenth century no one had seriously thought that there was any truth in these tales. But all this changed when a German archaeologist, Heinrich Schliemann, born in 1822, went to the place where he believed Troy had once stood and began to dig. His expectations were more than realized, for he found six cities, one of which was later conclusively proved to be the Troy of Homer. Homer had written about what was really true, and though legends and myths had been woven into his poem, the main events had really taken place, and a civilization which up to that time had, as it was thought, never existed, suddenly came out into the record of history. Because Troy was found to have really existed, everything found there was immediately connected with the Trojan heroes of the *Iliad*, and some things which were obviously legendary were treated as facts. Schliemann himself was not entirely free from these first exaggerations, but encouraged by what he had already discovered, he determined to find still more.

MYCENAE AND TIRYNS

Pausanias, an ancient Greek traveller, had written a book about his travels, and one of the places he had visited was Mycenae on the mainland of Greece. Here, he said, he had seen the tomb of Agamemnon, who on his return from Troy had been murdered by his wife, Clytemnestra, and hastily buried. Up to the time of Schliemann no one had seriously believed that there had ever been such a person as Agamemnon, but the spirit of discovery was in the air. Schliemann determined that having proved that Troy had once existed, he would find truth in still more legends, and he went to Mycena, in the southeast Peloponnese, and began to excavate. The early Greeks had not the same beliefs about the future life that the Egyptians had, but they did believe that death meant removing the dwelling place on earth to one beneath the earth, and so the early Greek tomb was built in much the same shape as the earthly house. They filled the tomb with everything that could add to the deceased's comfort, and if he were a king or great chief, he would be surrounded by things which would mark him out from other men and point to his great position. This being so, Schliemann thought that a king's tomb would be easily recognized, and he opened what he thought was probably the burial place of Agamemnon. Before doing anything else he sent a telegram to the King of Greece, which was speedily published throughout the world. The telegram said: "With great joy I announce to Your Majesty that I have found the tomb of Agamemnon!"

The sensation created by this news was tremendous. That it was really the tomb of the wide-ruling King of Argos was perhaps uncertain, but it was undoubtedly the tomb of a great lord who had lived at the same time, and at his death had been buried with a magnificent array of diadems, pendants, necklaces, ornaments of all kinds, goblets, plates, vases, all of pure gold, which were piled high in confusion in the tomb, and close by were other tombs also filled with untold treasure. In one grave alone Schliemann counted 870 objects made of the purest gold. This was only the beginning of excavations at Mycenae. Later on, a great palace was uncovered, and other work at Tiryns, nearer the sea, showed that another palace had existed there.

These buildings were very unlike the palace at Knossos; the latter had no fortifications, but these were strongly fortified. They had great walls, so mighty that in ancient times the Greeks thought the walls of Tiryns had been built by demons, and Pausanias considered them even more wonderful than the Pyramids. The fortress palace of Mycenae was entered by the gate of the Lionesses, which was reached by a rather narrow road, along which only seven men could march abreast– a precaution that made it more difficult for an enemy to approach the gates.

Mycenae and Tiryns are the best known today of the ancient fortress-palaces on the mainland of Greece, but at the time when they were built there were many others. The great lords frequently chose the hilltops for their dwellings, for the sake of better security and for the protection they could then in their turn afford the surrounding country people in times of danger. Most of these fortress-palaces were in the neighbourhood of the coast, for no true Greek was ever quite happy unless he were within easy reach and sight of the sea.

LIFE IN THE HOMERIC AGE

The Homeric Age was the age of the great hero-kings and chiefs. Most of these were supposed to be descended from the gods who, it was believed, came down from Olympus and mixed familiarly with human beings. Life was very different in this heroic age from the life of historic Greece, and it is evident from the excavations and discoveries that have been made, that it was a civilization with distinct characteristics of its own which preceded what is known as the Greece of history. It was an age when the strong man ruled by the might of his own strong arm, and piracy was quite common. Manners and customs were very primitive and simple, yet they were combined with great material splendour. Women held a high position in this society and they wore the most gorgeous clothes. A Mycenaean lady, arrayed in her best, would wear a dress of soft wool exquisitely dyed or of soft shining linen, and she would glitter with golden ornaments: a diadem of gold on her head, gold pins in her hair, gold bands round her throat, gold bracelets on her arms, and her hands covered with rings. Schliemann says that the women he found in one of the tombs he opened were "literally laden with jewellery."

The fortress-palaces were the chief houses and the huts of the dependents of the king or chief would be crowded round them, but these huts have, of course, disappeared. The palaces themselves were strongly built, with courtyards and chambers opening from them. Excavations have proved that the Homeric palaces did indeed exist: and well fortified though they were, their gardens and vineyards and fountains must have made of them very pleasant dwelling-places.

There was a gleam as it were of sun or moon through the high-roofed hall of great-hearted Alcinous. Brazen were the walls which ran this way and that from the threshold to the inmost chamber, and round them was a frieze of blue, and golden were the doors that closed in the good house. Silver were the door-posts that were set on the brazen threshold, and silver the lintel thereupon, and the hook of the door was of gold. And on either side stood golden hounds and silver, which Hephaestus had wrought by his cunning, to guard the palace of great-hearted Alcinous, being free from death and age all their days. And within were seats arrayed against the wall this way and that, from the threshold even to the inmost chamber, and thereon were spread light coverings finely woven, the handiwork of women. There the chieftains were wont to sit eating and drinking for they had continual store. Yea, and there were youths fashioned in gold, standing on firm-set bases, with flaming torches in their hands, giving light through the night to the feasters in the palace. And he had fifty handmaids in the house, and some grind the yellow grain on the mill-stone, and others weave webs and turn the yarn as they sit, restless as the leaves of the tall poplar tree: and the soft olive oil drops off that linen, so closely is it woven. And without the courtyard hard by the door is a great garden, and a hedge runs round on either side. And there grow tall trees blossoming, pear-trees and pomegranates, and apple-trees with bright fruit, and sweet figs, and olives in their bloom. The fruit of these trees never perisheth, neither faileth, winter nor summer, enduring through all the year. Evermore the West Wind blowing brings some fruits to birth and ripens others. Pear upon pear waxes old, and apple on apple, yea and cluster ripens upon cluster of the grape, and fig upon fig. There too hath he a fruitful vineyard planted, whereof the one part is being daily dried by the heat, a sunny spot on level ground, while other grapes men are gathering, and yet others they are treading in the wine-press. In the

foremost row are unripe grapes that cast the blossom, and others there
be that are growing black to vintaging. There too, skirting the furthest
line, are all manner of garden beds, planted trimly, that are perpetually
fresh, and therein are two fountains of water, whereof one scatters his
streams all about the garden, and the other runs over against it beneath
the threshold of the courtyard and issues by the lofty house, and thence
did the townsfolk draw water. These were the splendid gifts of the gods
in the palace of Alcinous.

Homer, *Odyssey*, VII

A blue frieze just like the one described above has been found
both at Mycenae and Tiryns.

The furniture in these houses was very splendid. We read
of well-wrought chairs, of chairs inlaid with ivory and silver; of
inlaid seats and polished tables; of jointed bedsteads and of a fair
bedstead with inlaid work of gold and silver and ivory; of close-
fitted, folding doors and of doors with silver handles; and of rugs
of soft wool. Rich and varied ornaments and vessels were used:
golden ewers and silver basins, two-handled cups, silver baskets
and tripods, silver mixing bowls. The most famous cup of all was
that of the clear-voiced orator Nestor; this had four handles on
which were golden doves feeding and it stood two feet from the
ground.

Metalwork at this time was very skilful and the warriors
went out arrayed in flashing bronze, bearing staves studded
with golden nails, bronze-headed spears and silver-studded
swords, their greaves were fastened with silver clasps, they
wore bronze-bound helmets, glittering girdles and belts with
golden buckles. Only a god could have fashioned a wondrous
shield such as Achilles bore, on which were depicted scenes

from the life of the time (the description of it can be read in the *Iliad*), but the tombs at Mycenae and elsewhere have yielded weapons and treasures very similar to those used by the heroes in Homer.

In the second century CE a Greek poet sang of Mycenae:

> *The cities of the hero-age thine eyes may seek in vain,*
> *Save where some wrecks of ruin still break the level plain.*
> *So once I saw Mycenae, the ill-starred, a barren height*
> *Too bleak for goats to pasture – the goat-herds point the site.*
> *And as I passed a greybeard said: "Here used to stand of old*
> *A city built by giants and passing rich in gold."*
> **Alpheus, translated by Sir Rennell Rodd**
> **in *Love, Worship and Death*.**

THE GREAT MIGRATIONS

The **Heroic Age** ended with a general migration among the tribes of Greece, which began with incursions of the Illyrians on its north-western frontier. The time of this movement was fixed by Greek historians at sixty years after the fall of Troy, *c.* 1124 BCE.

Though the Illyrians did not enter central or southern Greece, their southward movement produced a general change among the tribes of the peninsula. The Thessalians, who had previously been settled on the western coast of Epirus, now crossed the Pindus mountains, and cleared for themselves a place in the fertile basin of the Pineiós River, hitherto occupied by the Bœotians. The Bœotians, thus dispossessed of their ancient seats, moved southward, Vale of the Cephissus, whence they drove the Cadmians and Minyae. These tribes were scattered through Attica and the Peloponnesus. The Dorians, moving from the north, occupied the narrow valley between Oeta and Parnassus, which thus became *Doris*; while the Dryopians, earlier inhabitants of this region, took refuge in Euboea and the islands of the Aegean.

Twenty years later, a still more important movement took place. The Dorians, cramped by the narrow mountain limits of their homeland, united with their western neighbours, the Aetolians, to invade the Peloponnesus. It is said that they were pursuing the claims of their great ancestor, Hercules, who had been expelled from the southern peninsula a hundred years before. The Dorian migration is therefore often called the Return of the Heraclidae. Aristodemus was killed by lightning when about to cross the Corinthian Gulf. The victorious Dorians proceeded to divide the peninsula between themselves and their allies. The Aetolians received Elis, on the western coast; the rest of the peninsula, except its northern border on the Corinthian Gulf, remained to the Dorians, who continued for five centuries to be the dominant race in Greece.

The conquered Achaeans were forced either to emigrate to Asia or Italy, or to content themselves with the northern coast of their peninsula, from which they expelled its Ionian inhabitants, and gave it their own name, Achaia. The Ionians, after resting a few years in Attica, whose people were their kinsmen, sought more space in the Cyclades, in Chios and Samos, or on the neighbouring coasts of Asia Minor. In the fertile region between the Hermus and Maeander, and on the islands, twelve Ionian cities sprang up, and became rich and flourishing states.

The Aeolians had already been driven from their ancient home in central Greece, and had found refuge in Lesbos and the north-western coast of Asia Minor, between the Hermus and the Hellespont. They, also, formed twelve independent cities, but Mytilene, on the isle of Lesbos, was considered the metropolis. The Dorians, extending their migrations beyond the conquered peninsula, took possession of the south-western coast of Asia Minor, with the islands of Cos and Rhodes. Their six cities – sometimes called the Doric Hexapolis – were Cnidus and Halicarnassus, on the mainland; Ialyssus, Camirus, and Lindus, on the isle of Rhodes; and Cos, on the island of its own name.

THE TRIBES OF ANCIENT GREECE

This **excerpt** is from Strabo's *Geography*, Book VIII, Chapter 1:

There are many Greek tribes, but the chief people are equal in number to the Greek dialects with which we are acquainted, namely, four. Of these, the Ionic is the same as the ancient Attic; (for Iones was the former name of the inhabitants of Attica; from thence came the Iones who settled in Asia, and use the dialect now called Ionic;) the Doric was the same as the Aeolic dialect, for all the people on the other side of the isthmus except the Athenians, the Megareans, and the Dorians about Parnassus, are even now called Aeolians; it is probable that the Dorians, from their being a small nation, and occupying a most rugged country, and from want of intercourse [with the Aeolians], no longer resemble that people either in language or customs, and, although of the same race, have lost all appearance of affinity. It was the same with the Athenians, who inhabiting a rugged country with a light soil, escaped the ravages of invaders. As they always occupied the same territory, and no enemy attempted to expel them, nor had any desire to take possession of it themselves, on this account they were, according to Thucydides, regarded as Autochthones, or an indigenous race. This was probably the reason, although they were a small nation, why they remained a distinct people with a distinct dialect.

It was not in the parts only on the other side of the isthmus, that the Aeolian nation was powerful, but those on this side also were formerly Aeolians. They were afterwards intermixed first with Ionians who came from Attica, and got possession of Aegialus, and secondly with Dorians, who under the conduct of the Heracleidae founded Megara and many of the cities in the Peloponnesus. The Iones were soon expelled by the Achaei, an Aeolian tribe; and there remained in Peloponnesus the two nations, the Aeolic and the Doric. Those nations then that had little intercourse with the Dorians used the Aeolian dialect. (This was the case with the Arcadians and Eleians, the former of whom were altogether a mountain tribe, and did not share in the partition of the Peloponnesus; the latter were considered as dedicated to the service of the Olympian Jupiter, and lived for a long period in peace, principally because they were of Aeolian descent, and had admitted into their country the army of Oxylus, about the time of the return of the Heracleidae.) The rest used a kind of dialect composed of both, some of them having more, others less, of the Aeolic dialect. Even at present the inhabitants of different cities use different dialects, but all seem to Dorize, or use the Doric dialect, on account of the ascendency of that nation.

THE CULTURE OF
ANCIENT GREECE

The city-dwellers in Greece lived in the plains separated from their neighbours by mountains, and this caused the development of a large number of separate communities, quite independent of each other, each having its own laws and government, but there were three things which all Greeks had in common wherever they lived: they spoke the same language, they believed in the same gods, and they celebrated together as Greeks their great national games.

Because the Greek communities lived in the plains, separated from each other by mountains, instead of forming one large kingdom, they formed a great many small ones. There was in ancient times no King of Greece, but Athens, Sparta, Corinth, Thebes and countless other cities had their own independent forms of government, their own rulers, their own armies, their own ships, and except that they were all Greek and were all bound together by ties of language and religion, they were quite independent of each other. All these independent cities became known in time as City-States, for to the Greek the state meant the city; the territory immediately surrounding it was included in the state, but the city was the most important part of it.

LAND OF THE HELLENES

The **Greeks** called themselves Hellenes and their land Hellas. Like the Hebrews and the Babylonians, they believed that there had been a time when men had grown so wicked that the gods determined to destroy them. A terrible flood overwhelmed the earth, until nothing of it was left visible but the top of Mount Parnassus, and here, the old legend tells us, a refuge was found by two people, Deucalion and his wife Pyrrha, who alone had been saved on account of their righteous lives. Slowly the waters abated, until the earth was once more dry and habitable, but Deucalion and Pyrrha were alone and did not know what they should do. So they prayed to the gods and received as an answer to their prayer the strange command: "Depart, and cast behind you the bones of your mother." At first they could not understand what was meant, but at length Deucalion thought of an explanation. He said to Pyrrha: "The earth is the great mother of all; the stones are her bones, and perhaps it is these we must cast behind us." So they took up the stones that were lying about and cast them behind them, and as they did so the stones thrown by Deucalion became men, and those thrown by Pyrrha became women, and this race of men peopled the land of Greece anew. The son of Deucalion and Pyrrha was called Hellen, and as the Greeks looked upon him as the legendary founder of their race, they called themselves and their land by his name.

THE RELIGION OF ANCIENT GREECE

These **earliest Greeks** thought the world was flat and circular, and that Greece lay in the very middle of it, with Mount

Olympus, or as some maintained, Delphi, as the central point of the whole world. This world was believed to be cut in two by the Sea and to be entirely surrounded by the River Ocean, from which the Sea and all the rivers and lakes on the earth received their waters.

In the north of this world, were supposed to live the Hyperboreans. They were the people who lived beyond the North winds, whose home was in the caverns in the mountains to the North of Greece. The Hyperboreans were a happy race of beings who knew neither disease nor old age, and who, living in a land of everlasting spring, were free from all toil and labour.

Far away in the south, on the banks of the River Ocean, lived another happy people, the Aethiopians. They were so happy and led such blissful lives, that the gods used sometimes to leave their home in Olympus and go and join the Aethiopians in their feasts and banquets.

On the western edge of the earth and close to the River Ocean were the Elysian Fields, sometimes called the Fortunate Fields and the Isles of the Blessed. It was to this blissful place that mortals who were specially loved by the gods were transported without first tasting of death, and there they lived for ever, set free from all the sorrows and sufferings of earth.

THE GREEK PANTHEON

The gods in whom the Greeks believed were not supposed to have created the world, but they were themselves part of it, and every phase of this life that was so full of interest and adventure was represented by the personality of a god. First, it was the outside life, nature with all its mysteries, and then all the outward activities of man. Later, men found other things difficult to explain, the passions within them, love and hatred, gentleness and anger, and gradually they gave personalities to all these emotions and thought of each as inspired by a god. These gods were thought of as very near to humanity; men and women in the Heroic Age had claimed descent from them, and they were supposed to come down to earth and to hold frequent converse with them. The Greeks trusted their gods and looked to them for protection and assistance in all their affairs, but these gods were too human and not holy enough to be a real inspiration or to influence very much the conduct of those who believed in them.

The chief gods dwelt on Mount Olympus in Thessaly and were called the Olympians; others had dwellings on the earth, in the water, or in the underworld. Heaven, the water and the underworld were each under the particular sovereignty of a great overlord amongst the gods.

Zeus was the greatest of the gods. He was the Father of gods and men, the lord of the lightning and of the storm-cloud, whose joy was in the thunder. But he was also the lord of counsel and ruler of heaven and earth, and he was in particular the protector of all who were in any kind of need or distress, and he was the guardian of the home. The court of every house had an altar to Zeus, the Protector of the Hearth. A great statue of Zeus stood in the temple at Olympia. It was the work of Pheidias and was considered one of the Seven Wonders of the ancient world.

Hera was the wife of Zeus. She was "golden-throned Hera, an immortal queen, the bride of loud-thundering Zeus, the lady renowned, whom all the Blessed throughout high Olympus honour and revere no less than Zeus whose delight is the thunder." (Homeric Hymn to Hera)

Poseidon went to Olympus when he was summoned by Zeus, but he was the God of the Sea, and he preferred its depths as his home. His symbol was the trident, and he was often represented as driving over the waves in a chariot drawn by foaming white horses. All sailors looked to him for protection.

Athena, the grey-eyed Goddess, was the Guardian of Athens, and she stood to all the Greeks, but especially to the Athenians, as the symbol of three things: she was the Warrior Goddess, who led armies out to war and brought them home victorious; she was Athena Polias, the Guardian of the city and the home, to whom was committed the planting and care of the olive trees and who had taught women the art of weaving and given them wisdom in all fair handiwork; she was the wise goddess, rich in counsel, who inspired the Athenians with good statesmanship and showed them how to rule well and justly. Above all, she was Athena Parthenos, the Queen whose victories were won, and who was the symbol of all that was true and beautiful and good.

Apollo, the Lord of the silver bow, was the god who inspired all poetry and music. He went about playing upon his lyre, clad in divine garments; and at his touch the lyre gave forth sweet, music. Apollo was also worshipped as Phoebus the Sun, the God of Light, and like the sun, he was supposed to purify and illumine all things.

Following Apollo as their lord were the Muses, nine daughters of Zeus, who dwelt on Mount Parnassus. We are told that their hearts were set on song and that their souls knew no sorrow. It was the Muses and Apollo who gave to man the gift of song, and he whom they loved was held to be blessed. The Muse who inspired man with the imagination to understand history aright was called Clio.

The huntress Artemis, the sister of Apollo, was goddess of the moon as her brother was god of the sun. She loved life in the open air and roamed over the hills and in the valleys, through the forests and by the streams. She was the

Goddess of the loud chase, a maiden revered, the slayer of stags, the archer, very sister of Apollo of the golden blade. She through the shadowy hills and the windy headlands rejoicing in the chase draws her golden bow, sending forth shafts of sorrow. Then tremble the crests of the lofty mountains, and terribly the dark woodland rings with din of beasts, and the earth shudders, and the teeming sea.

Homeric Hymn to Artemis

Hermes is best known to us as the messenger of the gods. Hermes was the protector of travellers, and he was the god who took special delight in the life of the market place. But there was another side to his character: he was skilful in all matters of cunning and trickery, and legend delighted in telling of his exploits.

Hephaestus was the God of Fire, the divine metalworker. He was said to have been the first to discover the art of working iron, brass, silver and gold and all other metals that require forging by fire. His workshop was on Mount Olympus and here he used to do all kinds of work for the gods. Perhaps his most famous piece was the divine armour and above all the shield he made for Achilles. Some great quarrel in which he was concerned arose in Olympus, and Zeus, in rage, threw him out of heaven. All day he fell until, as the sun was setting, he dropped upon the isle of Lemnos.

Athena and Hephaestus were always regarded as benefactors to mankind, for they taught man many useful arts.

Hestia, the Goddess of the Hearth, played an important part in the life of the Greeks. Her altar stood in every house and in every public building, and no act of any importance was ever performed until an offering of wine had been poured on her altar.

Laughter-loving, golden Aphrodite was the Goddess of Love and Beauty. She rose from the sea born in the soft white foam.

To the ancient Greeks the woods and streams, the hills and rocky crags of their beautiful land were dwelt in by gods and nymphs and spirits of the wild. Chief of such spirits was Pan,

the goat-footed, the two-horned, the lover of the din of the revel, who haunts the wooded dells with dancing nymphs that tread the crests of the steep cliffs, calling upon Pan. Lord is he of every snowy crest and mountain peak and rocky path. Hither and thither he goes, through the thick copses, sometimes being drawn to the still waters, and sometimes faring through the lofty crags he climbs the highest peaks whence the flocks are seen below; ever he ranges over the high white hills and at evening returns piping from the chase breathing sweet strains on the reeds.

Homeric Hymn to Pan

GREEK WORSHIP

The centre of Greek worship was the altar, but the altars were not in the temples, but outside. They were also found in houses and in the chief public buildings of the city. The temple was looked upon as the home of the god, and the temple enclosure was a very sacred place. A man accused of a crime could flee there and take refuge, and once within the temple, he was safe. It was looked upon as a very dreadful thing to remove him by force, for it was believed that to do so would bring down the wrath of the god upon those who had violated the right of sanctuary.

In the houses the altars were those sacred to Hestia, to Apollo and to Zeus. The altar of Hestia stood in the chief room of the house, a libation was poured out to her before meals, and special sacrifices were offered on special occasions; always before setting out on a journey and on the return from it, and at the time of a birth or of a death in the house. The altar of Apollo stood just outside the door. Special prayers and sacrifices were offered at this altar in times of trouble, but Apollo was not forgotten in the time of joy: those who had travelled far from home stopped to worship on their return; when good news came to the house sweet-smelling herbs were burnt on his altar, and a bride took sacred fire from it to offer to Apollo in her new home.

The Greeks had no stated day every week sacred to the gods, but during the year different days were looked upon as belonging specially to particular gods. Some of these days were greater than others and were honoured by public holidays. Others caused no interruption in the everyday life.

Priests were attached to the temples, but sacrifices on the altars in the city or in the home were presented by the king or chief magistrate and by the head of the household. The Greeks did not kneel when they prayed, but stood with bared heads. Their prayers were chiefly for help in their undertakings. They prayed before everything they did: before athletic contests, before performances in the theatre, before the opening of the assembly. The sailor prayed before setting out to sea, the farmer before he ploughed and the whole nation before going forth to war. Pericles, the great Athenian statesman, never spoke in public without a prayer that he might "utter no unfitting word."

As time went on, the gods of Olympus seemed less near to mortal men, and they gradually became less personalities than symbols of virtues, and as such they influenced the conduct of men more than they had done before. Athena, for example, became for all Greeks the symbol of self-control, of steadfast courage and of dignified restraint; Apollo of purity; and Zeus of wise counsels and righteous judgments.

THE ORACLE

The greatest religious influence in Greece was probably that of the Oracle. This was the belief that at certain shrines specially sacred to certain gods, the worshipper could receive answers to questions put to the god. In very early times signs seen in the world of nature were held to have special meanings: the rustling of leaves in the oak tree, the flight of birds, thunder and lightning, eclipses of both the sun and moon or earthquakes. It is easy to understand how this belief arose. A man, perplexed and troubled by some important decision he had to make, would leave the city with its bustle and noise, and go out into the country where he could think out his difficulty alone and undisturbed. Perhaps he would sit under a tree, and as he sat and thought, the rustling of the leaves in the breeze would soothe his troubled mind and slowly his duty would become clear to him, and it would seem to him that his questions were answered. Looking up to the sky he would give thanks to Zeus for thus inspiring him with understanding. On his return home he would speak of how he had heard the voice of Zeus speaking to him in the rustling of the leaves, and so the place would gradually become associated with Zeus, and others would go there and seek answers to their difficulties, hoping to meet with the same experience, until at last the spot would become sacred and a shrine would be built there, and it would at length become known from far and near as an oracle. Plato said of these beginnings of the oracles that "for the men of that time, since they were not so wise as ye are nowadays, it was enough in their simplicity to listen to oak or rock, if only these told them true." Other places would in the same way become associated with other gods, until seeking answers at oracles became a well-established custom in Greece.

The great oracles of Zeus were at Olympia, where the answers were given from signs observed in the sacrifices offered, and at Dodona, where they were given from the sound of the rustling of the leaves in the sacred oak tree. But the greatest oracle in all Greece was that of Apollo at Delphi. It was at Delphi that Apollo had fought with and slain the Python, and it was thought that he specially delighted to dwell there, and had himself chosen it as the place where he would make known his will. A great shrine and temple was built there in Apollo's honour.

Whenever a Greek came to consult Apollo, he had first to offer certain sacrifices, and he always brought with him the richest gifts he could afford which were placed in the treasury of the god. Then he entered the temple and placed his request in the hands of a priest, who took it into the innermost sanctuary and gave it to the prophetess, whose duty it was to present the petition to the god himself and receive the answer. In ancient times it was believed that a mysterious vapour arose in this sanctuary through a cleft in the rocky floor, and that this vapour, enveloping the prophetess, filled her with a kind of frenzy in the midst of which she uttered the words of the answer given her by Apollo. This answer was written down by the priests and often turned into verse by them and then taken out to the enquirer. Sometimes these answers were quite plain and straightforward, such as the one which has remained true through all the ages. It was the oracle from Apollo at Delphi which said of the poet Homer: "He shall be deathless and ageless for aye." But sometimes the answers were like a riddle that required much thinking over to understand, and sometimes they were so worded that they might mean either of two things, each the opposite of the other.

The oracle at Delphi was frequently consulted by the Greeks at great crises of their history, and it had great influence. It was the priests who in writing down the answer really determined its nature. They were men who were in constant touch with distant places, they had had much experience with human nature, and they were well fitted to give guidance and advice in all kinds of difficult matters. The oracle at Delphi was thus a power in the worldly affairs of the Greeks, but it was more than that, it was also a source of moral inspiration. It encouraged all manner of civilization and the virtues of gentleness and self-control, it marked the great reformers with its approval, it upheld the sanctity of oaths, and it encouraged respect and reverence for women. On one of the temples were inscribed the sayings "Know thyself" and "Nothing in excess." It was said that these had been placed there by the ancient sages, and in later times they became famous as maxims in the teaching of the great philosophers.

The oracle was not always right in its interpretations; it sometimes failed in seizing the highest opportunities that lay before it, but as Greek history unfolds itself before us, we can see a gradual raising of moral standards, which was due in great measure to the influence of the oracle of Apollo at Delphi.

GREEK TEMPLES

A Greek temple was not a place where people met to worship, and it was never intended to hold a very large number of people. The religious ceremonies were carried on in the great spaces outside the temples, and sacrifices were offered on the altars which were always in the open air. The temple was the dwelling place of the god and the treasury where the gifts brought by the worshippers were kept.

Greek temples varied in size, but they were all built to the same general plan. The whole building was looked upon as the home of the god, and so the chamber in which the statue was placed was the central point, and all the other parts of the building were so constructed that they harmonized with the main purpose of the temple.

The earliest form of temple was the shrine, an oblong building with a portico, which had at first only two pillars in front, but which were later extended into a row of pillars across the whole front of the building. Then a portico was built at both ends of the temple, and lastly, in some temples a row of columns was built all round the building, with a double row in the portico at each end. Above the portico was a triangular gable called the pediment, which was usually filled with sculpture.

Greeks used three kinds of columns in their buildings. The Doric column was the simplest; it had no base and tapered very slightly up to the capital which consisted of a thick slab of stone. The Doric was the type most often used by the Greeks, and in its simplicity and perfection of form it symbolized the finest Greek spirit. The Ionic column stood on a base; it was more slender than the Doric, and the capital consisted of two very graceful spirals. The Ionic was a lighter type of column than the Doric and was used a great deal by the Greeks in Asia Minor. A third type was introduced later, called the Corinthian. The capitals of this column were richly carved in the form of leaves, but the Greeks never liked it as much as the simpler and more graceful types, and it was not very much used until Roman times. All the columns were fluted.

The Greeks never used ornament for the sake of ornament. The column was used as a support and ornament was felt to be entirely out of place on it, but the decoration on the capital served a purpose. As the eye followed the fluting upwards to where the vertical line met the horizontal, the simple decoration of the capital served to make the transition from one line to the other less abrupt. In Greek architecture no part of a building that bore any strain was ornamented, and wherever ornament was used it was always in harmony with the general purposes of the building.

THE OLYMPIC GAMES

The Greeks were bound together by their language, by their religion, and also by their great national games. The origin of these games is still somewhat in doubt. They probably began as some kind of religious ceremony in connection with burials, such as the Funeral Games described by Homer that were held in honour of Patroclus. But whatever may have been their origin, they were firmly established in the earliest times of historic Greece.

Greece was never free for long at a time from warfare. The very fact that the country was divided into so many small and independent states bred jealousies and hatreds, and state was often at war with state. This made it necessary that every Greek citizen should be ready at any moment to take up arms in defence of his home, and so he had to be physically always in good condition. This was brought about by regular athletic training which was an important part of the education of every Greek. It was considered just as bad to have an ill-trained body as it was to have an ill-trained mind, and one reason why the Greeks so despised the barbarians, as they called all those who were not of Greek race, was because the barbarian did not train his body to the same extent, and because he loved so much luxury.

All Greeks, then, received athletic training, and this training aimed at developing a beautiful body, for it was believed that to run gracefully was as important as to run swiftly, but though the Greeks loved contests and competition and strove hard for the victory, because they cared so much for grace of movement they did not lay much stress on record-breaking, and so they kept no records of exceptional athletic feats, which prevents us from knowing details of some of their great athletic achievements.

Games were held in nearly every Greek city and were a source of great pride to the citizens. The more important festivals were those held in honour of Poseidon at Corinth and called the Isthmian Games, those at Delphi which commemorated the slaying of the Python by Apollo and called Pythian Games, and the greatest of all, held every four years at Olympia in honour of

Zeus, and known as the Olympic Games. These games were the oldest in Greece and they were at all periods the most important. The first games in historic times were held in 776 BCE and the interval between each festival was called an Olympiad. These Olympiads constituted the Greek calendar, which took 776 BCE as its starting point.

OLYMPIA

This great festival at Olympia was held in August or September and lasted five days. It was a national affair and Greeks from all over the Greek world went to Olympia to take part in it. For a whole month a truce was proclaimed throughout Greece, all warfare had to stop, and all ordinary business and pleasure gave way to the greater business of going to Olympia. The games were usually held from the eleventh to the sixteenth day of this month of truce, the days before and after being given up to the journey to and from Olympia. All roads were declared safe for these days, and great was the punishment meted out to any who dared molest the pilgrims to Olympia, for they were going to pay honour to Zeus and were considered as specially under his protection. Visitors thronged every road and they came from every direction. They came from all the Peloponnesian states, from Corinth, Athens and Thebes. They came from the far-off Greek colonies, some from the shores of the Black Sea, looking almost like the nomads with whom they came so much in contact; some from Ionia, men clad in rich robes and of luxurious habits learnt from their Oriental neighbours; others from the western colonies, from Italy and Southern Gaul; and yet others, dark and warm-blooded men, from distant Africa. Yet all were Greeks, bound together in spite of their differences by the common ties of blood and religion.

The gathering together of so many visitors brought all kinds of people to Olympia: merchants with rich and rare goods for sale, for a regular fair was carried on during the festival, makers of small statues hoping for orders to be placed in the temples, poets who wanted to recite their poems, musicians ready to play on their lyres to any who would listen, gymnastic trainers from all over Greece who hoped to learn some new method that would improve their own teaching, people of all and every kind. Only there were no women. The games were considered too public a festival for it to be fitting for women to be present, and the journey was too long and difficult for them to undertake it. The women who lived near Olympia had a festival of their own, when they, too, raced and were awarded prizes, but it was at a different time from the great national festival.

There was no city at Olympia and but few buildings beyond the temples, so when the throng of visitors arrived, the first thing they did was to provide sleeping quarters for themselves. Certain people were allowed to sleep in some of the porticoes of the buildings connected with the temples, others had brought tents and a regular camp arose. Many announcements were made by heralds at this time; the terms of treaties between different Greek states were recited in public, for in those days of difficult communication between states, such a gathering as that at Olympia ensured that news made public then would be widely spread amongst the different states.

Then there were visits to be made to the great temple of Zeus and sacrifices to be offered. From the middle of the fifth century

BCE onwards every visitor to Olympia went reverently into the temple to gaze at the great statue of Zeus. This statue was said to be such a life-like image of the god, either Zeus must have come down from heaven and shown himself in a vision to the sculptor Pheidias, or Pheidias must have gone up to heaven and beheld him there.

The competitors in the games had all been at Olympia for the last thirty days undergoing a final and special training. Only men of pure Greek blood might compete, and no one who had been convicted of any crime or who was guilty of any impiety or disrespect to the gods. Each candidate had to prove that in addition to his regular athletic training, he had received special training for ten months before coming to Olympia.

The names of those who were to enter for the games were then written up on a white board, and should a man withdraw after that, he was branded as a coward. As soon as the competitor was finally enrolled, a boar was offered in sacrifice to Zeus, and then he had to take a solemn oath that he was a full Greek citizen, that he had fulfilled all the conditions necessary for the games, that he would abide by the rules of the contest, and that he would play fair, and such was the spirit of honour and fairness in which the games were played, that in more than a thousand years there appear the names of only six or seven competitors who were guilty of breaking their oath.

The first day of the festival was given up to sacrifices and processions. The different states always sent official representatives to the Games, and these would make public entrance in their chariots, richly arrayed and bearing costly gifts to place in the treasury of the temple. The next three days were devoted to the actual contests.

Long before the dawn on the first of these three days, every seat in the stadium was occupied. It was situated at the foot of a hill, and every available spot on the slope of this hill was used by the spectators. The sun beat down on their bare heads, for the Games were in honour of Zeus and he was looked upon as present, and no one might enter the presence of the Father of Gods and Men with covered head. Not until the setting sun gave the signal for the end of the day's contests, did they hurriedly rush off to their tents and snatch an hour or two of sleep before the coming of the dawn warned them to rise and secure their seats for the next day's spectacle.

The contests probably took place in the following order: First, there were the foot races: there were several of these varying in length from two hundred yards to three miles. The shortest race of two hundred yards was for a long time the race which brought greatest honour to the winner. Then followed the pentathlon which consisted of five contests: throwing the discus, throwing the spear, running, jumping and wrestling, and the winner was required to have won three out of the five. In the pentathlon, in particular, great importance was attached to the gracefulness of every movement, and the jumping, discus and spear throwing were generally accompanied by the music of the flute. Then came what was later regarded as the greatest and most exciting race of all, the four-horse chariot race. This was a race that poets loved to describe. Homer tells us how the charioteers

all together lifted the lash above their steeds, and smote them with the reins and called on them eagerly with words: and they forthwith sped swiftly over the plain; and beneath their breasts stood the rising dust like a cloud or whirlwind, and their manes waved on the blowing

*wind. And the chariots ran sometimes on the bounteous earth, and
other whiles would bound into the air. And the drivers stood in the cars,
and the heart of every man beat in desire of victory, and they called
every man to his horses, that flew amid their dust across the plain.*
Homer, *Iliad*, XXIII

The boxing and wrestling matches came last, and these were
the roughest and fiercest of all the contests.

On the last day of the festival the prizes were awarded. They
were very simple, but more highly valued than greater honours
could have been. Each prize consisted of a wreath of olive, which
had been cut from a sacred olive tree with a golden knife by a boy
especially chosen for the purpose, and an old tradition required
that both his parents should be alive. These wreaths used at one
time to be placed on a tripod in the sight of all the people, later,
a beautiful table of gold and ivory was made for them. A herald
announced the name of the victor, his father's name and the
city from which he came, and then one of the judges placed the
wreath on his head. This was the proudest moment of his life, and
though other rewards followed on his return home, nothing ever
quite equalled that glorious moment.

The last day of the festival was given up to sacrifices to Zeus,
followed by banquets and feasting which lasted late into the
night. Every kind of honour was shown the victors: poets wrote
odes celebrating their victories, and sculptors made models for
statues of them, for to every athlete who had won three victories
was granted the honour of being allowed to have his statue
erected in the open space outside the temple of Zeus.

The festival over, the victors and their friends and the great
throng of spectators returned to their homes. The victors were

not only proud on account of their own achievements, but for the glory they had brought to their city. The news of the approaching arrival of a victor was sent on ahead, and the day of his return to his native city was always honoured by a public holiday. In some places it was an old custom to pull down a part of the city wall and make a special entrance, in order that he who had brought the city such glory might enter by a path never before trodden by other men. Songs of triumph were sung to greet him, and he was led to his father's house along a road strewn with flowers. Rich gifts were presented to him, and in every way he was treated as a man whom the city delighted to respect and honour. At Athens the returning victors were honoured by being allowed to dine thenceforth at the public expense in the hall where the councillors and great men of the city took their meals.

Pindar, the Greek poet who has most often sung of the Olympic Games, summed up the feelings of every victor in the words: "He that overcometh hath, because of the games, a sweet tranquillity throughout his life for evermore."

THE STATUE OF OLYMPIAN ZEUS

This excerpt is from Pausanius' *Description of Greece*, Volume I, Book IV, Chapter XI:

The image of the god is in gold and ivory, seated on a throne. And a crown is on his head imitating the foliage of the olive tree. In his right hand he holds a Victory in ivory and gold, with a tiara and crown on his head: and in his left hand a sceptre adorned with all manner of precious stones, and the bird seated on the sceptre is an eagle. The robes and sandals of the god are also of gold: and on his robes are imitations of flowers, especially of lilies. And the throne is richly adorned with gold and precious stones, and with ebony and ivory. And there are imitations of animals painted on it, and models worked on it. There are four Victories like dancers one at each foot of the throne, and two also at the instep of each foot: and at each of the front feet are Theban boys carried off by Sphinxes, and below the Sphinxes Apollo and Artemis shooting down the children of Niobe. And between the feet of the throne are four divisions formed by straight lines drawn from each of the four feet. In the division nearest the entrance there are seven models, the eighth has vanished no one knows where or how. And they are imitations of ancient contests, for in the days of Phidias the contests for boys were not yet established. And the figure with its head muffled up in a scarf is they say Pantarces, who was a native of Elis and the darling of Phidias. This Pantarces won the wrestling prize for boys in the 86th Olympiad. And in the remaining divisions is the band of Hercules fighting against the Amazons. The number on each side is 29, and Theseus is on the side of Hercules. And the throne is supported not only by the four feet, but also by 4 pillars between the feet. But one cannot get under the throne, as one can at Amyclae, and pass inside, for at Olympia there are panels like walls that keep one off. Of these panels the one opposite the doors of the temple is painted sky blue only, but the others contain paintings by Panaenus. Among them is Atlas bearing up Earth and Heaven, and Hercules standing by willing to relieve him of his load, and Theseus and Pirithous, and Greece, and Salamis with the figurehead of a ship in her hand, and the contest of Hercules with the Nemean lion, and Ajax's unknightly violation of Cassandra, and Hippodamia the daughter of Œnomaus with her mother, and Prometheus still chained to the rock and Hercules gazing at him. For the tradition is that Hercules slew the eagle that was ever tormenting Prometheus on Mount Caucasus, and released Prometheus from his chains. The last paintings are Penthesilea dying and Achilles supporting her, and two Hesperides carrying the apples of which they are fabled to have been the keepers. This Panaenus was the brother of Phidias, and at Athens in the Painted Stoa he has painted the action at Marathon. At the top of the throne Phidias has represented above the head of Zeus the three Graces and three Seasons. For these too, as we learn from the poets, were daughters of Zeus. Homer in the *Iliad* has represented the Seasons as having the care of Heaven, as a kind of guards of a royal palace. And the base under the feet of Zeus (what is called in Attic θρανίον), has golden lions engraved on it, and the battle between Theseus and the Amazons, the first famous exploit of the Athenians beyond their own borders. And on the platform that supports the throne there are various ornaments round Zeus and gilt carving, the Sun seated in his chariot, and Zeus and Hera, and near is Grace. Hermes is close to her, and Vesta close to Hermes. And next to Vesta is Eros receiving Aphrodite just rising from the sea, who is being crowned by Persuasion. And Apollo and Artemis Athene and Hercules are standing by, and at the end of the platform Amphitrite and Poseidon, and Selene apparently urging on her horse. And some say it is a mule and not a horse that the goddess is riding upon, and there is a silly tale about this mule.

I know that the size of the Olympian Zeus both in height and breadth has been stated, but I cannot bestow praise on the measurers, for their recorded measurement comes far short of what anyone would infer looking at the statue. They make the god also to have testified to the art of Phidias. For they say when the statue was finished, Phidias prayed him to signify if the work was to his mind, and immediately Zeus struck with lightning that part of the pavement, where in our day there is a brazen urn with a lid.

And all the pavement in front of the statue is not of white but of black stone. And a border of Parian marble runs round this black stone, as a preservative against spilled oil. For oil is good for the statue at Olympia, as it prevents the ivory being harmed by the dampness of the grove. But in the Acropolis at Athens, in regard to the statue of Athene called the Maiden, it is not oil but water that is advantageously employed to the ivory: for as the citadel is dry by reason of its great height, the statue being made of ivory needs to be sprinkled with water freely. And when I was at Epidaurus, and enquired why they use neither water nor oil to the statue of Aesculapius, the sacristans of the temple informed me that the statue of the god and its throne are over a well.

THE GREEK CITY-STATE

The earliest form of government in Greece was that of the family, and the word of the head of the family was law to all those belonging to it. The land on which they lived belonged to the family as a whole, not to separate individuals, and the dead were always buried there, until in time the family claimed as their own that land, where they had lived for generations, and where their ancestors were buried.

After a time it became more convenient for families to join together and live in one community. By this means the labour of cultivating the land could be more evenly distributed, and in times of attack from enemies, larger and stronger forces could be used for defence. This grouping of families together made a *village* and the strongest and most capable man in the village would become its chief.

In time, just as families had found it more to their advantage to group themselves together and form villages, so did the villages living in the same neighbourhood find it a better thing to join together and form a still larger community, centred on a city, which became known as a kingdom, because instead of having a chief they were ruled by a king. At first the kings, like the chiefs, were chosen because of their ability and power; later the office became hereditary and was handed down from father to son. In time, these independent kingdoms became known as city-states, which comprised the city and territory immediately surrounding it.

The Greek philosopher Aristotle wrote a book in which the ideal of the city-state and the good citizen were set forth. He believed that the end for which the State existed was that all its citizens could lead what he called a "good life," and by that he meant the life which best gives opportunities for man to develop his highest instincts, and which makes it possible for every citizen to develop his own gifts whatever they may be, in the highest and truest way. To realize such a life there must be law and order in a state, and Aristotle considered that the first thing necessary to ensure this was that the state must not be too large. He believed that the greatness of a state was not determined by the size of its territory or the number of its population, but that though a certain size and certain numbers helped to make a state dignified and noble, unless these were combined with good law and order, the state was not great. States, he said, were like animals and plants or things made by human art which, if they are too large, lose their true nature and are spoilt for use. But how is one to know when the limit in size and population has been reached? Is there any test by which it can be discovered whether a state has grown or is in danger of growing too large?

Aristotle answered this question by saying that the state must be large enough to include opportunities for all the variety and richness of what he called the "good life," but not so large that the citizens could not see it or think of it in their minds as one whole of which they knew all the parts. He also thought it necessary that the character of all citizens should be well-known, an impossibility in too large a community, but how else, he asked, could men elect their magistrates wisely?

The duty of the State was, then, to ensure the possibility of a "good life" to all its citizens. What was the Greek ideal of citizenship? First of all, every citizen was expected to take a direct and personal share in all the affairs of the State. To the Greek there was no separation between private and public life, all things concerning the State were his affairs, and it was expected that everyone should have an opinion of his own, that he should think clearly on all matters of common interest and not allow himself to be swayed by his feelings without honestly thinking the matter out, and to a Greek, thinking meant straight thinking, the power to know right from wrong, to judge justly without prejudices or passion, to separate the important from the unimportant, and to follow undismayed wherever the truth might lead.

This belief in the duty of the citizen to be personally active in the affairs of the State tended to keep the State small, for if every citizen was to attend the meetings of the Assembly, the latter must be of such a size that everyone could be heard if he desired to speak, and it was necessary that a very short journey should bring the country-dweller into the city to attend to the State business, for frequent journeys and long absences from his farm or his flocks would be impossible for the countryman.

Further, the Greeks believed that wealth was allowed to a man only as a trust. Certain privileges and rights came to him because of its possession, but they were privileges and rights that required of their owner distinct duties. The more a man had, the more did the State require of him; he had to give his time to the making of laws, his wealth built ships, bore the expense of public festivals, adorned the city with beautiful buildings, it was spent not on himself alone, but shared with his fellow citizens, and given to that which was their common interest. This resulted in a passionate devotion of every Greek to his city, for every individual had a definite share in some way or other in the making of it, and by the sacrifice of his life in times of danger, he proved again and again that he was in very truth ready to die for it.

The ideal city demanded very high standards of her citizens, and no Greek State attained these perfectly. But in their search for what they conceived to be the highest perfection, the Greeks found out truths both concerning government and the real meaning of citizenship that have remained one of the priceless possessions of mankind.

SPARTA

Of all the city-states in Greece, two stand out from the others as having played the leading part in Greek history. These two are Athens, which most nearly approached the ideal city-state, and Sparta, the foremost military state in Greece.

Sparta was the chief city in the peninsula in the south of Greece called the Peloponnese, or the Land of Pelops, one of the ancient mythical heroes of that land. During the period of the Greek migrations, the Peloponnese was probably the last district to be settled, and the tribes which came down into it were called the Dorians. They invaded Laconia, of which the chief city was Sparta, and settled it and the surrounding country. Only the citizens of the city itself were called Spartans; those who owed allegiance to the city, but who lived in the country outside were known as Lacedaemonians.

Unlike most other Greek cities, which were well fortified and defended by a citadel built on high ground, Sparta, "low-lying among the caverned hills," had grown out of a group of villages and had no walls. But although there were no outward signs of security, Sparta had the mightiest warriors in Greece ready to defend it to the utmost. Lycurgus, the wise man of Sparta, was once consulted as to whether it would not be a wise thing to build a wall round the city, and he answered those who came to him with the words: "The city is well fortified which hath a wall of men instead of brick."

The Spartans were always afraid of attack from their slaves. These had been the former inhabitants of the land and had been conquered and made slaves by the Spartans. These slaves were called Helots; they were severely and often cruelly treated by their masters, and were always ready to revolt when opportunity came. This was one of the reasons that made the Spartans spend more time than other Greeks in military training. This common danger also had the result of drawing all Spartans very closely together, and of making them subordinate all other interests to the supreme duty of protecting the state.

THE LAWS OF LYCURGUS

The Spartans always held Lycurgus (died 720 BCE) to have been their great lawgiver, though they never agreed as to when he lived. It is probable that the laws were not made by one single lawgiver, but that many wise men, whose names were unknown to later generations, had helped to create the laws over a long period of time. As Lycurgus was the wise man whose name was known to the Spartans, they came to look back to him as their only lawgiver, because it was by the government he was supposed to have established and the laws he made that Sparta became so great a state. He was the brother of a King of Sparta who died leaving a child as his heir. Everyone thought that Lycurgus would take the opportunity to seize the throne and make himself King, but he declared that he would only rule until his nephew should be old enough to become King. Some people, however, would not believe this, and plots were made against his life. This decided Lycurgus to leave Sparta for a time and to visit some

other countries, with the intention of learning things from them
that might be of use to his own land.

On his way home he went to Delphi to consult Apollo, and
the oracle called him "beloved of God," and said to him:

Lo, thou art come, O Lycurgus, to this rich shrine of my temple,
Beloved thou by Zeus and by all who possess the abodes of Olympus.
Whether to call thee a god, I doubt, in my voices prophetic, God or a
man, but rather a god I think, O Lycurgus.

Herodotus: *Histories*, Book I

The oracle then went on to say "that his prayers were heard,
that his laws should be the best, and the commonwealth which
observed them the most famous in the world."

On his return to Sparta, the first thing Lycurgus did was to
reform the government. This was now to consist of three parts:
the Kings, the Senate or Council, and the Assembly. Sparta had
always had two Kings at a time, who succeeded each other from
father to son. It was they who had the right of commanding the
army in war, they were always accompanied by a bodyguard of
specially picked men, at the public sacrifices and games they
had special seats of honour, and at all banquets and feasts
double portions of everything were served to them. When it was
necessary for the State to consult the oracle, it was one of the
Kings who decided on the messenger to be sent.

The Senate or Council consisted of the two Kings who were
members by right of their birth, and of twenty-eight other men who
were elected as Senators for life. Every candidate had to be sixty
years old, for Lycurgus believed that until a man had reached that
age, he was not wise enough nor fit enough to be entrusted with

authority over his countrymen. The duties of the Senate were to prepare all the laws and matters of public interest which were to be brought before the general Assembly; it acted as a court of justice for criminal cases, and its deliberations carried great weight.

Every Spartan citizen over thirty years of age was a member of the Assembly. It was the duty of the Spartans in the Assembly to give or withhold approval of all the matters brought before them by the Senate. It was they who elected the Senators and all other magistrates, and they declared war and made peace. In spite of this Assembly of citizens, the government of Sparta was really in the hands of the Senate, for the members of the Assembly might not discuss the laws submitted for their approval, but only ratify or reject them. At no time were the ordinary citizens given much opportunity to speak at length in public. The Spartans did not like long speeches, and Lycurgus believed that no one should be allowed to talk much unless he could say a great deal that was useful and to the point in a few words. This way of talking became so characteristic of the men of Laconia, that it was called by their name, and even today speech that is short and sharp and to the point is called *laconic*.

Long after the death of Lycurgus, another special body of men was elected to help in the government. These men were called Ephors, and there were five of them. It was their business to watch the conduct of the Kings, to see that the laws were all carried out and that order and discipline were maintained in the state. Probably no other Greek state would have submitted to such oversight, but the Spartans were well-disciplined and did not look upon such an office as one that interfered in any way with their personal freedom. Plato, writing long after of their authority, said that it was, "exceedingly like that of a tyrant."

CUSTOMS IN SPARTA

Having established the government, Lycurgus next set himself to introduce what he considered good customs amongst the Spartans. The first thing he did was to re-distribute the land amongst the citizens. He found that some were very rich and others poor, and he determined that they should all live together sharing in everything alike. So he divided the land into lots and distributed it equally amongst all the citizens.

During his travels in other parts of the world, Lycurgus had had opportunities to compare rich states with poor ones, and he had concluded that the richest were not always the best governed, and that wealth did not always bring happiness. He was determined that the Spartans should become good soldiers and that they should be great in war, for he believed that simple habits and simplicity of living were more easily acquired by a nation of warriors than by one devoted only to peace. To this end he wanted to have neither rich nor poor in Sparta, but that all should be alike. Lycurgus, however, was wise enough to know that some people would always manage to make more money or to save more than others, so instead of dividing up all the money in the state equally between everyone, he commanded that all gold and silver coin should be called in, and that money made of iron, which had little worth, should be used as currency. Not only did this prevent any one man from becoming too rich, but it lessened the crime of theft in Sparta, for no one would want to steal what was of no value.

Everything needed in their houses had to be made by the Spartans themselves, with only the simplest tools, and the houses were roughly built. As a result, all Spartans grew accustomed to the plainest and simplest surroundings.

The last law made by Lycurgus to ensure simplicity of living was that all Spartan men and youths should eat at common dining-tables, and they were only allowed to eat such food as was permitted by the law. Each table seated about fifteen men, who shared in providing the food; each of them was "bound to bring in monthly a bushel of meal, eight gallons of wine, five pounds of cheese, two and a half pounds of figs and some very small sum of money to buy flesh and fish with." All the food was prepared in a very simple manner.

It was the custom that at any one table, only those should sit who were friendly to each other. When a newcomer wanted to join a certain table, all those already seated at it voted as to whether they would have him or not. An urn was passed round the table and everyone present dropped into it a small ball of bread. Those who voted for the newcomer dropped their balls without altering their shape, those who voted against him flattened the ball with their fingers before placing it in the urn. One flat ball was enough to exclude a man from the table.

SPARTAN EDUCATION

Lycurgus was determined that every Spartan should be so trained that he might become a good soldier, and some of his most important laws concerned the education of children. As soon as a child was born, he was carried to

the elders of the tribe to which he belonged; their business it was carefully to view the infant, and if they found it stout and well-made, they gave order for its rearing, but if they found it puny and ill-shaped, ordered it to be taken to a cavern on Mount Taygetus, where it was left to perish, for they thought it neither for the good of the child itself, nor for the public interest that it should be brought up, if it did not, from the very outset, appear made to be healthy and vigorous.

Plutarch: *Life of Lycurgus*

At the age of seven, Spartan boys left their homes and their mothers, and the State took charge of the rest of their education. Its chief goal was to make them good Spartan subjects and to teach them to endure pain and conquer in battle. As they grew older, Spartan boys were taught to undergo all kinds of hardships. They wore very little clothing, and were forced to steal their food. If they were caught, they were not only punished with whipping, but hunger too, for they were then reduced to their ordinary allowance, which was purposely kept very small, in order to force them to use cunning and skill if they wanted to add to it.

In every way the Spartan youths as they grew up were severely disciplined. Every year the older boys were whipped in public before the altar of Artemis, in order to teach them to endure pain without crying out, and it is said that some boys died under this whipping rather than utter a complaint.

Not very much time was spent by the boys in learning to read and write; most of their education was given to their gymnastic training, to running, jumping, boxing and wrestling, and to every kind of exercise that would fit them to be brave and hardy soldiers. They learnt some music, chiefly singing, but they only sang such songs as would put life and spirit into them, and their battle songs were sung with great enthusiasm.

During a war, the Spartan young men were treated a little less severely than when in training at home. They were allowed to curl and adorn their hair, to have costly arms and fine clothes. They had better clothes, too, and their officers were not so strict with them. They marched out to battle to the sound of music. "It was at once a magnificent and terrible sight to see them march on to the tune of their flutes, without any disorder in their ranks, any discomposure in their minds or change in their countenance, calmly and cheerfully moving with the music to the deadly fight."

Spartan discipline did not end when the boys and youths had become men. No one could live the life he chose; the city was a sort of camp in which each man took his share of provisions, and served the interest of his own country rather than his own ends.

The girls were educated at home, but, like the boys, they were given a gymnastic training, and they learned to run and wrestle, to throw the quoit and dart, and to be as strong and brave as their brothers. As the Spartan boys were trained to become good soldiers, ready to die for Sparta, so were the girls trained to become good wives and mothers of Spartan men, and if they could not themselves die for their country, to be willing to sacrifice those whom they loved the best. The Spartans held their women in great honour; they listened to their counsel and often acted upon it. A lady of another city once said to a Spartan, "You are the only women in the world who can rule men." "With good reason," was the answer, "for we are the only women who bring forth men."

Having established all these laws and customs, Lycurgus forbade the Spartans to travel, for he was afraid that contact with foreign people would teach them bad habits and make them discontented with their simple way of living.

At last the time came when Lycurgus felt that his laws and customs were firmly established, and that they were all familiar to the people, but he was afraid that after his death they might be changed. So he called a special Assembly of the people together and told them that everything was well-established, but that there was still one matter on which he would like to consult the oracle. Before he departed on this journey, he made the two Kings, the Senate and the whole Assembly take a solemn oath that they would observe his laws without the least alteration until his return. When he asked the god Apollo whether his laws were good and sufficient for the happiness and virtue of his people, the oracle answered that the laws were excellent, and that the state which kept them should be greatly renowned. Lycurgus sent this oracle in writing to Sparta, and then having once more offered a solemn sacrifice, he took leave of his friends, and in order not to release the Spartans from the oath they had taken, he put an end to his own life, thus binding them to keep his laws for ever. Nor was he deceived in his hopes, for Sparta continued to be one of the greatest of the Greek states, as long as it submitted the laws of Lycurgus.

THE RISE OF ATHENS

Athens was the most beautiful city in Greece. It grew up at the foot of the high rock, which in the earliest times was the citadel that defended the city, known as the Acropolis. The Acropolis had very strong walls, and the main entrance was guarded by nine gates, which must have made it almost impossible for an enemy to take, and there was a well within the fortress, so that there was always water for those who defended it. But history has told us almost nothing about the mighty lords who built this fortress or about the life of the people over whom they ruled.

According to legend, the earliest rulers of Athens were Kings, and of these one of the first was Cecrops. All kinds of stories gathered round his name, and it was believed that he was not altogether human, but a being who had grown out of the earth and was half-man and half-serpent. It was when he was King that the contest took place as to whether Athena, the Goddess of Wisdom, or Poseidon, Lord of the Sea, should be the special guardian of the city. The victory was awarded to Athena, who, taking her spear, thrust it into the ground, whereupon an olive tree marvellously appeared. Poseidon gave the horse as his gift to Athens, and legend adds that, striking the rock with his trident, he brought forth clear salt water, which he also gave to the Athenians. For all time the olive was associated not only with Athena, but with Attica and Athens her city, and to the Athenian, the sea became almost like a second home.

EARLY ATHENS

The ancient kings of Athens claimed descent from the gods. They were not only the lawgivers, but they acted as judges, as chief priests, and in time of war as generals. All who were oppressed had the right to appeal to the judgment seat of the King and his decisions were final. Though the King was the supreme ruler, there were assemblies of the chief men, always called the Elders, and of the People, who met whenever the King called them together. These gatherings are important, not because of any real power they possessed in early times, for they only met to hear what the King intended to do and never to discuss, but because it was from these assemblies that the power of the people to govern themselves developed.

The greatest of the early Kings was Theseus, he who slew the Minotaur and freed Athens from paying tribute to Minos the Sea-King of Crete. His greatest claim to be held in the remembrance of his countrymen was that it was believed to have been Theseus who united all Attica under the leadership of Athens. Before this time all the towns and villages in Attica had been independent, but he "gathered together all the inhabitants of Attica into one town, and made them one people of one city ... and gave the name of Athens to the whole state" (Plutarch: *Life of Theseus*). Legend tells of him that he was good and merciful to all who were in need, and a protector of all who were oppressed, but he offended the gods in some way, and died in exile far from Athens.

THE RULE OF THE FEW: THE OLIGARCHY

It is not known with any certainty how long the rule of the Kings lasted in Athens, but they seem to have slowly lost their power and at last other magistrates were appointed to help them rule. The earliest Kings had been hereditary rulers; when they became less powerful, though they were no longer the sole rulers of Athens, these hereditary Kings still kept their office for life. Later they ruled for life but were elected; the next change made was to elect a new king every ten years, and at last the greatest change of all took place when the old office of King was done away with, and the power that had once been in the hands of one man was entrusted to three: the Archon, a Greek title meaning *ruler*, who was the chief representative of the State and who gave his name to the year (in which he held office), the King-Archon, who was the chief priest and who had authority over all the sacrifices offered by the State, and the Polemarch, or War-Archon, who was the chief general. Six other archons were also elected whose duty it was to assist the others and to see that the laws of the State were obeyed.

Not everyone could be an Archon; only men from noble families could be elected, and so the power passed into the hands of a few men. The rule of a few is called an *oligarchy*, and it was the second step the Athenians took on their way to be a self-governing community.

At first this rule was good, for by experience the nobles learnt a great deal about the art of governing; they realized that order was better than disorder in a state, and they set high standards of devotion to public duty. But the nobles all belonged to one class of people, they were the best educated and the more wealthy, and instead of using their advantages of position and education and wealth as a trust for the good of the whole state (the ideal developed in later years by the Athenians), they grew to consider these things their own exclusive property and they became very narrow and intolerant. They considered themselves in every way superior to the common people, and began to make laws which benefited themselves alone, ignoring the rights of others, especially those of the poor.

Now the nobles had acquired their power because of their opposition to the rule of one man, but when the authority had been placed in their hands, they proved themselves equally unable to be just towards all, and their rule became as intolerant as that of the Kings. Then it was that their authority was questioned in its turn, and the people began to ask each other questions. What is the difference, they asked, between rich and poor, between the noble and the plain man, between the freeman and the slave? Who, they asked, are citizens, and what does it mean to be a citizen? The more the people questioned, the greater grew the oppression and injustice of the nobles, and conditions in Athens grew very bad. Many things helped to create this spirit of discontent: there had been wars, the harvests had been bad and famine had resulted, and there were very harsh laws which allowed debtors who could not pay their debts to sell themselves as slaves. Quarrels arose, and more and more the people questioned as to the justice of all this.

SOLON: THE WISE MAN OF ATHENS

It was at this time of confusion and distress that Solon (c. 630–560 BCE), one of the Seven Wise Men of Greece, appeared. By birth he was a noble, but he was a poor man and in the early part of his life he had been a merchant.

Just before this time Athens had been at war with Megara, a neighbouring state, over the possession of Salamis, which had formerly belonged to Athens, an island so near the Athenian harbour that it was absolutely necessary that it should belong to Athens. But the war had been long and unsuccessful, and no victory had been gained by either side. The Athenians were so "tired with this tedious and difficult war that they made a law that it should be death for any man, by writing or speaking, to assert that the city ought to endeavour to recover the island." Solon felt this to be a great disgrace, and knowing that thousands of Athenians would follow, if only one man were brave enough to lead, he composed some fiery verses which he recited in the market place.

> I come as a herald, self-sent, from Salamis, beautiful island,
> And the message I bring to your ears, I
>   have turned it into a song.
>
> Country and name would I change, rather
>   than all men should say,
> Pointing in scorn, "There goes one of the
>   cowardly, lazy Athenians,
> Who let Salamis slip through their fingers,
>   when it was theirs for a blow!"
>
> On then to Salamis, brothers! Let us
>   fight for the beautiful island,
> Flinging afar from us, ever, the weight of unbearable shame.

Poem of Solon, translated by Leslie White Hopkinson

Only parts of these verses have come down to us, but they so inspired the Athenians that it was determined to make one more effort to regain Salamis, and this time they were successful. Salamis was recovered, but conditions in Athens remained as unhappy as before. Solon was now held in such high honour that he was elected Archon in 594 BCE.

The first thing Solon did was to relieve the debtors. He did this by cancelling all debts and by setting free all who were slaves for debt, and by forbidding by law any Athenian to pledge himself, his wife or his children as a security for debt. This brought such relief to the state that the act was celebrated by a festival called the "Casting off of Burdens."

Solon wanted to bring order into the distracted city he loved, for he held that order was one of the greatest blessings a state could have, so he set to work to reform the government of the state, to reduce the power of the nobles and to give justice to the people. "First, he repealed all Draco's laws." (Draco had been an earlier lawgiver in Athens, whose laws were notorious for their severity, and for the harshness of their punishments – many offences were subject to the death penalty.)

Solon reformed the government of the state in such a way, that even the poorest citizens had political rights. They could not all be Archons, but Athens, like Sparta and other Greek states, had a general Assembly of the people, and they could all vote at this, and they could all take part in electing the magistrates. Whilst recognizing the rights of the poorer citizens, Solon believed in preserving a certain part of the power of the nobles, and he arranged the taxation and public service to the state in such a way that the greater the wealth of a man and the higher his position, the more the state demanded of him, both in service and money. Solon himself said of these laws:

I gave to the mass of the people such
rank as befitted their need,
I took not away their honour, and I
granted nought to their greed;
While those who were rich in power, who in
wealth were glorious and great,
I bethought me that naught should befall them
unworthy their splendour and state;
So I stood with my shield outstretched,
and both were safe in its sight,
And I would not that either should triumph, when
the triumph was not with the right.

Poem of Solon, from *Aristotle on*
the *Athenian Constitution*

Solon did not please everyone with his laws, and when

some came to him every day, to commend or dispraise them, and
to advise, if possible, to leave out, or put in something, and desired
him to explain, and tell the meaning of such and such a passage, he,
knowing that it was useless, and not to do it would get him ill will,
it being so hard a thing, as he himself says, in great affairs to satisfy
all sides, bought a trading vessel, and having obtained leave for ten
years' absence, departed, hoping that by that time his laws would have
become familiar.

Plutarch: *Life of Solon*

He stayed away the ten years and then returned to Athens.
He took no further part in public affairs, but was reverenced by
all and honoured until his death.

THE TYRANTS

Athens **did not attain** political freedom without a struggle. During this period of change, attempts were made from time to time by powerful leaders to get the rule entirely into their own hands. These leaders who wanted to seize the power and rule alone were called by the Greeks *Tyrants*. There was always the danger that such a ruler, with no authority in the state to control him, would become harsh, and oppressive, but this was not always the case. Though the rule of one man alone is never the best kind of rule, some of the Greek Tyrants made a real contribution to the states they governed. They were generally well-educated men, who encouraged art and literature; they were always ambitious men, and they often dreamed of extending their power beyond the limits of their own state, and though it was a purely personal and selfish ambition, the efforts at realizing it brought the Greeks into contact with things which had hitherto lain beyond their horizon, for in the Age of the Tyrants, no Greek had yet dreamed dreams or seen visions of empire.

A man was not always successful in his efforts to become a Tyrant. About forty years before Solon was made Archon, Cylon, a rich Athenian, of good family and popular as a winner at Olympia, tried to seize the power. He consulted the oracle, which told him to make the attempt at the time of the great festival of Zeus. He took this, as all Greeks would, as meaning the Olympic Games, so he waited until the time came for them, and then he and his friends attacked the Acropolis and actually took possession of the citadel. But it seemed that the oracle, giving one of those answers of which the meaning was uncertain, had referred to the festival held in honour of Zeus near Athens and not to that at Olympia, and Cylon's attempt was unsuccessful. Some of the conspirators fled, and others took refuge in the Temple of Athena. Here they were safe, for no one would dare touch anyone who had placed himself under the protection of the goddess in her sanctuary. But there was no food or drink in the temple, and as nobody brought them any, some of them died of hunger, and Cylon was forced to escape secretly.

Then the Archon told the remainder that if they would surrender, their lives should be spared. They consented, but not quite trusting the Archon, they fastened a long rope to the Statue of Athena and held it as they descended the hill, so that they might still be secure under the protection of the goddess. Half-way down the hill, however, the rope broke, and the Archon, declaring that this showed that Athena had withdrawn her protection, had the men put to death. This was looked upon as a great crime by the Athenians, for they considered it not only treachery, but also sacrilege, and it made the Archon many enemies. These declared that as a punishment for this act a curse would rest on him and on all his descendants. His family was descended from Alcmaeon, and so the curse was spoken of as the curse on the Alcmaeonids, and the enemies of this family always attributed to it any calamities that happened to the city.

The most famous Tyrant in Athens was Peisistratus. Whilst Solon was away on his travels, quarrels broke out again, and when he returned, though he took no active part in affairs, he tried by privately talking with the leaders of the various factions to restore peace, but he was unsuccessful. The smooth-talking and moderate Peisistratus gained the trust of the people, became very popular, and deceived people into thinking that he was only desirous of serving the state, when in reality he was doing all in his power to further his own ambition and to become sole ruler of Athens. In order to gain supporters, he appeared one day in the market place in his chariot, which was sprinkled with blood, and he himself appeared to be wounded. On being asked what was the matter, he said his enemies had inflicted these injuries upon him. One of his friends then declared that the Athenians should not permit such a thing to happen, and advised that a bodyguard of fifty men should accompany him to protect him from any further assault. This was done, whereupon with their help, Peisistratus took possession of the Acropolis. But his power was not great enough to hold it, and he and his followers were driven out of Athens.

Peisistratus soon returned, however, having thought of a curious plot by which he might deceive the Athenians into believing it to be the will of the gods that he should rule. During a festival, accompanied by a large number of youths, he entered Athens in his chariot, and at his side stood a tall and beautiful woman, dressed as Athena herself and carrying a shield and spear. The people shouted that the goddess herself had come from Olympus to show her favour to Peisistratus, and he was received as Tyrant. But again he was driven out by his enemies. He stayed away ten years, and then once more he collected an army and advanced on Athens. Once more he was successful and entered the city. This time no one opposed him, he became sole ruler and remained so until his death some ten years later.

Peisistratus showed himself to be a wise ruler; he improved the city and brought water into it by an aqueduct, and he built new roads. Along these roads, especially in places near springs and fountains, were placed small statues of Hermes, and on the pedestals under some of them verses were engraved, perhaps similar to the following lines, to cheer the traveller on his way:

> I, Hermes, by the grey sea-shore
>   Set where the three roads meet,
> Outside the wind-swept garden,
>   Give rest to weary feet;
> The waters of my fountain
>   Are clear and cool and sweet.

Written by Anyte, a poetess, probably in the fourth century BC

It was Peisistratus who made the law that men wounded in battle and the families of those who were killed should be cared for by the state. He built a new Temple to Athena and made her festival more splendid, and he had the ancient poems of Homer collected and written down, so that they might be more carefully preserved. But good ruler as he was, he was still a Tyrant, and during his rule the people were deprived of their right to govern themselves, but so long as he lived, no one opposed him.

GREEK COLONIES

The **Greeks** were a sea-faring, adventurous people. Their own land was small, but the islands of the Aegean formed stepping-stones, as it were, to the coast of Asia Minor, and the Aegean world was very familiar to the Greek sailor. Greek galleys were found in most ports, and the Greek trader became a formidable rival of the Phoenician.

As they sailed from island to island and on to the mainland, the Greeks came to realize that some of these places would make suitable homes, and by degrees they began to colonize them; that is to say, parties of settlers went from their mother-cities to found new homes overseas. Pioneers, adventurous explorers, had always gone out first and brought back reports of the new land. A suitable site required a good water supply, and fertile land where corn could be grown, and the vine and the olive cultivated. The settlers needed timber from which they could build their ships, and of course a good harbour was necessary. They also hoped to find friendly natives who would help them in their farm-work and who would in no way oppose them or interfere with their plans. The natives must have looked with eyes of wonder upon the newly arrived Greeks. The only foreign traders they knew were the Phoenicians, and they came only to trade, to exploit the people and to exhaust the resources of the place in order to gain gold.

THE FOUNDING OF A COLONY

All kinds of considerations took the Greeks over the sea to found new homes for themselves: some of them were discontented with their government and wanted to go where they could establish a new one; some had experienced overcrowding in their home cities, which created difficulties in the supply of food; many thought a new land would give them greater and better opportunities; others found that the trade of the colonies was a source of wealth; and others went just for the love of adventure.

Whenever a body of men decided to sail away and found a colony, they first consulted the oracle at Delphi as to whether they would be successful, and whether Apollo approved of the place they had chosen and would bless their enterprise. They then chose a leader, whose name was always held in honour and handed down as the founder of the colony. On leaving the mother-city, the colonists went in procession to the Town Hall and there they received fire from the sacred hearth, which they took with them, and from which they kindled the fire on their own sacred hearth in their new home.

The Greek poet Euripides has described this Greek adventure over the sea, and the wonder of those who received the strangers:

> A flash of the foam, a flash of the foam,
>   A wave on the oarblade welling,
> And out they passed to the heart of the blue:
> A chariot shell that the wild waves drew.
> Is it for passion of gold they come,
>   Or pride to make great their dwelling?

Euripides: *Iphigenia in Tauris*, trans. G. Murray

These colonies were quite independent of the mother-city as far as government was concerned, but the colonists looked back to the home from which their race had sprung with great affection; wherever they went they were still Greeks, they spoke the Greek language and they worshipped the Greek gods.

Colonies were founded not only in the islands of the Aegean, but along the coasts of the Black Sea, which the Greeks called the Euxine. These latter colonies, of which Byzantium (the ancient name for Constantinople) was the greatest, became very important to the Greeks, for they supplied them with grain which grew abundantly on the northern shores, and with iron from the Hittite land in the South-East.

The greatest of all the colonies in the East were the Ionian colonies, those in the eastern part of the Aegean and on the coast of Asia Minor. The Greeks who colonized them were descended from the Ionian tribes who had settled in Greece, and so this whole region became known as Ionia. Herodotus tells us that the "Ionians had the fortune to build their cities in the most favourable position for climate and seasons of any men whom we know." Miletus was the greatest of the Ionian cities, and it developed a very rich civilization some time before the great days of Athens.

Great thinkers came out of Ionia. Thales, one of the Seven Wise Men of Greece, the philosopher and man of science, studied the heavens, and he foretold an eclipse of the sun in a certain year, which came to pass. The Babylonians before him had made similar studies, but he carried on their work and made greater advances. He questioned in his mind what his discoveries might mean, and for the first time in the world he declared that the movements of the sun and moon and stars were determined by laws, and that the eclipse of the sun was due to certain movements of the heavenly bodies, and had nothing to do with the anger of the Sun-God. This was the first step in away from superstition, and, it was Thales of Miletus and other Ionian philosophers in the sixth century BCE who first set people to thinking about the real meaning of the things they saw about them in the world of nature. What we to-day call science was born in Ionia more than two thousand years ago.

Another wise man of science who lived in Miletus was Anaximander. He was one of the earliest mapmakers, and he and Hecataeus, who wrote a Geography as a "text to Anaximander's map," were amongst the first thinkers who developed the science of Geography.

The Ionian colonies could claim poets as well as men of science. Chios is said to have been the birthplace of Homer, and Lesbos, one of the largest of the island colonies, was famous as the home of Sappho, not only the first woman whose poetry has come down to us, but one of the great poetesses of the world. Unfortunately we have only a few fragments of her poems.

> THE GIFTS OF EVENING
> *Thou, Hesper, bringest homeward all*
> *That radiant dawn sped far and wide,*
> *The sheep to fold, the goat to stall,*
> *The children to their mother's side.*
> **Poem of Sappho, tran. Sir Rennell**
> **Rodd in *Love, Worship and Death*.**

The face of Greece was turned towards the East, but adventurous spirits have always turned towards the unknown

West; they founded colonies in the south of Italy, and these became so flourishing that the whole region was known as Magna Graecia. These Greeks brought their writing, their art, and their poetry and planted them securely in the land that was one day to be ruled by a city, which was then only a little settlement at the foot of seven hills. Rome became mightier than Greece in the art of governing a great empire, and the day was to come when Rome would rule Greece, but would always acknowledge the teachings of Greece in the development of Roman civilization.

Other Greek colonies were founded at Syracuse in Sicily, and along the north coast of the Mediterranean to what is now Marseilles, and in the south a few were established along the shores of Africa to Naucratis in Egypt. The colonies in the south of Spain and along the north coast of Africa from the Pillars of Hercules to Carthage were in the hands of the Phoenicians, but by the end of the sixth century BCE the prevailing civilization in the Mediterranean was Greek.

IONIA AND LYDIA

The Ionian colonies occupied the coast land of Asia Minor, but the mainland behind them was the Kingdom of Lydia. For a long time the Ionians lived in peace, developing their science, thinking out their ideas, and growing in power. But at the beginning of the sixth century BCE a new race of kings came to the Lydian throne. They were vigorous and ambitious, and did not approve of the important coast towns with good harbours being in the hands of Greeks. So they attacked them, beginning with Miletus, which was besieged. The siege lasted eleven years, but the city did not surrender. At last the Lydians realized that Miletus was being saved by its harbour, and though it could get no food or supplies of any kind by land, everything needed was brought to the city by water. So the King of Lydia gave up the idea of conquering Miletus, and he made a treaty of peace with the Ionian city.

It was probably not only the impossibility of conquering a seaport that made the King of Lydia give up the siege of Miletus, but the knowledge that a war cloud had arisen in the east which was steadily drawing nearer his land. This was the army of the Medes, a nation which had already helped to destroy Assyria. Several battles took place with no very decisive result, but at length the two armies met in a battle

in which it happened, when the fight had begun, that suddenly the day became night. And this change of the day Thales the Milesian had foretold to the Ionians. The Lydians, however, and the Medes, when they saw that it had become night instead of day, ceased from their fighting and were much more eager both of them that peace should be made between them.

Herodotus: *Histories,* **Book I**

So peace was made, and soon after the King of Lydia died, and Croesus succeeded him.

Now the Ionian cities, when they saw their independence threatened, ought to have combined together and made a joint stand against their enemies, but each separate city so prized its independence and so feared anything that might even seem to lessen it, that they stood alone, and when Croesus, being at peace with the Medes, determined to get possession of these Ionian cities, he was able to attack them one by one and to overpower them. He allowed them to keep their own independent government, but he required them to pay him a regular yearly tribute. This was the first time in Greek history that Greeks had paid a tribute to anybody; before the reign of Croesus, all Greeks everywhere had been free. Croesus left a certain amount of independence to the Ionian cities, because of his admiration for the Greeks and their civilization. He sent rich and splendid gifts to Apollo, and in return was made a citizen of Delphi, and at the Pythian Games his envoys were given special seats of honour.

By this time Cyrus, the Mede, had become King of Persia, and Croesus watched his increasing power with great anxiety. He saw that war was bound to come, so he sent a message to the oracle at Delphi asking if he should march against the Persians. What Herodotus called a "deceitful" answer came back, that if he crossed the river Halys a great empire would be destroyed. Thinking, of course, that this meant the destruction of the Persian empire, Croesus crossed the river and met Cyrus in battle. The Lydians were famous for their horses, and horsemen were an important part of their army. Cyrus knew this, so he thought of a plan whereby he might defeat them. He ordered all the camels which were in the rear of his army carrying the provisions and baggage, to be unloaded and the camels brought to the front, and there well-armed men were mounted on them. He did this "because the horse has a fear of the camel and cannot endure either to see his form or to scent his smell; and so soon as the horses scented the camels and saw them, they galloped away to the rear, and the hopes of Croesus were at once brought to nought." (Herodotus, I.)

The Lydians were defeated and withdrew into Sardis, the capital. But after a short siege Cyrus took the city, and Croesus lost his kingdom. He did not want to fall into the hands of the Persians, so he had a great pyre erected, and after pouring out a libation to the gods, he mounted it and bade his slaves set it on fire that he might perish in the flames, rather than fall alive into the hands of his conqueror. But suddenly clouds arose in the sky and rain fell, extinguishing the flames. It was thought that this must be the doing of Apollo, to whom Croesus had always shown much honour, and hearing of it, Cyrus commanded that he should be taken down from the pyre and brought into his presence. "Croesus," he asked him, "what man was it who persuaded thee to march upon my land and so to become an enemy to me instead of a friend?" And Croesus answered,

O King, that I did this was to your gain and my loss, and the fault lies with the god of the Hellenes who led me to march against you with my army. For no one is so senseless as to choose of his own will war rather than peace, since in peace the sons bury their fathers, but in war the fathers bury their sons. It was the will, I suppose, of the gods that these things should come to pass thus.

Herodotus: *Histories*, Book I

Lydia was now added to the Persian Empire and only the Ionian cities were still independent. But even in the face of the great danger from Persia, they did not unite, and one by one Cyrus conquered them until Ionia had been reduced to subjection, and when the cities on the mainland had been conquered, then the Ionians in the islands submitted to Cyrus. This was how the Greeks who lived in Asia lost their independence, and became subject to the Great King of Persia.

PAUSANIAS' IONIA

This **excerpt** is from Pausanias' *Description of Greece*, Volume II, Book I, Chapter V:

The Ionians have a most magnificent country for the fruits of the earth, and temples such as there are nowhere else, the finest that of Ephesian Artemis for size and opulence, and next two to Apollo not quite finished, one at Branchidae in Milesia, the other at Claros in Colophonia. Two temples in Ionia were burnt down by the Persians, one of Hera in Samos, and one of Athene in Phocaea. They are still wonderful though the fire has passed upon them. And you would be delighted with the temple of Hercules at Erythrae, and with the temple of Athene at Priene, the latter for the statue of the goddess, the former for its great antiquity. And at Erythrae is a work of art unlike the most ancient of Aeginetan or Attic workmanship: its design is perfect Egyptian. It is the wooden raft on which the god sailed from Tyre in Phœnicia, why the people of Erythrae do not say. But to prove that it came into the Ionian sea they say it was moored at the promontory called Mid, which is on the mainland about half-way from the harbour of Erythrae to the island of Chios. And when this raft was at the promontory, the people of Erythrae and the Chians too had no small trouble in trying to get it on shore. At last a native of Erythrae, who got his living from the sea by catching fish, but had lost his eyesight through some disease, Phormio by name, dreamed that the women of Erythrae were to cut off their hair, and that the men making a rope out of this hair were to drag the raft ashore. The women who were citizens wouldn't hear of it: but all the women who were slaves of Thracian race, or who being free had yet to earn their own living, allowed their hair to be cut off, and so at last the people of Erythrae got the raft to shore. So Thracian women alone are allowed to enter the temple of Hercules, and the rope made of hair is still kept by the people of Erythrae. They also say that the fisherman recovered his sight, and saw for the rest of his life. At Erythrae there is also a temple of Athene Polias, and a huge wooden statue of the goddess seated on a throne, in one hand a distaff in the other a globe. We conjecture it to be by Endœus from several circumstances, especially looking at the workmanship of the statue inside, and the Graces and Seasons in white marble, which used to stand in the open air. The people of Smyrna also had in my time a temple of Aesculapius between the mountain Coryphe and the sea which is unmixed with any other water.

Ionia besides the temples and the salubrity of the air has several other things worthy of record. Near Ephesus is the river Cenchrius, and the fertile Mount Pion, and the well Halitaea. And in Milesia is the well Biblis: of the love passages of Biblis they still sing. And in Colophonia is the grove of Apollo, consisting of ash trees, and not far from the grove the river Ales, the coldest river in Ionia. And the people of Lebedus have baths which are both wonderful and useful to men. The people of Teos also have baths at the promontory Macria, some natural consisting of sea-water that bursts in at a crevice of the rock, others built at wonderful cost. The people of Clazomenae also have baths. Agamemnon is honoured there. And there is a grotto called the grotto of Pyrrhus' mother, and they have a tradition about Pyrrhus as a shepherd. The people of Erythrae have also a place called Chalcis, from which the third of their tribes takes its name, where there is a promontory extending to the sea, and some sea baths, which of all the baths in Ionia are most beneficial to men. And the people of Smyrna have the most beautiful river Meles and a cave near its springs, where they say Homer wrote his Poems. The Chians also have a notable sight in the tomb of Œnopion, about whose deeds they have several legends. The Samians too on the way to the temple of Hera have the tomb of Rhadine and Leontichus, which those are accustomed to visit who are melancholy through love. The wonderful things indeed in Ionia are not far short of those in Greece altogether.

THE PERSIAN WARS

The **Persians** were hardy warriors, accomplished horsemen and skilled warriors with bow and spear who overran the Near East from Egypt to the River Oxus. Their rule of conquered lands was savagely repressive, and they accumulated booty and tribute from subject states all over Asia. They had established tyrants in all the Greek cities, and required the assistance of their soldiers and sailors in their wars, things which were very bitter to the freedom-loving Greeks. The allied Greek resistance to Persian invasion from 490–479 BCE was a defining moment in Greek history, confirming to the Greeks that their free institutions were infinitely superior to Persian despotism and reinforcing a sense of Greek unity. The Battle of Marathon when the outnumbered Greek defenders stood, undaunted, against might of the Persians, was a decisive defeat, and a defining moment in the formation of a confident and powerful Greece. Ultimately the Persian Wars saw the emergence of the two great powers of fifth-century-BCE Greece: Sparta, which stood at the head of the Peloponnesian League and the growing naval power of Athens.

DARIUS AND THE IONIAN REVOLT

When **Darius** had become King, he determined, like the Great Kings before him, to add yet more lands to his empire, and so made ready an army which was to invade Scythia, the region north of the Black Sea. As the Persians themselves were not naturally sailors, the Greeks in the Ionian cities were forced to send a large number of ships to the help of this expedition.

Darius and his army set out, and, arriving at the River Ister (now known as the Danube), were joined by the Ionian ships. Here Darius commanded that a bridge of boats should be built, and then taking a cord in which he tied sixty knots, he called the Ionian leaders together and instructed them that, each day he was in Scythia, they should untie a knot. If he did not return before all the knots were untied they should sail back to their own lands.

Scythia was a land totally unknown to the Persians, and strange tales were told in after years of the adventures of the King and his army. The Scythians were a nomad people, and they believed themselves to be invincible. When they heard that Darius was in their land with the intention of conquering it, they planned not to fight a pitched battle openly, but to "retire before the Persians and to drive away their cattle from before them, choking up with earth the wells and the springs of water by which they passed and destroying the grass from off the ground." For some time Darius pursued this mysterious people, but he could never come up with them. When he finally was able to confront the King of the Scythians, and demand why he was not willing to fight he received the following answer:

"My case, O Persian, stands thus: Never yet did I fly because I was afraid, either before this time from any other man, or now from thee; nor have I done anything different now from that which I was wont to do also in time of peace: and as to the cause why I do not fight *with thee at once, this also I will declare unto thee. We have neither cities nor land sown with crops, about which we should fear lest they be captured or laid waste, and so join battle more speedily with you; but know this that we have sepulchres in which our fathers are buried; therefore come now, find out these and attempt to destroy them, and ye shall know then whether we shall fight with you for the sepulchres or whether we shall not fight. Before that, however, we shall not join battle with thee. About fighting let so much as has been said suffice; but as to masters, I acknowledge none over me but Zeus my ancestor and Hestia the Queen of the Scythians. To thee then in place of gifts of earth and water I shall send such things as it is fitting that thou shouldest receive; and in return for thy saying that thou art my master, for that I say, woe betide thee."*

Herodotus: *Histories*, Book IV

The King of Scythia sent gifts to Darius as he had promised, strange and mysterious gifts. He sent him a bird, a mouse, a frog and five arrows. At first the Persian could not imagine what these gifts might mean, but one of his wise men interpreted them as meaning, according to Herodotus, that "unless ye become birds and fly up to the heaven, or become mice and sink down under the earth, or become frogs and leap into the lakes, ye shall not return back home, but shall be smitten by these arrows."

The Scythians continued to lead the Persians from place to place in this strange campaign, until at last they brought them back again to the Ister where the Ionians were guarding the bridge of boats. The Scythians arrived first, and they tried to persuade the Ionians to break up the bridge, so that Darius would find no means of escape and would then fall into their hands. Some of the Greeks were in favour of doing this, but the Tyrant of Miletus, who wanted to keep on good terms with Darius, advised against such treachery and his word prevailed. In order to get the Scythians away, they pretended, by moving a few of the boats, that they were going to destroy the bridge, but when Darius came, after a moment's fear that he had been deserted, he found the bridge still there, and he crossed safely and returned to his own land.

When Darius learned that it was owing to the advice of the Tyrant of Miletus that the bridge had been saved, he sent for him and praised him highly for what he had done, telling him he knew him to be a man of understanding and well-disposed towards him, and that in consequence he wished him to go with him to Susa, to eat at his table and to be his counsellor. Darius did this because in reality he distrusted him and preferred that he should be near him in Susa, where his movements could be watched.

In the meanwhile a kinsman of this Tyrant had been left in his place at Miletus, and when a rebellion broke out in Naxos, he undertook to put it down, hoping that this would bring him favour from the King. Unfortunately for him, he was unsuccessful, and as he very much feared the wrath of the King, he decided that as he could not put down the rebellion, he would himself join it. The Greeks in Miletus were more than willing to revolt from the Persian yoke and they were joined by other Ionian cities. But they did not feel strong enough to stand alone against Persia, so they sent ambassadors to Greece asking for help from their kinsmen there.

Sparta was asked first. The ambassador appealed to the King and told him that the Ionians felt it was a disgrace not only to themselves but also to the Spartans, who were looked upon as the leaders of all men of Greek birth, that they should be slaves instead of freemen. He then went on to describe the Persians whom he might conquer, the wealth of their land and all the benefits that would come to him if he would help the Ionians to become free:

"Marvel not, Cleomenes, at my earnestness in coming hither, for the case is this. – That the sons of the Ionians should be slaves instead of free is a reproach and a grief most of all indeed to ourselves, but of all others most to you, inasmuch as ye are the leaders of Hellas. Now therefore I entreat you by the gods of Hellas to rescue from slavery the Ionians, who are your own kinsmen: and ye may easily achieve this, for the Barbarians are not valiant in fight, whereas ye have attained to the highest point of valour in that which relates to war: and their fighting is of this fashion, namely with bows and arrows and a short spear, and they go into battle wearing trousers and with caps on their heads. Thus they are easily conquered. Then again they who occupy that continent have good things in such quantity as not all the other nations of the world together possess; first gold, then silver and bronze and embroidered garments and beasts of burden and slaves; all which ye might have for yourselves, if ye so desired. And the nations moreover dwell in such order one after the other as I shall declare: – the Ionians here; and next to them the Lydians, who not only dwell in a fertile land, but are also exceedingly rich in gold and silver," – and as he said this he pointed to the map of the Earth, which he carried with him engraved upon the tablet, – "and here next to the Lydians," continued Aristagoras, "are the Eastern Phrygians, who have both the greatest number of sheep and cattle of any people that I know, and also the most abundant crops. Next to the Phrygians are the Cappadokians, whom we call Syrians; and bordering upon them are the Kilikians, coming down to this sea, in which lies the island of Cyprus here; and these pay *five hundred talents to the king for their yearly tribute. Next to these Kilikians are the Armenians, whom thou mayest see here, and these also have great numbers of sheep and cattle. Next to the Armenians are the Matienians occupying this country here; and next to them is the land of Kissia here, in which land by the banks of this river Choaspes is situated that city of Susa where the great king has his residence, and where the money is laid up in treasuries. After ye have taken this city ye may then with good courage enter into a contest with Zeus in the matter of wealth. Nay, but can it be that ye feel yourselves bound to take upon you the risk of battles against Messenians and Arcadians and Argives, who are equally matched against you, for the sake of land which is not much in extent nor very fertile, and for confines which are but small, though these peoples have neither gold nor silver at all, for the sake of which desire incites one to fight and to die, – can this be, I say, and will ye choose some other way now, when it is possible for you easily to have the rule over all Asia?" Aristagoras spoke thus, and Cleomenes answered him saying: "Guest-friend from Miletos, I defer my answer to thee until the day after to-morrow."*

Herodotus: *Histories*, Book V

The King told him he would think it over and give him an answer on a day following. When the day came, the King asked the ambassador from Miletus how many days' journey it was from the sea of the Ionians to the residence of the King. Now it must be remembered that no part of Greece was far from the coast, and that no Greek, not even a Spartan who was a soldier rather than a sailor, was happy if he felt out of reach of the sea. So the feelings of the Spartan King can be understood, when he was told that to reach the city of the King of Persia was a journey of three months from the sea. His mind was quickly made up. "Guest-friend from

Miletus," he said, "get thee away from Sparta before the sun has set; for thou speakest a word which sounds not well in the ears of the Lacedaemonians, desiring to take them a journey of three months away from the sea."

The ambassador then went to Athens, where he was more successful. The Athenians sent twenty ships to help the Ionians, and the Eretrians, out of gratitude for help once received from Miletus when they were in need, added five. With this assistance, the Greeks marched to Sardis and seized it. But a house accidentally caught fire, and the fire began to spread over the whole town. This gave the Persians time to rally from the surprise of the attack and they drove out the Greeks, who scattered in dismay. Some were overtaken and slain, and the rest retreated to their ships.

Darius was in Susa at this time, and the news of the burning of Sardis was taken to him there. He did not take much account of the Ionians who had taken part,

because he knew that they at all events would not escape unpunished for their revolt, but he enquired who the Athenians were; and when he had been informed, he asked for his bow, and having received it and placed an arrow upon the string, he discharged it upwards towards heaven, and as he shot into the air he said: "Zeus, that it may be granted me to take vengeance upon the Athenians!" Having so said he charged one of his attendants, that when dinner was set before the King he should say always three times: "Master, remember the Athenians."

Herodotus: *Histories*, **Book V**

Darius remembered the Athenians, but he had first to punish the Ionian cities for their share in the revolt. One by one he attacked them, and they fell before him, until at last only Miletus was left. The only hope of safety lay in the sea-defences, and all the ships the Ionians could collect were gathered at Lade, an island just outside the harbour of Miletus. Now the Ionians had copied many of the customs of their Lydian neighbours, and they were more luxurious and led softer lives than their kinsmen on the mainland. Efforts were made by one of the Greek leaders to make the Ionians drill and exercise themselves every day, that they might all be in good condition when the day of battle should come. For a time they submitted, but they were lazy and unaccustomed to such toil, and the hard work and exercise so exhausted them, that they declared they would prefer slavery to such hard work as was being forced upon them. So they refused to drill any more.

There could only be one result to this. The Persians gave battle and the Ionians were defeated, some of them even disgraced themselves by sailing away without fighting at all. The men of Chios refused to play the coward and fought to the end, but there were too few of them to turn the tide of battle and the Persians overcame them completely. Miletus was taken by storm, the city was destroyed by fire, the men were all put to death, and the women and children sent as slaves to Susa.

The news of the fall of Miletus was a terrible blow to the Greek world. Up to that time Miletus had been the greatest of the Greek cities – rich, not only in material wealth, but in all that concerned the intellectual life. It was, above all, a blow to the Athenians, for Athens and Miletus were closely bound by ties of kinship.

The Ionians had been punished to the utmost for daring to revolt from his power, and there was no fear that they would do it again. Darius was now free to remember the Athenians.

MARATHON

In 492 BCE Darius sent Mardonius, a general who was high in his favour, across the Hellespont with orders to march through Thrace and Macedonia, and having firmly secured their allegiance, to march on to Greece, where Athens and Eretria were to be severely punished for their share in the burning of Sardis. Darius had several reasons for this expedition: the punishment of Athens and Eretria was the one about which most was said, but as it never entered his mind that he could be defeated, Darius probably intended so to destroy the cities on the mainland that the Greeks in Ionia would see that it would be useless to rely on the help of their kinsmen should they ever think of another revolt, and so to punish the European Greeks that they would never dare to interfere again in the affairs of the Persian Empire. But underneath all these reasons were dreams of conquest. The Great King had visions of subduing the whole of Greece and of extending his empire into Europe.

Preparations were made and Mardonius set out. A fleet was to sail close to the coast and to keep in constant touch with the army. All went well until Mount Athos was reached and here a great storm arose; it was said that 300 ships were destroyed and more than 20,000 men perished.

The army fared little better, for it was attacked by some Thracian tribesmen, and though Mardonius forced them to submit to him, he suffered so much loss in the fighting, that as his fleet also had been almost entirely destroyed, he was obliged to depart back to Asia having gained no honour in this undertaking.

Two years went by, and then another expedition was planned. Before it started, Darius sent messengers to Athens and Sparta and other Greek states demanding of them earth and water, the symbols of submission to the Great King. Some states agreed to the demand, either because they were struck dumb with terror at the mere thought that the Great King might invade their land, or because they thought that he was certain to conquer and that by submitting at once they would secure themselves and their land from destruction. Athens and Sparta, however, refused uncompromisingly. The messengers were thrown by the Athenians into a pit, and by the Spartans into a well, and told that if they wanted earth and water they could get them for themselves. On hearing what had happened to his messengers, Darius gave orders to the generals to set out at once for Greece, and to punish every state which had refused submission by enslaving all the inhabitants and bringing them bound to Susa. In particular, Athens and Eretria, for their other misdeeds, were to receive the severest treatment. So the expedition started.

This time the Persian fleet sailed across the Aegean, touching at Naxos, the first of the Ionian cities that had revolted, and which now received its punishment by being burnt and its people enslaved. Then the Persians went on to Delos, where they offered sacrifices to Apollo, and from there they sailed to Eretria which they immediately attacked. The city held out for six days and then traitors within the walls opened the gates to the Persians who entered and took the city. They burnt it to the ground and carried off all the inhabitants into slavery. And so Eretria was punished for its share in daring to burn a city of the Great King.

News of these movements of the Persians had, of course, reached Athens, but up to this time the Athenians had not considered themselves vulnerable to dangerous consequences. But Eretria was not very far from Athens, and when the news of the utter destruction of this city arrived, the Athenians realized the full extent of their peril. Now Hippias, the exiled Tyrant, had taken refuge with the Persians, but he had never given up hope of one day returning to Athens. He was at this very time plotting with friends in the city, and the Persians, knowing this, hoped for their aid in taking Athens. So the Athenians were threatened with dangers both from within and without.

It is easy to imagine the dismay of the Athenians when they heard that Eretria had been destroyed, and that the Persians, the conquerors of the world, were even then on their way to Athens. How could they hope, with their small army, to stand against the great empire? Help must be had, and that quickly. To whom should they turn, if not to Sparta, the foremost military state in Greece, and which, should Athens fall, would be the next state attacked? Self-defence, if no other reason, would surely bring them with speed to Athens. So the Athenians sent Pheidippides, a swift runner, with a message imploring help. The distance from Athens to Sparta is a hundred and fifty miles, and the hours must have seemed very long to the Athenians as they waited for his return with the answer. But so swiftly did he run that he was back before they had dared expect him. He had reached Sparta in less than forty-eight hours, rushed into the midst of their Assembly with but scant ceremony, and passionately entreated them to come to the help of Athens.

But to this cry for help the Spartans gave but a cool answer. They would come, certainly, but must wait five days until the moon was full when it was their custom to sacrifice to Apollo, and to break this custom would be to slight the god. When the full moon had come, then they would send help to the Athenians. Pheidippides only waited long enough to receive the answer, and then with despair in his heart, he started back to Athens. Over the hills and the plains, through woods and across streams he raced, appealing in his heart to the gods to whom Athens had ever shown honour, yet who seemed to have deserted her in her utmost need. Was there no help? Suddenly he stopped; whom did he see, sitting in a cleft of a rock? It was Pan, the Goat-God.

According to Herodotus, the god spoke graciously and kindly to him, and bade Pheidippides go home and tell Athens to take heart, for Pan was on her side. If Pheidippides had run swiftly before, now he ran as if wings had been given to him. He burst upon the waiting Athenians who had not dared expect him so soon, with the news that Sparta indeed had failed them, but that Pan, mighty to save, would fight for them.

But now grave news was brought: the Persians were landing in Attica. It was September of the year 490 BCE, and the hot summer days had not yet passed away. The Athenians could not wait for the Spartans, they must go out alone and meet the foe. They marched twenty-four miles in the heat over a rough and rugged road, until they reached the plain of Marathon. There they found the Persians.

The Persians had probably never intended to fight at Marathon. They hoped that the friends of Hippias in Athens would in the end betray the city to them, and their plan in landing where they did was to bring the Athenian army away from the city, and if possible to keep it away, until they should have received the expected signal from the traitors. The plain of Marathon is surrounded by hills except where it slopes down to the sea. The Athenians occupied the stronger and higher positions, the Persians were encamped near the sea, and their ships were anchored close to the coast. For several days the armies watched each other and waited. The Athenians counted the days until the moon should be full, when there was hope that the Spartans might come; the Persians knew that every added day gave the conspirators more time to do their treacherous work in the city. And so both sides waited.

Suddenly help came to the Athenians from an unexpected quarter, help which cheered and inspirited them. Through a cloud of dust on one of the roads leading down into the plain, they saw the gleam of spears and helmets. It could not be the Spartans, for they would not come from that direction. As the men drew nearer, they were found to be an army from Plataea, a little city in Boeotia, to which, when some years before Thebes had threatened its independence, Athens had sent succour. Now, though not thought of by the Athenians as an ally, because it was small and not powerful, Boeotia had remembered those who had offered help in the hour of need, and had come down to Marathon to help Athens.

Miltiades was the Athenian general at Marathon. He knew why the Persians were waiting, and when messengers brought him word that they were embarking some of their men, he knew that this meant their intention to sail round to Athens, because the conspirators in the city were ready to act, so he gave the signal to attack. There were probably two Persians to every Greek, so the Greek army had been arranged in the best way to face these odds. The centre line was thin, but the wings were very strong. On the first onslaught from the Persians this centre gave way, but the wings immediately wheeled round and attacked the Persians with such force that these gave way before them and fled down to the shore. The Greeks pursued, and there was terrific fighting and slaughter. Seven of the Persian ships were destroyed by fire, but the others escaped. The Persians fled to these remaining ships, leaving over six thousand dead on the plain and quantities of rich plunder. They set sail for Athens, and knowing that the Athenian army was still on the plain of Marathon, they hoped to find the city undefended and that the traitors would open the gates to them. But the Athenians who had won at Marathon were not going to let their city fall into the hands of the enemy, so when they saw the Persian ships setting sail, wearied as they were with the strain of battle, they marched over the twenty-four miles of rough road to the defence of their beloved city, leaving only a small force behind to guard the bodies of the slain and to prevent thieves from carrying off the plunder.

On his return from Sparta, Pheidippides had been asked what reward should be given him for the race he had run. All he asked was to be allowed to fight for Athens. It was given him as he asked. He fought in the fight at Marathon, but when the victory had been gained, one more race was asked of him. Over the rough road he ran to Athens to shout in the ears of the waiting Athenians: "Athens is saved!" But his heart could not contain such great joy, and having delivered his message, he died.

The Athenian army reached Athens before the enemy, and when in the moonlight the Persian ships sailed into the bay near Athens, there, ready to meet them, were the same men who had defeated them at Marathon earlier in the day. The Persians were not willing to meet them again so soon; they realized that they had indeed suffered grievous defeat, and commands were given for the broken army and crippled fleet to set sail for Asia.

The Spartans came as they had promised, but too late to take any part in the battle. The Athenians lost about two hundred men in the battle. They were buried where they had fallen, a great mound was erected over their graves, and their names were inscribed on tall pillars nearby. Much rich plunder was left by the Persians on the plain, some of which was offered to Apollo as a thank-offering for the victory. The Athenians built a beautiful little temple, known as the Treasury of the Athenians, at Delphi, and Pan was not forgotten. A grotto on the side of the Acropolis was dedicated to him, where sacrifices were offered in memory of his help and encouragement when both had been sorely needed.

The Greeks who had fought at Marathon had many tales to tell of the battle, and many a wondrous deed was said to have been performed. It was thought that the gods themselves and the ancient heroes of Athens had taken part. Pan, they said, had struck such fear into the hearts of the Persians that they had fled in disorder and terror, a terror ever after known as a panic. Some even said that Theseus and other heroes had been seen, and for a long time the spirits of those who had been slain were thought to haunt the battlefield.

The battle of Marathon was one of the great events in history. For the first time the East and the West had met in conflict, and the West had prevailed. Never before had a little state faced the world empire of the Persians and conquered. The Greek soldiers had shown themselves capable of facing the Persians, long looked upon as the conquerors of the world, and of prevailing against them. The civilization of the East had met with a check on the very threshold of Europe, and Athens had saved Greece. But the Great Kings of Persia were not accustomed to defeat; would they accept this, and was Greece and, through Greece, Europe, safe, or would the Persians come again?

When the report came to Darius of the battle which was fought at Marathon, the King, who even before this had been greatly exasperated with the Athenians on account of the attack made upon Sardis, then far more than before displayed indignation, and was still more determined to make a campaign against Hellas. He at once sent messengers to the various cities of the Empire and ordered that they should get ready their forces. Each city or community was called upon to send more men than at the former time, and to send also ships of war, and horses, provisions and transport vessels. When these commands had been carried all round, all Asia was moved for three years, for all the best men were being enlisted for the expedition against Hellas, and were making preparations. But before the expedition was ready, a rebellion broke out in Egypt, and soon after Darius died, to be succeeded by his son, Xerxes.

THE INVASION OF XERXES

Mardonius, the general who had been forced to retire from Thrace after the wreck of the fleet off Mount Athos, was anxious to persuade the King to undertake another invasion. He probably wanted to retrieve the reputation he had lost on the former occasion, and hoped that if Greece became a Persian province, he would be made governor. Xerxes did not need much persuasion. He came of a race of kings whose word was the law of the Medes and Persians, and his wrath was great against the states that had not only refused to submit to the Persian King, but had actually defeated his army in battle. He would wreak his vengeance upon them for what they had done, and he declared that he would march an army through Europe against Greece.

Our knowledge of the preparations made for this invasion by Xerxes comes from the *Histories* of Herodotus. He may have exaggerated some things in his account, but his history was written for the Greeks of his own time and he wanted to make clear to them how great was the difference between the East and the West; how much better their freedom and independence were than the slavery endured by states which were ruled by the Great King. For these states had no voice in the affairs of the Empire; if the King went to war, they had to follow him and lay down their lives for causes in which they had no concern, and which generally only ministered to the greed and avarice of their rulers.

Having decided on the invasion of Greece, Xerxes sent heralds throughout the Empire proclaiming the war and bidding all fighting men make ready and join the King at Sardis. There the troops were mustered, and in the spring of 480 BCE, ten years after the battle of Marathon, Xerxes and his army were ready to set out. They were to march to the Hellespont, and then, by way of Thrace and Macedonia, to descend into Greece. The fleet was to join the army at the Hellespont, and by sailing close to the shore, to keep in constant touch with the army on land.

At last all was ready and the day came for the army to leave Sardis. First the baggage-bearers led the way together with their horses, and after these, half the infantry of all the nations who followed the Great King. Then a space was left, after which came the King himself. Before him went first a thousand horsemen, chosen from amongst the noblest Persians, and then a thousand spearmen; these were followed by ten sacred horses with rich trappings, and behind the horses came the sacred chariot of the great Persian god, drawn by eight horses, with the reins held by a charioteer on foot, for no human creature might mount upon the seat of that chariot. Then followed Xerxes himself, attended by spearmen chosen from the best and most noble of all the Persians. They were in turn followed by a body of men known as the Immortals, of which there were always ten thousand. They bore this name, because if any one of them made the number incomplete, either by death or illness, another man filled his place, and there were never either more or fewer than ten thousand. These were the very flower of the Persian army; nine thousand of them carried spears ending with silver pomegranates, and the spears of the thousand who guarded the front and rear were ornamented with pomegranates of gold.

The Medes and Persians wore tunics and trousers, for which the Greeks always felt the greatest contempt because they were worn by the Barbarian and not the Greek, and soft felt caps on their heads. They carried wicker shields and had short spears and daggers and bows and arrows. Besides these, a host of nations followed the Great King: Assyrians; Bactrians; Scythians; Caspians; Arabians; Ethiopians. All these and many more made up the army of the Great King, which marched in magnificent array from Sardis to the shores of the Hellespont, where the fleet was to meet them. When Xerxes reached the strait, he had a throne of white marble built for him and there he took his seat and gazed upon his army and his ships. Now Xerxes had given orders that a bridge should be built across the Hellespont over which his army should pass into Europe. But when the strait had been bridged over, a great storm arose which destroyed the bridge. When Xerxes heard of it, he was enraged and command was given to cut off the heads of those who had had charge of building the bridge. A new bridge was then built, stronger and more secure than the first, and over this the army passed in safety.

In order that no accidents might happen, honour was paid to the gods, and incense and fragrant perfumes were burnt upon the bridge and the road was strewn with branches of myrtle. The crossing was to take place early in the morning, and all were ready before the dawn broke. As the sun was rising, Xerxes poured a libation from a golden cup into the sea, and prayed to the Sun that no accident might befall him till he had conquered Europe, even to its furthest limits. Having prayed, he cast the cup into the Hellespont and with it a golden mixing bowl and a Persian sword, as gifts to the powers of the sea. When Xerxes had done this, the great army passed over the bridge in brilliant array. It took seven days and seven nights without any pause for the whole army to pass over.

When the whole army had crossed over safely, Xerxes inspected it. When he had done this, the ships were drawn down into the sea, and Xerxes, changing from his chariot to a ship of Sidon, sat down under a golden canopy and sailed along by the prows of the ships and inspected his fleet. The ships then set sail, and were to go along the coast to Therma where the land army was to meet them again.

Xerxes and the army then proceeded on their march through Thrace and Macedonia. Messengers had been sent on ahead some time before to make arrangements for provisioning this great host. All the towns through which the Persians passed were compelled to provide food and drink for the men and the animals with them. It was a tremendous undertaking, and scarcity and want were left behind as the invaders passed on. The inhabitants had to provide great quantities of wheat and barley, they were made to give up the best of the fatted cattle, their birds and fowls, and to provide everything in the way of gold and silver needed for the service of the table. All this was a great hardship to the people of the land, and in one place they went in a body to their temple and entreated the gods that for the future they would keep them from such evil.

The fleet sailed safely to Therma and was joined there by the army as had been arranged. So far all had gone well for the Persians. They had succeeded in a great achievement, for apparently without any serious mishaps, this tremendous army had been transported from Sardis right round the Aegean and had been fed and cared for on the way. The difficulties must have been very great, and only splendid organization could have done it successfully. But it had been done, and now Xerxes, in order to wreak his vengeance on one Greek city, stood with his army composed of the fighting men of forty-six nations on the very threshold of Greece. From Therma he could look across to the mountains of Thessaly, he could see snow-topped Olympus, the home of the gods who watched over the fortunes of the freedom-loving Greeks. The Athenians had withstood the Persians at Marathon, but now the whole of the eastern world was marching against them. Could they withstand that mighty host, or would they be forced to submit?

GREEK PREPARATIONS FOR WAR

Ten years had passed between the battle of Marathon and the arrival of Xerxes on the borders of Greece. Since then the Athenians had enjoyed a great reputation for their military power. Myths and legends had woven themselves round the name of Marathon with the result that the power of the Athenians was reputed greater than perhaps it actually was, and that of Persia was certainly depreciated. If Persia had been as formidable as had always been supposed, how could the Athenians have defeated the mighty Empire almost unaided? So for a number of years the Greeks had felt less terror at the name of Persia, and they had been enjoying a certain feeling of security, little realizing how false it was.

But suddenly they were shaken out of their calm. Rumours of the Persian preparations for an invasion of Greece reached them, rumours which were doubtless exaggerated, but which nevertheless had much truth in them. It is amazing how in spite of slow and difficult communication news was swiftly carried in those days from place to place. So the Greeks were fairly well-informed as to what the Persians were doing. At this crisis the Athenians took the lead, and gathered the peoples of Hellas together.

The first thing the Greeks did was to hold a conference at Corinth, which was attended by envoys from all the leading states except Argos and Thebes, which stood aloof. At this conference the Greeks made three important decisions. They resolved that they would reconcile all their own differences and bring to an end the wars they had with one another; as Hellenes they would unite against the common foe. Then they determined to send spies to Asia, who should bring back accurate reports of the preparations and power of Xerxes. And lastly, they would send messengers to the colonies in Sicily, Corcyra and Crete asking for assistance.

Three spies set out, but they were captured in Sardis and condemned to death. When Xerxes, however, heard what had happened, he sent for the spies, who were brought into his presence. To their surprise, instead of being led out to immediate execution, Xerxes commanded that they should be led round and shown the whole army, both foot and horse, and when they had seen everything, they were to be set free to return home. He did this, because he said that when the men returned to Hellas they would tell the Greeks of his power, and he thought it likely that they would submit to him. Little did Xerxes know the kind of freedom-loving people with whom he had to deal. So the spies looked at everything and then returned to Greece.

Meanwhile the messengers to the colonies returned. The answers to the appeal for support were very disappointing. Neither Sicily, Corcyra nor Crete would help. They either refused outright or made uncertain answers. They seem to have thought more of their own preservation than of the safety of Greece as a whole; they thought the Persian would probably win, and they preferred either to be on the winning side, or to be in such a position that they could make good terms with the Persian, did he conquer.

The Greeks now made ready to go out with their armies to meet the Persian foe. The chief command was given to Sparta, the greatest military state in Greece, and they marched to the Vale of Tempe in the north of Thessaly, where they hoped to meet Xerxes and prevent him from coming into Greece. When they got there, however, they found that it would not be possible to hold the pass against the enemy, for it was so situated that the Persians could attack them by sea as well as by land, and there was another path over the mountains by which the Persians could attack them in the rear. So the Greeks withdrew to Corinth, in order to deliberate further where they would meet the enemy. This retreat from Thessaly took place while Xerxes and his army were crossing the Hellespont, and it had important consequences for the Persians, for the Thessalians, hitherto never very loyal to Greece, seeing the other Greeks leave their land, took the side of the Persians and proved very serviceable to the King.

The Greeks now decided on making a stand much further south at Thermopylae. This was a narrow pass and easier to defend, so they resolved to guard it and not permit the passage of the Persian army. At Thermopylae the Greeks awaited the Persians.

THERMOPYLAE

It was midsummer in the year 480 BCE when the Persian host left Therma and marched down through Thessaly to the Pass of Thermopylae. The Persians encamped before the Pass and a scout was sent forward to bring back information as to what the Greeks were doing. Only a small force of Greeks was defending the Pass, the main part of the Greek army was kept back further to the south to defend the Isthmus. A small body of about three hundred Spartans had been sent under their King Leonidas to defend the Pass of Thermopylae, and, if possible, to prevent the Persians from advancing further into Greece. These three hundred men were the picked body-guard of the King, a force in which only fathers of sons might serve, so that their families might not die out of Sparta.

The Persian scout went cautiously forward, and to his great surprise saw some of the Spartans practising athletic exercises and others combing their long hair. He could not see the rest, as an ancient wall built across the Pass hid them from sight. He returned to Xerxes and reported on what he had seen. The King sent for a Greek who was in his camp and asked him what this behaviour of the Spartans might mean. He told him that they were following an ancient Spartan custom, for "whenever they are about to put their lives in peril, then they attend to the arrangement of their hair." The Spartans knew against what odds they had to fight, but their duty had placed them where they were, and no Spartan ever retreated or turned his back upon his foe.

The Great King intended to attack at the same moment both by land and by sea. The fleets were at Artemisium, and there were four times as many Persian ships as Greek. A hot and sultry summer's day had passed, and the signal to attack was expected in the morning. But at early dawn the sea began to be violently agitated and a strong east wind arose, thunder rumbled in the distance, and soon a terrible storm broke. The Greek ships were in safety, but a large number of Persian ships were wrecked and great treasure was lost. For three days the storm continued, and for three days Xerxes had to wait before he could attack the Pass. When on the fourth day the storm died down, the sea fight began. Three times over the Greeks attacked the Persian ships, and each time they prevailed against them. After the third fight, news was brought to Themistocles, the Athenian admiral, that two hundred Persian ships, sailing to the Greek rear, had been lost in the storm, so that there was nothing more to fear from an attack in that direction. The Greeks succeeded in throwing the Persian ships into confusion and so crippled the fleet, that they finally won the battle. It was then that Xerxes gave the order to his army to attack the Pass.

For the whole of a hot summer's day the Persians attacked. First the Medes tried to force the Pass, but it was narrow, and as they met the Spartan spears, down they went, man after man. Hour after hour this continued, but every attack was repulsed and hardly a Spartan fell. Then the Medes withdrew and the Immortals took their place. They were fresh and greatly superior to the Spartans in numbers, but neither could they prevail against them. At times the Spartans would make a pretence of turning to flight, but when the Medes followed after them with shouting and clashing of arms, then they turned and faced them and slew large numbers of them. The Spartans lost a few men, but at the end of the day the Persians drew back, exhausted and defeated, and the Spartans still held the Pass.

The next day, the same thing happened. So great was the slaughter of the Persians on this day that three times Xerxes leapt up from the seat from which he was watching the fight, in deadly fear for his army. But by the end of the day the Pass had not been taken, and again the Persians withdrew, exhausted and driven back, leaving large numbers of their companions lying dead before the Pass.

Xerxes was in great straits as to what he should do next, when he was told that a man desired audience with him. He was a Greek who lived in that region, and he offered, if the Persian would reward him with enough gold, to lead his army by a path known to him, but of which the Spartans were ignorant, over the mountain to a spot from which the Pass might be attacked in the rear. It was a long and difficult path, but the traitor knew it well and would guide them surely. The reward was promised, and about the time when the lamps were lit in the camp, the Immortals with their commander set out under the guidance of the traitor. All through the long black night they climbed by a steep and rocky path, and when dawn appeared they had reached the summit of the mountain. In this region a thousand men of Phocis were stationed to protect their own country and the path which led down to the valley below. They could not see the Persians as they climbed, for the sides of the mountain were covered with oak trees, but in the great silence which falls upon nature just before the dawn, suddenly these men heard an unexpected sound. It was the Persians stepping on the dried oak leaves which lay thickly on the ground beneath their feet. The Greeks started up and when the Persians, coming suddenly upon them, discharged their arrows at them, they retreated to a higher position close at hand, where they waited for the expected attack. To their surprise, however, the enemy turned away and left them. On went the traitor followed by the Persians, until they were on the road in the rear of Leonidas.

While it was still night, scouts came down from the mountains where they had been keeping watch, and told Leonidas that the Pass was turned, and that the enemy was approaching it from the rear. Leonidas knew what that meant, the end had come, but he commanded Spartans and he knew that whilst one remained alive, the Pass would not be taken.

At sunrise, according to the arrangement made with the traitor, Xerxes attacked. The Spartans, knowing that they were going forth to death, now advanced further out into the broader space in front of the Pass, where there was more room. And then followed a fight which will never be forgotten. The Medes made attack after attack, and the Spartans slew them and drove them back every time. Many were driven into the sea and perished, and many more were trodden down while still alive and trampled to death, and there was no reckoning of the number that perished. Two brothers of Xerxes fell fighting, and then Leonidas fell. The Spartans fought for the body of their King; most of their spears were by this time broken, so they fought and killed the Persians with their swords. Four times the Persians had almost taken the body of the King, and four times they were driven back by the Spartans, when word came that the Immortals were attacking the Pass in the rear. Then the remaining Spartans placed themselves with the body of Leonidas behind the wall, and there they made their last defence. On this spot those who still had them defended themselves with daggers, and those who had no weapons left, fought with their hands and teeth, until, overwhelmed by the Barbarians who were now assailing them both in the front and in the rear, they were surrounded and cut down, until not a Spartan was left alive.

And so the Persians took the Pass, and the road to Athens lay clear before them. The Spartans were buried where they fell, and a pillar was erected to the memory of those who had died so great a death in defending the Pass. On it was inscribed the simple words:

> *Stranger, bear word to the Spartans that we*
> *lie here obedient to their charge.*

THEMISTOCLES

The Persians had taken the Pass of Thermopylae; Thebes, the chief city in Boeotia, was anxious to be on the winning side; there was nothing to save Athens from the conquering Persian army.

But in this dark hour, a statesman arose in Athens who was to restore confidence and to make the place of Athens secure among the free nations of the world. This man was Themistocles, already known to the Athenians as the admiral who had defeated the Persians at Artemisium. He came of a humble family, but the laws made by Solon and later law-givers made it possible for him, in spite of his birth, to rise to the highest position in the state:

From his youth Themistocles had been of a vehement and impetuous nature, of a quick intelligence, and a strong and aspiring bent for action and great affairs. The holidays and intervals in his studies he did not spend in play or idleness, as other children, but would be always inventing or arranging some oration or speech to himself, so that his master would often say to him: "You, my boy, will be nothing small, but great one way or other, for good or else for bad." He received reluctantly and carelessly instructions given him to improve his manners and behaviour, or to teach him any pleasing or graceful accomplishment, but whatever was said to improve him in sagacity or in management of affairs, he would give attention to beyond one of his years. And when in company he was obliged to defend himself because he could not play on any stringed instrument, he would retort that though he could not do that, yet were a small and obscure city put into his hands, he would make it great and glorious. It is said that Themistocles was so transported with the thoughts of glory, and so inflamed with the passion for great actions, that though he was still young when the battle of Marathon was fought, upon the skilful conduct of the general Miltiades being everywhere talked about, he was observed to be thoughtful, and reserved, alone by himself; he passed the nights without sleep, and avoided all his usual places of recreation, and to those who wondered at the change, and inquired the reason of it, he gave the answer that "the trophy of Miltiades would not let him sleep."

Plutarch, *Life of Themistocles*

This was the man who was now to help Athens, and he possessed the very qualities most needed in this serious position: acuteness; good judgment; the ability to communicate with others; competence; foresight. This foresight was shown in the belief held by Themistocles, that the battle of Marathon was just the beginning of far greater conflicts.

Themistocles believed that the chief thing necessary for Athens was a fleet, and he persuaded the Athenians, though with great difficulty for they could not at first see the necessity, to build ships. There was not very much money in Athens just then, and without money ships could not be built. But at this critical time, an unexpectedly large sum of money was paid into the public treasury. This was the revenue from the silver mines at Laurium in the south of Attica, which the Athenians were intending to divide amongst themselves. Themistocles persuaded them to give up this plan of division and to dedicate the money to ship-building. This they did, and they also improved the harbour of Athens, and

henceforward, little by little, turning and drawing the city down towards the sea in the belief that with their ships they might be able to repel the Persians and command Greece, Themistocles, so Plato tells us, turned the Athenians from steady soldiers into mariners and seamen and gave occasion for the reproach against him, that he took away from them the spear and the shield and bound them to the bench and the oar.

Plutarch, *Life of Themistocles*

Themistocles did not accomplish this without opposition. He had a rival in Athens, Aristeides, a man who had grown up with him and played with him as a boy, but who had always taken the opposite sides in whatever they were doing. Unlike Themistocles, Aristeides belonged to a noble family, and whenever Themistocles took the side of the people, Aristeides favoured the nobles. Staid and settled in temperament, he was intent on the exercise of justice, and utterly opposed to falsehood and trickery. Of all his virtues, it was the *justice* of Aristeides which most appealed to the people; it never failed under any circumstances, and so they gave him the surname of the *Just*.

Aristeides believed that the building of a navy for Athens was too great a change from the former policy of the city. The Athenians had won the battle of Marathon and had thereby secured their reputation as soldiers, and he thought it very ill-advised and dangerous to depart from the old traditions and to put all their strength into war ships. Themistocles thought otherwise, and the two leaders came into violent conflict with each other.

There was at Athens a custom known as Ostracism. This was a law which once a year allowed the Athenians to banish for ten years any citizen who had, as they thought, assumed too much power or had become too popular. They were always afraid that such power might lead to a return of the Tyranny, and in their passionate desire to prevent that, they were often led to banish those who deserved a better reward for their services. In times of national danger, those who had been ostracized were sometimes recalled before their term of exile was over; otherwise they were not allowed to return until ten years had passed. The sentence of ostracism could not be passed unless at least six thousand votes were cast. Each vote was written on a piece of broken pottery, called an ostrakon and then placed in an urn set up in a special place for the purpose. The conflict between Themistocles and

Aristeides grew so great that the Athenians decided that one or the other of them must give way and leave Athens, and they decided to hold an ostracism. This resulted in the banishment of Aristeides, and Themistocles was left to carry out his aims for Athens without opposition.

Aristeides was a noble and a conservative, and opposed to the changes which Themistocles felt to be so necessary if Athens was to keep her freedom, but he was a man whose honour has never been called in question, who gave of his best to his country without ever asking for reward, and who, when he was later recalled to power and his great rival was falling into disgrace, never, as far as is known, by word or deed, treated him in any way that was mean-spirited or ungenerous.

Thanks to Themistocles, the Athenians now had a navy and a good harbour, but that would not protect them from the army of Xerxes which was advancing through Boeotia towards Attica. In their alarm, they sent messengers to Delphi to ask the advice of the oracle, but the answer they received filled them with despair. They were told to leave their home, for all was doomed to destruction, that fire and the War-God were about to bring ruin upon them, that there was no hope for them, but that they would steep their souls in sorrow. The Athenians could not believe that such a fate awaited them, and they sent again to the oracle, entreating Apollo to look upon them with favour. At last they received the following answer, with which they returned to Athens: "Zeus, wide-gazing, permits to keep in honour of Pallas walls of wood unshaken to shelter thee and thy children. Wait not for horse nor for foot that come to ruin thy country, out of the mainland afar; but rather yield to the foeman, turning thy back in flight, for yet shalt thou meet him in battle."

With this answer the Athenians returned home, and there great discussion arose as to the meaning of the oracle. Some interpreted it as meaning that they should build a fence of wood round the city, others that the "walls of wood" could only mean ships, and that they should leave everything and betake themselves to their fleet. Themistocles was the side of those who held that the wooden walls were the ships, and he persuaded the Athenians to remove to a place of safety out of Attica their wives and children, and as much of their property as they could. This they did, and then leaving only a few men to guard the Acropolis, the fighting men betook themselves to their ships and anchored near the island of Salamis.

All this was done none too soon, for the Persian army had arrived in Attica and laid the land to waste. When they reached Athens they took the lower city, then proceeded to besiege the Athenian defenders in the temple on the Acropolis. At length, the Persians found an obscure and arduous ascent to the Acropolis, and after entering the gates the killed the defenders, plundered the temple and set fire to the whole of the Acropolis. Athens had fallen into the hands of the invaders.

SALAMIS TO THE END

Athens was burnt, its walls had been destroyed, but the Athenian men had not yet been defeated; they were with the fleet at Salamis, and ready to fight to the death for the freedom of their state. They were joined there by ships from the other Greek states, but when the news of the burning of Athens reached the

Greek commanders, those who came from the Peloponnese, especially the Spartans, were unwilling to remain at Salamis any longer, but wanted to sail to their homes, and should the enemy pursue them, make their last stand there. Themistocles opposed this policy with all his might, and a hot discussion followed. In spite of his passionate appeal, the commanders of the other Greek ships decided to set sail and leave the Athenians to fight the Persians alone.

In these desperate straits, Themistocles thought of a stratagem by which he might force a battle, before his allies had time to desert him. He sent a secret messenger, whom he could trust, in a boat to the encampment of the Persoamss and charged him to give a message to Xerxes informing him that the Hellenes were planning to take flight, and were not forming a united front against him. For that reason, it would be possible for Xerxes to win a great victory, as his foes would be occupied with conflict amongst themselves.

Xerxes received this message with joy and immediately acted upon it, and began to surround the Greeks so that not one might escape. Whilst this was being done, Aristeides, the banished rival of Themistocles, whose sentence had been lifted in this hour of peril when Athens needed all her sons, suddenly returned from Aegina to the Athenian fleet, with the news that it was impossible for any of the Greeks to sail away because they were even then surrounded by the enemy. Aristeides gave this news first to Themistocles, saying to him that if at other times they had been rivals, there was only one kind of rivalry in which they could now engage, a rivalry as to which should do more service to his country. The news he brought was true, and the Greeks could not now escape a battle.

The sea-fight began as the day dawned. Xerxes had erected a great throne for himself from which he could watch the events of the day. Aeschylus, a great Athenian poet, who was himself present at the battle, wrote a play called *The Persians* in which a messenger takes the news of Salamis to the mother of Xerxes, waiting at Susa for the return of her son. Never before had he been defeated, but now she must listen to a tale of woe:

> 'Twas this began all our disaster, Queen:
> A demon or fell fiend rose – who knows whence? –
> For from the Athenian host a Hellene came,
> And to thy son, to Xerxes, told this tale,
> That when the mirk of black night should be come,
> The Greeks would not abide, but, leaping straight
> Upon the galley thwarts, this way and that
> In stealthy flight would seek to save their lives.
> Soon as he heard, discerning neither guile
> In that Greek, nor the jealousy of heaven,
> This word to all his captains he proclaims,
> That, when the sun should cease to scorch the earth,
> And gloom should fill the hallowed space of sky,
> In three lines should they range their throng of ships
> To guard each pass, each sea-ward surging strait;
> And others should enring all Aias' Isle:
> Since, if the Greeks should yet escape fell doom,
> And find their ships some privy path of flight,
> Doomed to the headsman all these captains were.
> Thus spake he, in spirit over-confident,
> Knowing not what the gods would bring to pass.

With hearts obedient, in no disarray,
Then supped our crews, and every mariner
To the well-rounded rowlock lashed his oar.
But when the splendour faded of the sun,
And night came on, each master of the oar
A-shipboard went, and every man-at-arms.
Then rank to rank of long ships passed the word:
And, as was each appointed, so they sailed.
So all night long the captains of the ships
Kept all the sea-host sailing to and fro.
And night passed by, yet did the Hellene host
Essay in no wise any secret flight.
But when the day by white steeds chariot-borne,
Radiant to see, flooded all earth with light,
First from the Hellenes did a clamorous shout
Ring for a triumphant chant; and wild and high
Pealed from the island rock the answering cheer
Of Echo. Thrilled through all our folks dismay
Of baffled expectation; for the Greeks
Not as for flight that holy paean sang,
But straining battleward with heroic hearts.
The trumpet's blare set all their lines aflame.
Straightway with chiming dip of dashing oars
They smote the loud brine to the timing cry,
And suddenly flashed they all full into view.
Foremost their right wing seemly-ordered led
In fair array; next, all their armament
Battleward swept on. Therewithal was heard
A great shout – "On, ye sons of Hellas, on!
Win for the home-land freedom! – freedom win

For sons, wives, temples of ancestral gods,
And old sires' graves! this day are all at stake!"
Yea, and from us low thunder of Persian cheers
Answered – no time it was for dallying!
Then straightway galley dashed her beak of bronze
On galley. 'Twas a Hellene ship began
The onset, and shore all the figure-head
From a Phoenician: captain charged on captain.
At first the Persian navy's torrent-flood
Withstood them; but when our vast fleet was cramped
In strait-space – friend could lend no aid to friend, –
Then ours by fangs of allies' beaks of bronze
Were struck, and shattered all their oar-array;
While with shrewd strategy the Hellene ships
Swept round, and rammed us, and upturned were hulls
Of ships; – no more could one discern the sea,
Clogged all with wrecks and limbs of slaughtered men:
The shores, the rock-reefs, were with corpses strewn.
Then rowed each bark in fleeing disarray,
Yea, every keel of our barbarian host,
They with oar-fragments and with shards of wrecks
Smote, hacked, as men smite tunnies or a draught
Of fishes; and a moaning, all confused
With shrieking, hovered wide o'er that sea-brine
Till night's dark presence blotted out the horror.
That swarm of woes, yea, though for ten days' space
I should rehearse could I not tell in full.
Yet know this well, that never in one day
Died such a host, such tale untold, of men.

Aeschylus: *The Persians*, translated by A.S. Way

Xerxes, the Great King, was defeated, and his one desire now was to return home to Asia. He left his general, Mardonius, in Thessaly with a picked body of men, who should carry on the war in the spring, but he himself, with what was left of his army, marched back through Macedonia and Thrace, to the Hellespont and so back to his own land. It was a very different march from the triumphant one he had made earlier in the year. The inhabitants of the lands through which they had passed had no fear of a defeated King, and it was difficult to obtain provisions. The Persians seized what crops there were, tearing the grass from the ground, and devouring bark and leaves from the trees. The army was beset by plague and the King left some of his soldiers behind. In such manner did Xerxes return home.

In the meanwhile, Mardonius and his army spent the winter in Thessaly. When the spring came (this was the spring of 479 BCE), he sent a messenger to the Athenians who spoke these words to them:

The Spartans heard that this message had come, and they sent messengers to Athens imploring the Athenians to make no terms with the Persians, for they feared that if Athens became subject to Persia, there would be no safety left for them. They offered to send supplies to Athens to make up for the loss of their harvest, destroyed by the Persians, to support the families of those Athenians who had been slain, to do almost anything, in fact, if only the Athenians would stand firm.

The Spartans need not have feared. The freedom-loving Athenians were not likely to submit to a Persian foe. They sent back this answer:

So long as the sun goes on the same course by which he goes now, we will never make an agreement with Xerxes, but trusting to the gods and heroes as allies, we will go forth to defend ourselves against him.

Herodotus: *Histories,* **Book 8**

To the Spartans they said:

It was natural, no doubt, that you should be afraid lest we should make a treaty with the Barbarian; but it was an unworthy fear for men who knew so well the spirit of the Athenians, namely that there is neither so great quantity of gold anywhere upon the earth, nor any land so beautiful, that we should be willing to accept it and enslave Hellas by taking the side of the Medes. ... Be assured of this, that so long as one of the Athenians remains alive, we will never make an agreement with Xerxes. We are grateful for your thought toward us, but we shall continue to endure as we may, and not be a trouble in any way to you. But send out an army as speedily as you may, for the Barbarian will be here invading our land at no far distant time.

Herodotus: *Histories,* **Book 8**

This was the Athenian answer, and upon hearing it the envoys went away back to Sparta.

PLATAEA

When the messengers returned to Mardonius with the answer from Athens, the Persian general marched out of Thessaly down through Boeotia into Attica, and for the second time Athens was burnt. Xerxes had left but little to burn, Mardonius left nothing. He then marched back into Boeotia and set up his camp in the region between Thebes and Plataea. Here he waited for the Greeks. There was some delay before they came, for the Spartans made various excuses for not setting out, but at length under their King, Pausanias, they marched out and joined the Athenians. And then at Plataea was fought the last great battle in this great war. All day long it raged, and at first it seemed as if the Persians were gaining, but whilst the outcome of the battle was still in doubt, Mardonius was killed, and with him fled all the hopes of the Persians. They took to flight, but were pursued and overtaken by the Greeks and very few were left alive.

The Greeks then entered the camp of the Persians, and they gazed in astonishment at the riches they found there. There were "tents furnished with gold and silver, and beds overlaid with gold and silver, and mixing bowls of gold, and cups and other drinking vessels." One tenth of this rich plunder was sent to Delphi and the rest divided amongst those who had fought the battle. A bronze statue of Zeus was sent as an offering to Olympia, and one of Poseidon was sent to the Isthmus. It was further resolved that the land belonging to Plataea should be held sacred for ever, and that never again should fighting take place on it.

After the Persians had taken the Pass of Thermopylae, the body of Leonidas had been taken and cruelly used in revenge for his having dared to withstand the Great King, and to slaughter so many of his Persian soldiers. It was suggested to Pausanias that he should take vengeance for this barbarous act by mutilating the body of Mardonius who had fallen in the battle. Pausanias rejected this suggestion as unworthy of a Hellene, arguing that Leonidas had already been greatly avenged by the number of Persian lives that had been taken.

In the Persian camp, the Greeks found the tent of Xerxes himself, which he had left for Mardonius, not wishing to be cumbered with too much baggage in his flight from Greece. When Pausanias saw

> the couches of gold and of silver with luxurious coverings, and the tables of gold and silver, and the magnificent apparatus of the feast, was astonished at the good things set before him, and for sport he ordered his own servants to prepare a Laconian meal; and as, when the banquet was served, the difference between the two was great, Pausanias laughed and sent for the commanders of the Hellenes; and when these had come together, Pausanias said, pointing to the preparation of the two meals severally: "Hellenes, for this reason I assembled you together, because I desired to show you the senselessness of this leader of the Medes, who having such fare as this, came to us who have such sorry fare as ye see here, in order to take it away from us." Thus it is said that Pausanias spoke to the commanders of the Hellenes.

Herodotus: *Histories*, Book 9

After the battle of Salamis, the Persian ships had withdrawn to Samos, and those of the Greeks to Delos, where they had spent the winter. In the spring, when the armies were marching out to meet at Plataea, the fleets moved slowly towards the Ionian coast, and on the same day as the battle of Plataea, so Herodotus tells us, they met in a fierce sea-fight, in which the Persians were completely routed. Thus on the same day, by land and sea, the Persians were defeated and Greece was free. Greece had proved that right was greater than might, and that in the cause of freedom the weaker might stand against the stronger and prevail.

THE ATHENIAN EMPIRE

The Persian had been defeated, and Greece was free. The Athenians had suffered more than any other state, for they had been forced to leave their city to be occupied by the enemy, and twice it had been burnt to the ground. Now, however, they were free to return. The city was utterly destroyed, but a great hope for the future filled their hearts when they found that the sacred olive tree on the Acropolis, which had been burnt by the Persians, was not dead after all, but had sent up fresh green shoots. Athena had not deserted them.

With the foundation of the Delian League whose object was the freeing of all Hellenes in Asia Minor and the islands of the Aegean from the Persians, Athens gained dominance over neighbouring states and eventually moved the League Treasury, in which taxes from all member states were stored, to Athens. As the leading state of the Confederation, Athens was now effectively an empire and was recognized as such. The island states in the Aegean as well as the Ionian cities on the mainland of Asia Minor were bound to her by ties of allegiance. The heart of the empire was Athens, and settlers from many different places were welcomed there, if they brought with them something that contributed to the welfare of the city: the sculptor, the worker in gold, silver or other metals, the potter, the dyer, the leather-worker, and the merchant who brought costly wares from distant lands, all these and many more were welcomed.

THE FORTIFICATIONS OF ATHENS

Themistocles was now the acknowledged leader of Athens, and the hero of all Greece, endorsed by a prolonged ovation at the next Olympic Games. He was by nature a great lover of honours and glory, and he liked to appear superior to other people. It was this man who had given Athens her navy by means of which she had defeated the Persians, and he now realized that if she was to keep her independence, the city must be well fortified. The Athenians were more than willing to follow his advice, and everyone in the city, men, women and even children worked hard to rebuild the walls.

The Spartans were becoming more and more jealous of the increasing power of the Athenians, and when they heard of the new walls that were rising all round Athens, they sent envoys there to tell the Athenians that they held any such fortification of their city unnecessary. They thought it wiser that there should be no strongly-walled city in Attica, for should an enemy ever capture it, the citadel could be used as a base from which the enemy would go out and conquer other places. If war should come again, and the Athenians should feel insecure in their city, Sparta would gladly welcome them in the Peloponnese. Themistocles suggested that he should go to Sparta and talk everything over with the Spartan leaders, and he set out accordingly. He left instructions that during his absence the work on the walls should go on with all possible speed and that messengers were to be sent to tell him when the work was finished. But the Spartans were not satisfied with the excuses and explanations given them by Themistocles, so he suggested that they should send messengers to Athens to find out the truth for themselves. They had hardly started when the Athenian messengers arrived with the news that the walls were built. Themistocles then told the whole truth to the Spartans, telling them that Athens was in every way the equal of Sparta and would take no orders from Sparta as to what should not be done in Athenian territory. The Spartans were angry, but they did not show it at that time, and Themistocles returned home to Athens.

Themistocles next set to work to fortify the harbour of the Peiraeus. Athens is a few miles inland from the sea, and the Peiraeus is the Athenian harbour. It is a peninsula with a deep bay on one side, in which ships can lie safely at anchor. A strong wall was built all round this peninsula, and the narrow entrance to the harbour was made secure by chains which could easily be drawn across in such a way as to prevent, whenever necessary, the entrance of any ships. The city and the harbour were then connected by Long Walls, which practically formed a fortified road down to the sea. This gave Athens all the advantages of a seaport, and an enemy would find it as difficult to take Athens as it had been to take Miletus.

The Persians had been defeated in Greece, but the Ionian Greeks in Asia Minor were still subject to the Great King. Now that the war was over, these Greeks appealed to the states on the mainland to help them. Athens took a special interest in these Ionian colonies as they had been settled by men of close kinship to the Athenians. So the

Hellenes deliberated about removing the inhabitants of Ionia, and considered where they ought to settle them in those parts of Hellas of which they had command, leaving Ionia to the Barbarians: for it was evident to them that it was impossible on the one hand for them to be always stationed as guards to protect the Ionians, and, on the other hand, if they were not stationed to protect them, they had no hope that the Ionians would escape from the Persians. Therefore it seemed good to these of the Peloponnesians who were in authority that they should remove the inhabitants of the trading ports which belonged to those peoples of Hellas who had taken the side of the Medes, and give that land to the Ionians to dwell in; but the Athenians did not think it good that the inhabitants of Ionia should be removed at all, nor that the Peloponnesians should consult about Athenian colonies; and as these vehemently resisted the proposal, the Peloponnesians gave way.

Herodotus: *Histories*, Book 9

The Spartans not only gave way, but when an Athenian fleet set sail for the Hellespont, the Spartans sent twenty ships with Pausanias, the general who had commanded at Plataea, to join the expedition. The combined fleets took Sestos and then in the following year Byzantium. Pausanias was left in command at Byzantium, and soon after a strange change was observed in him. His manner became overbearing and proud, and he gave up his Spartan habits of simple living, and adopted Persian ways, even dressing as a Persian. All this was so suspicious that he was recalled to Sparta, but as nothing was proved against him, he returned to Byzantium. Here he entered into correspondence with Xerxes and offered, in return for gold and the Great King's daughter as his bride, to betray Greece to the Persians. At last one of his slaves gave evidence against him. For some time Pausanias had been sending messengers to Asia Minor, and this particular slave had noticed that none of these messengers ever returned. When in time it became his turn to be sent, instead of bearing the message to the East, he took it to one of the Ephors, who opened it and found in it proofs of treachery and betrayal of Greece to the Persians, with instructions to kill the slave who brought the message. The news that his messenger had been intercepted reached Pausanias, who immediately took refuge in a chamber adjoining the shrine in one of the temples. The Ephors, in order to prevent his escape, gave orders that the doorway should be blocked up, and, imprisoned in the little chamber, Pausanias slowly starved to death. He was only taken out when he was just at the point of death, in order that the body of a traitor might not profane the temple.

Meanwhile, Themistocles had been at the head of affairs in Athens. He had many enemies amongst the Athenians, and they accused him of many wrong acts. These were never definitely proved against him, and the records of the end of his career are so scanty that it is difficult to know how much truth there was in the accusations, but there were undoubtedly a number of suspicious facts of which his enemies made use. Amongst other things he was accused of taking bribes. He denied it, yet when he left Athens, he possessed a strangely large fortune, the sources of which were never explained. A last serious accusation brought against him was that he was in communication with the Persians and was about to play the traitor. There was no proof of this, but Themistocles believed in the policy of making peace with the Persians; he saw that wealth and prosperity would most surely come to Athens through trade, and so he advocated peaceful relations with the great empire of the East. This was a very unpopular policy to hold in Athens, and feeling grew more and more bitter against Themistocles, until at last he was ostracized.

He left Athens and wandered from place to place. No city would give him a welcome, partly because he was feared, and partly because Athens was now a powerful state, and no one wanted to cause offence by giving shelter to an Athenian exile. Sometimes he was forced to flee for his life, or go into hiding and eventually, this homeless wanderer from city to city, the man who had saved Greece and had laid the foundations of the greatness of Athens, came to Susa, and prostratd himself before Artaxerxes, who had succeeded Xerxes as King, saying:

"O King, I am Themistocles the Athenian, driven into banishment by the Greeks. The evils that I have done to the Persians are numerous, but I come with a mind suited to my present calamities; prepared alike for favours or for anger. If you save me, you will save your suppliant; if otherwise, you will destroy an enemy of the Greeks."
Plutarch: *Life of Themistocles*

The King rejoiced greatly over the arrival of Themistocles and made him welcome. At the end of a year Themistocles was able to speak the Persian language quite easily and he became very intimate with the King, who honoured him above all strangers who came to the court.

Tradition has handed down to us the hope that at the end his ancient love and loyalty to Athens triumphed, for it is said that the Great King summoned him to help the Persians in an expedition against Greece, but that Themistocles, rather than sink to such a depth of shame, drank poison, and so put an end to his own life. Though almost certainly innocent of the worst of that of which he was accused while still in Athens, his later actions place him, if not with those who became actual traitors to their country, at least with those whose loyalty and honour have been indelibly stained.

Athens could never have a great state without the contribution of Themistocles, and Plutarch tells us that long years after the death of Themistocles, there was a tomb near the haven of Peiraeus, where the sea is always calm, which was reputed to be that of the great Athenian statesman, and that it was said of it:

> Thy tomb is fairly placed upon the strand,
> Where merchants still shall greet it with the land;
> Still in and out 'twill see them come and go,
> And watch the galleys as they race below.
> **Plutarch:** *Life of Themistocles*

Was it, perhaps, possible that the Athenians of a later generation, recognizing what Themistocles had done for Athens, forgave him, and brought his body home to rest near the great harbour which he himself had made?

THE CONFEDERACY OF DELOS

The recall of Pausanias from Byzantium left the Spartans in Asia Minor with no commander. Sparta had never been very much in earnest about freeing the Ionians, and the Ionians, very naturally, felt more confidence in a sea-power than in one whose strength lay chiefly in her army, and so they turned to Athens for leadership.

Themistocles was in exile, and his old rival Aristeides was now the most powerful leader in Athens. He believed that it was the duty of the Athenians to do all in their power to free their kinsmen in the Ionian cities from the Persian rule, and to this end, he and the Ionian leaders formed a league, known as the Confederacy or League of Delos. It took its name from the island of Delos where the meetings were held, and where the treasury of the League was kept. Delos was chosen because it could easily be reached by all the members of the League, and also because it was a place specially honoured by Apollo, for legend said he had been born there, and before Delphi had become so important, his chief sanctuary had been in his island birthplace.

The object of the League was the freeing of all Hellenes in Asia Minor and the islands of the Aegean from the Persians, and, having secured their liberty to help them maintain their independence. For this purpose money and ships were needed. "By the good will of the allies, the Athenians obtained the leadership. They immediately fixed which of the cities should supply money and which of them ships for the war against the Persians. Aristeides was given command to survey the countries and to assess the tax for which they were liable. He made the people of Greece swear to maintain loyalty to the League.

The contributions were collected every spring by ten specially appointed men, called Hellenic Stewards, who brought the money to Delos where it was placed in the treasury of the League. The League began its work at once, and one by one the Greek cities in Asia Minor and the islands in the Aegean were set free, until at length not one was left under the rule of Persia. As each city became independent, it joined the League, which grew in strength and importance as its numbers increased. Athens was its acknowledged leader; not only did she determine the amount each member should contribute, but the Hellenic Stewards were all Athenians, and affairs of the League were governed by Athenian law. Slowly the relationship of Athens to the other members of the League changed. At first the states had regarded themselves as allies of each other and of Athens, but as the power of Athens grew, she began to look upon these Greek states less as allies than as subjects who were bound to follow her lead and do her bidding. At length this relationship was so well-recognized that in some states Athens exacted this oath of allegiance from those who enjoyed her protection as members of the Delian League.

In name, Athens together with all the island states in the Aegean and the Ionian cities in Asia Minor, were allies and independent. Their envoys still met at Delos, supposedly to take counsel with each other, but in fact they were subject to Athens and obeyed her commands. The League had been formed in 477 BCE and for twenty-three years Delos was its headquarters. Then it was suggested that the treasury should be moved to Athens, and that the meetings should in future be held there. No longer was Athens merely the leading state amongst her allies. The removal of the treasury from Delos Athens in name as well as in fact not simply the leading state of a Confederation, but the Athenian Empire.

THE ATHENIAN EMPIRE UNDER PERICLES

Themistocles had been exiled, Aristeides was dead, and a statesman named Pericles now took the leading part in Athenian affairs. His boyhood had been spent during some of the most thrilling years of Athenian history. As a child he had become a hero-worshipper of the men who had fought at Marathon; he must have been amongst the older children who were forced to flee from Athens on the approach of Xerxes; and though not old enough to fight, he was old enough to understand how much hung upon the outcome of the battle of Salamis, and he probably spent that great day in sound, if not also in sight, of the conflict between the two hostile fleets. His father was the commander of the fleet which in the following year defeated the Persian on the same day on which was fought the battle of Plataea and one can imagine the youth, returning to his beloved Athens, glorying in the deeds of his father and his countrymen, and resolved to take his part in making Athens a great and glorious city.

Pericles belonged to a noble family, and he had been educated by some of the great philosophers of his day. Like Thales of Miletus, these men believed that nature was governed by laws that had nothing to do with the good-will or anger of the gods, and one of them, though still believing in the existence of many gods, held the belief that the world had been created by one Mind alone, and he taught Pericles to share this belief. This helped to free the mind of Pericles from superstition, and on several occasions he tried to free others from the fears which superstition brings.

Although by birth belonging to the nobles, Pericles took the side of the people in Athens, partly, at first, because he did not want to do anything that might make it even seem that he was aiming at the sole power of a Tyrant. He soon became the acknowledged leader, and he then withdrew himself from public life, only intermittently attending the Assembly and reserving himself for great occasions.

In many ways Pericles showed himself superior to the men around him, and because of this superiority and for his great power in public affairs he was given the surname of the Olympian. Like Zeus, and according to Plutarch, he was said to speak with "thunder and lightning, and to wield a dreadful thunderbolt in his tongue."

Under the leadership of Pericles, Athens rose to be a great state. The Age of Pericles was a short one, lasting only for about fifty years in the last part of the fifth century BCE, but it was a period which was great not only in material prosperity, but also in every form of intellectual and artistic beauty. The most memorable work of Pericles was the construction of public and sacred buildings – for more than two thousand years they have testified to the greatness of the people who built them.

By the laws Pericles made, it became possible for every free-born Athenian citizen, no matter how poor he was, to take an active part in the government of the State, thus completing the work of the earlier lawgivers and making Athens a democracy, a state ruled by the many.

It was the custom in Athens, that the bodies of Athenians who had been slain in battle should be brought home, and buried in special tombs which were situated in a very beautiful spot outside the walls. Only after the battle of Marathon were the dead, in recognition of their great valour against the Barbarian, buried on the field. All others were brought home and given a public funeral. There was always buried with them an empty coffin, as a symbol of all those whose bodies were missing and could not be recovered after the battle. It was believed that this wish to do honour to the dead and to give them fitting burial would ensure their happiness in the life after death, which every Greek believed to be imperilled if there was lack of proper burial. At the close of the funeral ceremonies, some great orator was always asked to deliver a suitable oration. On one such occasion, Pericles was the orator, and in the great Funeral Speech he made, he set forth to the Athenians what he considered Athens stood for in the world. There are no better words in which to describe the greatness of Athens at this time and the ideals at which she aimed, so listen to the words of Pericles, describing the city he loved:

Our form of government does not enter into rivalry with the institutions of others. We do not copy our neighbours, but are an example to them. It is true that we are called a democracy, for the administration is in the hands of the many and not of the few. But while the law secures equal justice to all alike in their private disputes, the claim of excellence is also recognized; and when a citizen is in any way distinguished, he is preferred to the public service, not as a matter of privilege, but as the reward of merit. Neither is poverty a bar, but a man may benefit his country whatever the obscurity of his condition... A spirit of reverence pervades our public acts; we are prevented from doing wrong by respect for authority and for the laws, having an especial regard to those which are ordained for the protection of the injured as well as to those unwritten laws which bring upon the transgressor of them the reprobation of the general sentiment.

And we have not forgotten to provide for our weary spirits many relaxations from toil; we have regular games and sacrifices throughout the year; at home the style of our life is refined; and the delight which we daily feel in all these things helps to banish melancholy. Because of the greatness of our city the fruits of the whole earth flow in upon us; so that we may enjoy the goods of other countries as freely as of our own... We are lovers of the beautiful, yet simple in our tastes, and we cultivate the mind without loss of manliness. Wealth we employ, not for talk and ostentation, but when there is a real use for it. To avow poverty with us is no disgrace; the true disgrace is in doing nothing to avoid it. An Athenian citizen does not neglect the state because he takes care of his own household; and even those of us who are engaged in business have a very fair idea of politics. We alone regard a man who takes no interest in public affairs, not as a harmless, but as a useless character; and if few of us are originators, we are all sound judges of a policy... In doing good, again, we are unlike others; we make our friends by conferring, not by receiving favours.... To sum up, I say that Athens is the school of Hellas ... for in the hour of trial Athens alone among her contemporaries is superior to the report of her... We have compelled every land and every sea to open a path for our valour, and have everywhere planted eternal memorials of our friendship and of our enmity. Such is the city for whose sake these men nobly fought and died; they could not bear the thought that she might be taken from them; and every one of us who survives should gladly toil on her behalf... Day by day fix your eyes on the greatness of Athens, until you become filled with the love of her; and when you are impressed by the spectacle of her glory, reflect that this empire has been acquired by men who knew their duty and had the courage to do it... And now, when you have duly lamented, everyone his own dead, you may depart.

Thucydides, II

THE CITY OF ATHENS

Almost in the centre of Attica lies a plain surrounded in the distance by hills: towards the East, Mount Hymettus, the home of goats, purple with thyme and filled with the murmur of bees; and to the North, Mount Pentelicus, famous for its shining white marble, that gleamed a rosy-red when the sun went down. Rising straight out of the plain is a great oval-shaped rock, the famous Acropolis of Athens, once its citadel and fortress, but transformed by Pericles into a great shrine for Athena. From this rock the land sloped gently to the sea. The plain was watered by the Cephisus, the only stream in Attica which did not run dry in the summer, and along its banks were olive groves, adding their touch of dark grey-green to the landscape. In the centre of this plain, at the foot of the Acropolis, was Athens.

Roads from all directions led to Athens, but the Greeks, unlike the Romans, were not great road-makers, and except for those used for processions on festivals, such as the Sacred Way that led to Eleusis, the roads in Attica were not in good repair, and foot-passengers when they went on a journey generally preferred the shorter paths over the hills. In the early morning, the roads outside the city were thronged with people coming in from the country on various kinds of business. Chief of these were the farmers, bringing their fruit and vegetables and other produce to sell in the market, but merchants from distant lands were also to be seen bringing their wares along the road from the Peiraeus.

The city was entered by gates in the great wall which had been built by Themistocles after the Persian Wars, and from the gates, the streets all led to the Market Place, or Agora, as it was called by the Greeks. The streets were narrow, crooked and dark, and were not paved, and the houses on each side presented a very dull appearance, for the windows rarely faced the street. The streets were dirty, too, for all kinds of refuse were thrown into them. This absence of light and air did not make for health, and so very often pictures of Apollo, the Bringer of Health, were painted on the walls. The Athenians spent their wealth on their great public buildings, and there was very little to distinguish one private house from another.

The water in Athens came from wells and springs and fountains, many of which were at the street corners, and it was the task of the slave maidens to draw the water from the fountain and to carry it home in vessels which they carried on their heads.

It is evident that Athens was a city very different from a well-equipped modern city, and that it lacked a great deal of what we consider necessary. But the Athenians of the fifth century BCE had extraordinarily little use for *things*, and laid no stress on comfort. They could tell the time without a clock, wear sandals without stockings or even go barefoot. They judged law-suits in the open air on a cold winter's morning, studied poetry without books, learned geography without maps, and politics without a newspaper. The Athenians were civilized without being comfortable. Of course much of this simple life was possible because of the climate; nevertheless it is the glory of the Athenians that they not only believed but practised the belief, that the things of the mind and spirit are greater than those of the body.

The daily life of Athens centred in the Agora. If the streets approaching it were mean and dirty, the Agora itself, the centre of public life, was wide and spacious and surrounded by dignified and beautiful buildings. In shape it was a great open square, two sides of which were taken up with public buildings and temples. On the remaining sides were the Stoas or Porches. These consisted of a roof supported by a row of columns in front and a wall at the back. Each stoa was a covered walk, protected from the glare of the sun, the biting of the cold wind, and from the rain, and whatever the weather might be. One of these Porches was known as the King's Porch. It was used as one of the law-courts, and on the wall at the back were inscribed the laws of Solon, and it was here that every archon had to take his oath of office. The most frequented of the stoas was the *Painted Porch*, so called because its wall was decorated with frescoes, one of which was a great painting of the battle of Marathon.

The centre of the Agora was a great open space, part of it free for the public to walk in, and part of it full of booths and stalls where was sold everything needed by the Athenians.

There were three classes of people in Athens: the citizens, who were all free-born Athenians; the foreign residents who were called metics; and the slaves. In outward appearance there was often very little difference between them, but only the citizens might vote, and they alone had any privileges. The metics were generally well-to-do; they were merchants and bankers and helped very largely to create the wealth which made Athens great.

The morning life of Athens centred in the Agora, but when the afternoon came, this was gradually deserted, and the Athenians who had gathered there earlier in the day went along the roads that led out of the city to the different Gymnasia. These were originally places devoted to the games practised by all Athenians, but they gradually became used more as parks, where the young men played games and the older men watched and talked. The Academy was the greatest of the gymnasia, and philosophers used to frequent it, and with their pupils discuss all the many things in which the keen and adventurous minds of the Athenians were interested. Plato, one of the greatest of the philosophers, was a well-known figure at the Academy.

Rising above the city, watching over it and guarding it, was the Acropolis, crowned by temples and statues. A great statue of

Athena looked down upon the city at her feet, at the busy Agora and the public buildings in which the government of the state was carried on, at the narrow streets lined with the houses of the citizens, and, beyond the walls, at the pleasant roads leading, on one side, out to the gymnasia and the country beyond, and, on the other, down to the harbour busy with the trade of Athens and where the galleys went in and out on their voyages all over the Mediterranean world.

THE ACROPOLIS IN THE TIME OF PERICLES

The greatest Athenian temples were on the Acropolis, the ancient citadel of Athens, which had been transformed by Pericles into a dwelling-place for Athena.

The fittest place for a temple or altar was some site visible from afar, and untrodden by foot of man, since it was a glad thing for the worshipper to lift up his eyes afar off and offer up his prayer.
Socrates in Xenophon's *Memorabilia*

The Acropolis was approached by a flight of steps leading to the Propylaea or Entrance Porch. Six great Doric columns stood at the entrance, and opening out to right and left of the main hall were other porticoes, the walls of which were decorated with paintings showing the deeds of ancient heroes. The roof was of white marble, and standing at this entrance one could catch a glimpse of the sea in the distance. Tradition held that it was on this spot that Aegeus stood to watch for the ship that should being back Theseus, and that it was from this high rock that he cast himself down in despair when he saw the ship returning with black sails, a sign, as he thought, that his son was dead.

To the right of the Propylaea, in the south-west corner of the Acropolis, was the little temple of Athena Nike, Athena of Victory. In this temple the goddess herself represented Victory, so she had no wings, which were always given by the Greeks to statues of Victory, and the temple came to be known as that of the Wingless Victory. A wonderful view is to be had from this temple, and the site for it was chosen, because from where it stands Salamis is in sight, and it was to be for ever a thanks-offering to Athena for the victory gained there over the barbarian foe.

Passing through the Propylaea, one came out upon the Acropolis, where rising up in majesty was the great bronze statue of Athena Promachos, Athena the Warrior Queen, Foremost in Fight, who went out to war with the armies of Athens and brought them home victorious. Pheidias, the great Athenian sculptor who had made the image of Zeus in the temple at Olympia, had made this statue, using for it the bronze which had been found amongst the Persian spoils after the battle of Marathon. The goddess stood upright, clad in armour and holding a spear in her hand. The tip of this spear was gilded, and it was said that sailors as they drew near the land could see it gleaming in the sunshine, and when they saw it they knew that home was near.

A little further, on the north side of the Acropolis, was the Erechtheum, called after the mythical King of Athens, Erechtheus. It was a very beautiful temple, and one of the porches has always been known as the Porch of the Maidens, because instead of being supported by columns, it is supported by the figures of six maidens. When the figure of a woman is used for this purpose, it is called in architecture a Caryatid.

A temple to Athena had always stood on this spot since memory began, and it was hallowed by all kinds of associations. Near the temple was the sacred olive tree of Athena, and within its walls was the old and most holy wooden statue of Athena, said to have dropped from heaven. It was in this temple that the goddess was worshipped in a more intimate way, for this was Athena Polias, the Guardian of the City and the Home. It was for this ancient wooden statue that specially chosen Athenian maidens wove the beautiful robe called the peplos, which was carried at the time of the festival held every four years to the temple and presented to the goddess.

THE PARTHENON

But greater than all else on the Acropolis was the Parthenon, created by Ictinus the architect, and Pheidias the sculptor. This most beautiful Greek temple in the world stood on the south side of the Acropolis. It was a Doric building surrounded by forty-six great pillars, and to the Athenian this building was the very soul of Athens. Elsewhere on the Acropolis it was Athena the goddess who was worshipped: Athena the Warrior, Athena the Guardian of the City, and in one place, though without a temple, Athena the Inspirer of all Arts and Crafts. But here in the Parthenon Athena was more than the goddess, she symbolized Athens itself, all the achievements of Athens in war and peace, and the spirit that guided the Athenians.

The sculpture on the east pediment represented the birth of Athena. It was the old Homeric poem interpreted in stone.

Her did Zeus the counsellor himself beget from his holy head, all armed for war in shining golden mail, while in awe did the other gods behold it. Quickly did the goddess leap from the immortal head, and stood before Zeus, shaking her sharp spear, and high Olympus trembled in dread beneath the strength of the grey-eyed Maiden, while Earth rang terribly around, and the sea was boiling with dark waves, and suddenly brake forth the foam. Yes, and the glorious son of Hyperion checked for long his swift steeds, till the maiden took from her immortal shoulders her divine armour, even Pallas Athena; and Zeus the counsellor rejoiced.

Homeric Hymn to Athena

Zeus rejoiced not only because Athena was born, but because she symbolized the birth of Athens; as she sprang from the head of Zeus arrayed in all the symbols of power, so surely was it the will of the gods that Athens should be great and powerful.

The sculpture on the west pediment represented the contest of Athena with Poseidon for the possession of Athens. Poseidon represented material prosperity. His gift to Athens was the sea, over which sailed her ships, colonizing and trading and bringing wealth to the state. But Athens, which was to account the things of the mind and spirit of greater value than those of material prosperity, was not to be ruled by Poseidon; the victory was given to Athena.

The pediments symbolized the will of the gods for Athens. All round the building under the cornice were smaller groups of sculptures called metopes, and these represented in stone the way in which Athens had fulfilled the will of the gods for her. First, there were battles between gods and giants, the conflict between order and disorder, and in every case order had triumphed; then there followed battles between the ancient heroes of legend and tradition and all kinds of evil forces in nature, and in these battles Theseus, the hero-king, fought for Athens and prevailed.

The Parthenon was built after the Persians had been driven out of Greece. The Greeks called all who were not of Greek blood Barbarians, and they believed that it was the will of the gods that in every conflict between Greek and Barbarian, the Greek should in the end prevail. The Greek of the fifth century BCE thought of all history as the working out of the great drama of the victory of the Greek spirit over that of the Barbarian, and the records of this drama are seen in political history in the development of the Athenian Empire, in literature, in the history of Herodotus, and in art in the building of the Parthenon.

But the Parthenon symbolized more than the history of Athens, it was also the symbol of her religious life. On the outer wall, under the colonnade, was the great frieze symbolizing the Panathenaic procession, that great procession which every four years wound its way up to the Acropolis. This was the festival of Athena, and at the east end of the building was a group of gods and goddesses waiting for her coming. They were waiting for her in her own city, where she would take the foremost place. In the solemn procession all classes of Athenians were represented: noble maidens, bearing baskets with offerings for the sacrifice; youths with offerings, and youths on horseback; chariots; grave elders and priests; and cattle for the sacrifice. Aliens, too, were there, for it was not only Athens that was symbolized, but the Athenian Empire; symbol of what Athens hoped would be a united Greece. It is very difficult to distinguish between Athenian patriotism and religion. To the Athenian, the city was Athena, and Athena the city, and the Parthenon was the crown of both.

The Parthenon was entered by the eastern porch. The light inside was dim, but as the eye grew accustomed to the dimness, the statue of Athena slowly became clearly visible. There she stood, a great figure nearly forty feet high. She was clad in a sleeveless garment that reached to her feet, bracelets in the form of serpents were on her arms, the aegis with the head of Medusa covered her breast. In her right hand the goddess bore an image of Victory, and her left hand rested on a shield, inside of which was coiled a snake. The statue was made of gold and ivory, and it was to the Athenians the symbol of all that was best in the Athenian ideals. Their passionate desire for freedom, their unfaltering search for truth, their great love of beauty were all personified for them in the calm and queenly figure of her whose battles were won, of Athena Parthenos. Having offered their sacrifices outside, they entered her temple with awe, believing that "he who enters the incense-filled temple must be holy; and holiness is to have a pure mind."

ATHENIAN DRESS

The morning crowd in the Agora consisted almost entirely of men; to see Athenian women a stranger would have to be invited to their houses, a rare privilege but seldom accorded, or to have visited Athens during a festival, when women were allowed to take part in the great processions which went up to the shrine of Athena on the Acropolis. But men of all classes could be seen every day in the Agora.

The chief garment worn by all these men was the *chiton* or tunic. It was made by taking an oblong piece of cloth, cutting it the required length and then folding it round the body, so that it hung from the neck to the knees. It was fastened at the neck with a pin, sometimes beautifully wrought in gold, in such a way that arm-holes were made, and one side was always left open. A girdle kept the folds of the chiton in place, and it was generally tight enough to disguise the fact that one side was open. A man's chiton seldom came below his knees, but the wearer could always regulate the length, and workmen and all those engaged in active occupations were generally *well-girded*, that is, they pulled up the chiton, so that it was short, with part of it hanging over the girdle. Older men usually allowed the chiton to hang to its full length.

In the house, the chiton was the only garment required, and workmen and all young men engaged in active pursuits seldom wore anything else out of doors, but out of the house, the older men generally added a mantle known as the *himation*. This was another oblong piece of cloth, but larger than that used for the chiton, which was thrown over the left shoulder, brought round under the right arm to the front of the body, and then thrown again over the left shoulder. The himation was not, as a rule, pinned and so it had to be very carefully adjusted in order that its folds might hang well. It was a very difficult thing to put on a himation gracefully, and it was often the work of a special slave to arrange it before his master went out of doors. The folds had to hang well, and it had to be of the right length, for if it was too short, the Athenian thought the wearer looked like a rustic come to the city for the first time, and to wear it too long was a sign of ostentation and needless display.

The only other garment sometimes worn by men was the *chlamys*, a short cloak worn by the young men. It was circular, gathered round the neck and fastened by a pin or clasp, and hung over the back and left shoulder reaching to the waist. The chlamys was generally of a bright colour; the chiton and himation were more often white, though sometimes colours were used, but beautifully designed borders were frequently embroidered in colours on both the chiton and himation.

Athenian men seldom wore anything on their heads, unless they were travelling, when they wore a close-fitting cap, either with or without a brim, but they generally wore sandals on their feet, though this was not considered absolutely necessary.

The dress of the Athenian women consisted, like that of the men, of a chiton and himation, but the woman's chiton was longer; it reached to her feet and was fuller, and it often had short sleeves. No Athenian woman could ever appear out of doors without her himation, and this was often so arranged that it was drawn over her head, forming a hood. This was generally the only form of head covering worn by Athenian women, though if they went out in the sun they sometimes took parasols.

Athenian women probably used more colours in their dress than the men; a particularly beautiful saffron-yellow was a favourite colour, especially for their bridal dresses, and on such occasions their dress was enriched by gold ornaments, necklaces, bracelets and rings. Ornaments of various kinds were freely used by the Athenian women in their dress, but the Greeks disliked anything that had no purpose but show, and their jewels were so arranged as to enrich their appearance without taking away from its simple dignity and beauty.

THE ATHENIAN HOUSE

Athenian men, for they gave very little time to their houses. These were the places where the women of the family spent nearly all their hours, but where the men did little more than sleep and have their meals. In the summer time an Athenian house was probably a pleasant place, though we should have found it lacking in nearly everything that we consider necessary, but in the winter it would have been uncomfortably chilly and draughty.

It has already been noticed that an Athenian house usually presented a blank wall to the street, for it was built round a court on to which all the rooms opened. The houses were generally of one story only, though a few occasionally had more, and the rooms drew all their light and air from the court. Socrates once said that a perfect house should be one that was cool in summer and warm in winter, and of such a convenient size that the owner could keep all his possessions in it with ease and security.

The front door was always kept carefully shut and bolted, but a knocker, often in the form of a ring in a lion's mouth, announced the visitor, who was admitted by the porter, a slave who sat in a small room just inside the door. The door opened into a courtyard, which in a good-sized house would be fairly large, but badly paved. This was the men's court. A row of columns all round the sides supported a roof which made a kind of verandah, from which small rooms opened. These rooms do not seem to have had any light or air except that which entered from the court, and they must have been dark and uncomfortable. They were used only by the grown sons of the family and by the male slaves.

In the middle of the court stood an altar to Zeus the Protector of the Home, on which fragrant incense always burned, and fresh garlands of flowers and leaves would be placed on it every day.

Leading out of the men's court was the dining-hall. There would be no table, for the guest did not go to the table, but the table, a low one, was brought to him as he sat or reclined on a beautifully carved couch. The most sacred spot in the house was in this room, the altar of Hestia, on which burned the sacred fire of the family hearth. There might be a row of large vases against one wall, and if one of them bore the inscription, "I am from the Games at Athens," the family would take care to preserve it as one of their greatest treasures, for the words meant that the vase had been a prize won by some member of the family in the Athenian Games.

A door opposite that which led from the men's court into the dining room, opened into another court, that of the women. This was similar to the men's court, but more often planted with flowers and shrubs. The women's rooms, nearly as small and dark and uncomfortable as those of the men, opened from the women's court, and the kitchen was probably at the back of it. On one side of this court there was a large chamber, the best furnished in the house, where the master and mistress slept.

All the furniture in these rooms was simple, but of beautiful design. The chief things used were couches, footstools, low chairs and tables and chests. The latter took the place of closets and cupboards. There were lamps and bronze candelabra, and large numbers of cases used by the Athenians as ordinary water-jugs, wine jars and drinking cups, all of the most graceful shapes and forms and beautifully painted.

The life of the Athenian house centred in the women's court, though during the daytime when the men of the house were absent, the women used the men's court almost as much as their own. The moment, however, they heard the sound of the knocker on the front door, they fled to their own part of the house, lest they should be caught unawares by a male visitor.

ATHENIAN TRADE

The earlier Greeks believed that a state should be self-supporting, that the farmers should produce enough food, and the craftsmen everything needed in daily life. But from the time of Solon onwards this became increasingly difficult in Athens, for owing to the arrival of settlers who came from many different places, attracted by the possibilities of work in the growing state, the population increased, and it became impossible to produce enough food. This had a very important influence on Athens, for instead of being self-sufficing and secure within its own walls, it became dependent for her life on the food supplies, and especially on the corn, that came to her from Egypt and the Black Sea colonies, and in the time of war it was absolutely necessary that the routes to these places should be kept open. Very strict laws were passed to regulate the corn trade and to make sure that enough would always be brought to Athens. No Athenian merchant might take corn to any other harbour than the Peiraeus, and none might leave Egypt or the Black Sea ports unless he had a certain amount of corn on board his ship.

The fact that the Athenian merchant had to go to distant places for corn increased his trade in other articles. He was at home on the sea, and his many-oared ship passed swiftly over the waters of the Aegean, stopping at many places: at the ports of Ionian colonies, where he found his kinsfolk, eager to hear the latest news from the mainland and especially from Athens; at foreign ports, where he rejoiced that he was a Greek and did not dwell amongst these strangers.

The Athenian merchant sailed in his own ship, and beyond his final destination, generally had no definite route in mind.

He was guided by the favourable winds, or by rumours of suitable trading ports where he would find good opportunities for exchanging his goods. He left Athens with oil, honey from Hymettus, and the far-famed Athenian pottery, the chief exports, and he exchanged these for the corn and fish of the Black Sea ports, the wool of Miletus, the perfumes and spices of Syria, the linen and papyrus and the all-important corn of Egypt, the wine of Chios, the cypress wood of Crete, the dates of Phoenicia, the rugs and cushions of Carthage; while in such ports as Carthage and Miletus he found articles which had reached these places by caravans from still more distant lands. In Carthage he obtained ivory and ebony from Africa, and in Miletus richly woven carpets and rugs from Babylon.

All this trade brought wealth to Athens, and it taught the quick Athenian mind, always alert and interested in any new thing, "new ways of enjoying life."

ATHENIAN POTTERY

The industry for which Athens was best known throughout the Mediterranean world was that of the potter, and Athenian vases were exported in very large quantities. But these vases were not mere ornaments; each had its own particular use as a household utensil, an offering to a god, or as an offering at a tomb.

Vases for different purposes were made of different shapes; each was beautiful in form, but with its beauty it combined usefulness. The handles on the water jars are placed just where they are most needed, the oil pours out of the narrow neck of the oil jug drop by drop so that the quantity could be easily regulated, and the drinking cup has a slight curve to the rim, so that one can drink out of it quite easily without spilling the liquid.

There are certain well known forms of these vases: the Amphora is a large two-handled vase which was used for storing oil and other liquids; the Hydria has three handles and was used for carrying water; the Krater is a large vase in which wine and water were mixed; the Lekythos is a jug with a narrow neck used for pouring out oil slowly in small quantities; and the Kylix is a wide and shallow drinking cup. A large amphora, often full of oil, was given as a prize for some of the athletic contests at the Panathenaic games held in Athens. Such an amphora can always be recognized, as it bears on one side the figure of Athena with the inscription: "I am from the Games at Athens," and on the other a painting depicting the contest for which the vase was a prize.

The quarter in Athens given up to the potters was known as the Cerameicus, and here there were a number of workshops owned by different vase-makers. At the head of each establishment was the master; but he was a craftsman as well as manager and was able to do everything connected with the industry: he could not only make the vase, but also design and paint it. His workmen, however, did most of the turning, shaping and polishing of the vases. When the vase had been made, it was given to the artist who painted the design on it, after which it had to be dried, baked and glazed. The black glaze that was used in Athens was one of the great discoveries of the ancient potters' art. Time never spoiled it, and it seems as fresh today as when it was first put on the vases. In some cases it has peeled off in small flakes, but that only happens when the clay beneath is damp; otherwise it remains unchanged.

The earlier vases were painted in black on the red background of the clay; later, the artist sketched his design on the red clay and gave the vase back to the workman, who painted in the background in black and then returned it to the artist, who retouched his design and in some cases added here and there a touch of colour.

Besides the rooms for the workmen and artists, and the court where the ovens were placed, a potter's workshop required storerooms where the finished vases were kept, and a room where the master received his customers and sold his pottery.

In all their art the Greeks were chiefly interested in representing the human form. The subjects of the paintings on the vases were always carefully chosen and were suited to the use to which the vase was to be put. The large vases had graver and more serious subjects, the kylix had more animated scenes. This cup was used at banquets and on festive occasions, and so the artists painted gay and merry scenes on it, and as they tried to attract buyers by the novelty of their designs, the kylix paintings show a great deal of originality. The subjects were taken from mythology, or showed battle scenes, or subjects connected with daily life. If all our other sources of knowledge of life in Athens were suddenly lost to us, the vases would still be a rich mine of information, as in one way or another they represent all the varied experiences of human life.

The craftsmen and vase-painters themselves were in no way regarded as the equals of the great sculptors. The Athenians regarded them as quite lowly workers, but they were artists nevertheless, proved so by the fact that though there was often copying of a general design, the artist never copied mechanically, but put into his work something that was his own. In all the great quantity of Greek vases in the world today no two have been found exactly alike, and so the craftsmen, though they were unconscious of how later ages would regard their work, knew the satisfaction that comes from creating beauty in any form.

EVERYDAY LIFE IN ATHENS: MEN

The day began early in Athens, and as soon as the sun was up everyone was stirring: the workman was off to his work, the schoolboy to school, and every booth and stall in the Agora was laden with articles to attract the buyers who were expected in the market.

Upper class men enjoyed a stroll in the Agora, where they could meet their friends, or go to the barber's shop, and hear the latest news of the day. However, wealthy citizens had definite duties required of them by the State: for example, they were required to fit out and keep in good order one or more triremes for the navy, or to take turns to provide for one of the choruses in the regular dramatic festivals.

Then there were other duties towards the State that were demanded of every free-born citizen. He must sit on the jury and judge law-suits whenever he was called upon to do so, and as the Athenians were very fond of such suits the demand came very often. In some way or other every Athenian citizen took part in the actual government of the state, and in the time of Pericles about nine thousand men held, during the year, some kind of state position. These officials were chosen by the people and were seldom re-elected, so that not only was everybody in turn responsible for certain functions, but everyone was capable of intelligently discussing the affairs of the state, and this was done at great length every day whenever Athenian citizens met together.

About once every ten days, the Agora was deserted in the morning, and every free-born Athenian citizen over thirty years of age, both rich and poor, was expected to go to the Pnyx, the meeting place of the Assembly. In times of war, or when some very important question in which everyone was interested had to be settled, no one stayed away, and there would be great hurrying in the early morning in order to get a good place.

The Pnyx was a great open-air place of assembly, west of the Acropolis and not far from the city wall. In shape it was a sloping semi-circle, part of which was supported by a wall. There were no seats, and the citizens had to make themselves as comfortable as they could on the bare ground. Facing the slope was a rock cut in the form of a platform and mounted by steps on each side. This was called the Bema, and here the orators stood when they addressed the Assembly. In front of the Bema was the altar on which was offered the sacrifice that always opened the Assembly, and behind it on a rock were seats for the state officials who had charge of the meeting.

There were doubtless many days when the business in hand was not very interesting, but there were times when excitement ran high and no one was absent. Not far off rose the rock of the Acropolis, symbol of the strength and glory of Athens and of the guardianship of Athena; in the dim distance was the sea, the great bond of union between Athens and the islands of the Aegean and the East, and a symbol of the protecting power of Poseidon. It was in the Pnyx that the decision was made to march to Marathon and to face the unnumbered Persian foe; that

Themistocles pleaded passionately for a navy; that the messengers from Delphi brought back the answer about the "wooden walls"; that Aristeides persuaded the Athenians to free the Ionians from their Persian masters and to form the Delian League which led Athens to become an Empire; and it was there, too, that Pericles in stately and measured tones urged the Athenians to beautify their city as no other city in the world had ever been beautified before.

After a light meal in the middle of the day, Athenian men would go to the Academy or one of the other gymnasia, where they would spend the cool of the day exercising, or in watching the youths at their games; in walking in the pleasant groves talking over the events of the day with his friends; or in discussing with some philosopher all kinds of questions concerning new interpretations of old beliefs and new ideas about man, whence he comes and whither he goes. Some of these were questions which were discussed for the first time in the history of the world, and never before and but seldom since has there been such an eager desire to know the truth about all things, as there was in this Athens of the fifth century BCE.

But as the evening drew on and it grew dusk, the Athenians left the gymnasia and returned to the city. All day long they had been in company, and in the evening the most was made of every opportunity to meet again, so it was very likely that the day would end by a banquet. If that were so, the guests would all have been invited in the morning, either by the host himself when he met them, or by a message carried by a slave. Preparations were usually made for more than the invited number of guests, as it was a common custom for guests to bring some additional friends of their own, and uninvited guests would often come without any special bidding. Since leaving the gymnasia, all the guests would have been at their homes. There they would have bathed and clad themselves in fresh chitons and mantles, and slaves would accompany them to the house of their host.

At a banquet the guests reclined on couches, and the food was brought to them on low tables. The evening meal was the chief meal of the day in Athens. It began with fish or meat and vegetables, and when this course was over, the tables were removed, water was poured over the hands of the guests, and garlands were often passed round. Then came the second course of fruits, confectionery and various kinds of sweetmeats, after which the tables were again removed, and replaced by smaller ones on which stood beautifully shaped drinking cups. The guests were given more garlands and wreaths, and the slaves brought in the large kraters, in which the wine and water were mixed, and the after-dinner entertainment of the evening began.

This entertainment was called the Symposium, and it began with the pouring out of three libations: to the Olympian gods, to the Heroes, and to Zeus. Then the health of the hosts and of his guests was drunk; after which began the entertainment. This consisted of conversation, singing, listening to music, watching dancers, in playing games, telling stories or passing round jests. Just what was done at the Symposium depended on the kind of guests present. Serioius-minded guests were content with one another's conversation. More often, however, the guests were less serious. They enjoyed chatting and listening to the music of the flute and other instruments, they played games, and watched dancing.

When the party came to an end, a libation was offered to Hermes, the slaves were called, who attended their masters home, lighting their way with torches or lamps. The older men would go sedately home, the younger would keep up their merriment and go noisily and boisterously through the streets until, having knocked at the doors of their houses, the sleepy porter would wake up and let them in, and silence would at length reign in the streets of the city.

EVERYDAY LIFE IN ATHENS: WOMEN

Women's lives were based in the home, where they managed g all the household affairs and bringing up the children. Women educated theirr sons until they were seven years old, when they went to school, and theirr daughters until they were about fifteen, when they were considered old enough to be married.

The Greek writer Xenophon wrote an account of what were considered the duties of an ideal Athenian wife. He imagines the husband of a young bride telling her what he expected of her, and in what way he hoped the household affairs would be managed. She was consigned to the house, where she looked after the budget, the carding of wool, the making of clothing, the provision of food, and the care of the sick. She was responsible for teaching other young women her domestic skills, for the care of her children and support of her husband.

Added to all these occupations was the education of the children. The Athenian lady had nurses for them, Spartan slave-women, if they were to be had, for their discipline was sterner than that of other Greeks, and the Spartan nurses had the reputation of being able to keep their young charges in particularly good order. All kinds of toys were provided for the children, hoops and balls, spinning-tops and go-carts, dolls and toy animals. The Athenian mother learnt to be a good story-teller, for it was in these early days that the children wanted stories told them, and many a tale would she relate of the gods and heroes of old, of the nymphs and spirits of the forests and mountains, of the sea and of the air. And when night came and the children must go to bed, then she would sing them to

The girls had to be trained to all the duties of an Athenian wife, and there was much to learn in the short years of their girlhood. It was a domestic training that they were given; of other things they learned as much or as little as their mother knew herself and was able to teach them, probably not more than a little reading and writing. A girl was not encouraged to take up any kind of intellectual pursuits

When the Athenian girl married, she took upon her young shoulders the training of her own household, even as she had seen her mother do. Her marriage had usually been arranged for her, and she often knew but little of her future husband. Before the marriage day, she offered all her girlhood toys to Artemis, the goddess who had watched over her childhood.

When these symbols of her youth had passed from her keeping into that of the goddess, she was dressed in beautiful raiment, crowned with a wreath and covered with the bridal veil for the marriage ceremony. This took place in the evening on a day when the moon was full; the marriage took place in the court, a sacrifice was offered and a libation poured out to the gods, and then the marriage feast followed, at which cakes of sesame were always eaten. This was the only occasion on which women were allowed to be present at a feast, but through it all the bride remained closely veiled. When the feast was over, the bridal chariot was driven up to the door, and the bride took her seat in it beside her husband, her mother walked behind it bearing the marriage torch with which the fire on the hearth of her new home would be lighted, the guests surrounded it and with flute-playing and singing escorted the bride to her new home.

If the bridegroom lived in a distant place, the bridal procession broke up at the gates of the city, but if he lived in Athens, he and his bride were escorted to the door of his house, where they were met by his mother, and then, to the music of a marriage song, the bride was led into her new home.

The well-born Athenian lady seldom left the house, and never unless attended by a female slave. She had practically no society but that of her slaves. She saw no men, except those of her own family. If her husband dined at home alone, she shared his meal, but if he had guests she was unseen. From time to time she took part in the great religious festivals and processions, and occasionally she was permitted to be present in the theatre when a tragedy was performed, but she was never permitted to see a comedy for the wit and humour were often coarse and were considered unfitting for her ears.

But whatever was the actual life of the Athenian lady, the Athenian ideal of womanhood was very high. In the wondrous temple that stood high above the city, looking down upon it and guarding it, was the figure that symbolized to the Athenians all that was good and beautiful and true, and it was the figure of a woman. It was always the figure of a woman that represented Victory, and nearly all the great Greek dramas deal with the fate of a woman, who was generally the wife or daughter of a King.

The Sacred Mysteries of Eleusis centred round the story of the love and sorrow of a woman.

Despite her subordinate position in the background, the Athenian woman was of real influence in Athens. The Athenian ideal of service was that the man should give it wholly to the state, and the woman wholly to her home. She reigned supreme in the household, and as her sons grew up, they recognized in her those qualities which every Greek and especially the Athenian, was taught to value so highly: that quiet courage which by its very steadfastness overcomes all the little anxieties and annoyances of daily life; and that self-control and self-mastery which, putting self in the background, sets free the individual for service to others.

ATHENIAN EDUCATION

The chief aim of Athenian education was the building of character. The Athenians were more concerned that their sons should grow up to be good citizens, loving what was beautiful and hating all that was ugly, than that they should know any great number of facts.

Like the Spartans, the Athenians believed in the training of the body, and in making patriotic citizens who would count it a glory to die in defence of their city, but they also believed that it was a glory to live for their city, and to this end they trained the mind and the imagination as well as the body. To an Athenian a good man was a good citizen, one who, being physically perfect, would be able to defend his city in time of war, who, being able to think, would be capable of governing, and loving all that was beautiful would set high standards of taste in art, in letters, and in conduct. Praxiteles gave outward form to this ideal in his statue of Hermes, and though the Athenian ideal was not complete, Athenian education produced a warrior like Miltiades, statesmen like Themistocles and Pericles, a poet like Sophocles, artists like Pheidias and Praxiteles, philosophers like Socrates and Plato, and a historian like Thucydides.

The Athenians believed that training which aimed only at money-making, or bodily strength, or mere cleverness apart from intelligence, was mean and vulgar and did not deserve to be called education. True education, they held, made a child long to be a good citizen and taught him both how to rule and to obey. It must not be supposed that the Athenians despised wealth or the power of wealth. Only a wealthy state could have built the Parthenon or celebrated the great Panathenaic Festival, but the Athenians despised mere money-making, and they believed that a man's success was not to be measured by the amount of money he had made, but by the use to which he put it, and they believed that an education which taught a boy to be industrious and thrifty, to despise self-indulgence and luxury, to think straight and see clearly, would make him a better citizen than one which aimed only at making him a successful man of business. So they aimed at giving every boy a good education.

The Athenian boy went to school when he was seven years old. At this age he was placed in the charge of a pedagogue, a trusted slave who accompanied him when he went to school, carried his books for him, and helped him, when necessary, with his lessons. The pedagogue was also expected to keep him in good order, to teach him good manners, to answer all his many questions, and to punish him whenever he thought fit, which was probably very often.

Schools opened early, so early that Solon made a law forbidding schoolmasters to open their schools before sunrise and requiring them to be closed before sunset, so that the boys should not have to walk about the dark and empty streets. He walked to school followed attendants and pedagogues, who carried writing-tablets, books if he was going to a music-school, his well-tuned lyre.

Once they arrived at the school, the pedagogues remained in an ante-room, where they waited together until morning school was over. The boy entered a larger room beyond, where he settled down to his lessons. The boys sat on low benches with their writing-tablets on their knees, and the master sat on a higher chair in front of them. Lyres and other musical instruments, a book-roll or two, or perhaps some drinking-cups hung on the walls.

Athenian boys were taught three main subjects: letters, music and gymnastics. The first thing connected with letters was to be able to read and write. The first writing lessons were given on wooden tablets covered with wax, and for a pen a stylus with a sharp metal point was used. With this stylus the letters were scratched on the wax. When a boy had learnt to write better, he was allowed to write on papyrus with a reed dipped in a kind of sticky substance which took the place of ink.

Athenian boys had no books for children – they began by reading great poetry and literature. Much of the literature they learnt by heart, standing in front of the master who recited it to them, and they learnt it by repeating it after him line by line. In this way they mastered passages from the *Iliad* and the *Odyssey*, and though it must have been unusual, it was not an unknown feat for a boy to be able to recite the whole of those poems by heart. Reciting poetry in an Athenian school was by no means a dull affair, for the boys acted as they recited. The art of reciting poetry was held in high esteem not only in Athens, but all over Greece, and in all places where the Greek tongue was spoken and where Greek ideals prevailed.

A certain amount of arithmetic was also taught, for it was considered a good training for the mind and a valuable preparation for household management, politics, crafts, sciences and professions.

Part of the day was given to the study of letters, and then the boys went to the music school, where they learnt to play the lyre and to sing. A song accompanied by the music of the lyre was a favourite part of the entertainment after a banquet, and every Athenian gentleman was expected to be able to sing and play whenever he was called upon. So much was it the mark of a gentleman, that "He who doesn't know the way to play the lyre" became a proverbial expression for an uneducated person.

Very little is known about Greek music, but it was considered very necessary that the music taught should be of an ennobling and inspiring kind. The Lydian melodies were held to be altogether too soft and sentimental, and the Athenians preferred those known as Dorian, because they were simpler and sterner and of a kind to inspire men to noble and manly deeds. Aristotle who wrote so much about the ideal state, wrote also about the education an ideal state should give to its children. He held that "music is neither a necessary nor a useful accomplishment in the sense in which letters are useful, but it provides a noble and worthy means of occupying leisure time," and Aristotle, like all Athenians, believed that it was the part of a good education to teach not only how to work well, but also how to use leisure well. The Athenians thought music was a good medicine for all ills.

In the afternoon the boys were taken by their pedagogues to the palaestra or wrestling-school, where they learned gymnastics. It was as important that the boy should have a well-trained, graceful body, as that he should have a clear and well-furnished mind, and so he spent a good part of each day running, jumping, wrestling, and throwing the discus under a special master.

According to Plato, this education turned the Athenian boy from being "the most unmanageable of animals" into "the most amiable and divine of living beings." This change had not taken place without many a punishment of the boy, and it was a proverb that "he that is not flogged cannot be taught." Not long ago an old Greek papyrus was discovered which gives a vivid account of the discipline that was thought necessary by both parents and teachers, for the schoolboy who preferred, as he probably often did, to play games instead of learning his lessons.

Children were not always well behaved in other ways, it seems, and complaints were made by their parents that the children contradicted them and did not always rise when their elders came into the room, that they chattered too much before company, crossed their legs when they sat down, and completely tyrannized over their pedagogues.

But in spite of all his misdemeanours and punishments, in letters, music and gymnastics, the Athenian boy was educated until he was eighteen years old. The stories of the ancient heroes who had fought at Troy, and those of more recent times who had defeated the Persians filled him with enthusiasm for his race and a love of freedom for his city. Having to learn many things without the aid of books, his mind grew quick, alert and observant, and his music and gymnastics taught him the beauty of self-control and dignified restraint.

At eighteen, the Athenian youth left school. The state did not give him the full rights of a citizen until a few years later, and until then he was required to perform certain military duties, but he was no longer a boy, and he was considered old enough to understand the meaning of citizenship, and to know what were its duties and privileges. So it was then, at the time of leaving his boyhood behind, and entering upon the richer and fuller life before him, that the youth took the oath of the Ephebi or young men. He was given the shield and spear of the warrior, and then in the temple, before Zeus, the Lord of Heaven, and in the presence of the highest Athenian magistrates, he swore:

"Never to disgrace his holy arms, never to forsake his comrade in the ranks, but to fight for the holy temples, alone or with others: to leave his country, not in a worse, but in a better state than he found it; to obey the magistrates and the laws, and defend them against attack; finally to hold in honour the religion of his country."

THE ATHENIAN THEATRE

The tragedies and comedies that emerged in the heyday of Classical Athens in the fifth century BCE were innovative, challenging and thought-provoking. They were also harbingers of a new form of mass entertainment, which would spread throughout the Greek world, and become the foundation upon which all modern theatre is built.

Greek drama began as a religious observance in honour of Dionysus. To the Greeks this god personified both the spring and the vintage, the latter a very important time of year in a vine-growing country, and he was a symbol to them of that power there is in human beings to rise out of themselves, to be impelled onwards by an inward joy that they cannot explain, but which makes them go forward, walking, as it were, on the wings of the wind, of the spirit that fills them with a deep sense of worship. We call this power *enthusiasm*, a Greek word which simply means *the god within us*.

From very early times, stories of his life were recited at the religious festivals held in honour of Dionysus, and then stories of the other gods and of the ancient heroes were told as well. It was from these beginnings that the drama came. Originally, the story was told in the form of a song, chanted at first by everyone taking part in the festival, and later by a chorus of about fifty performers, and at intervals in the song the leader would recite part of the story by himself. By degrees the recitation became of greater importance than the song; it grew longer, and after a time two people took part in it and then three; at the same time the chorus became smaller and of less importance in the action of the drama, until at last it could consist of only fifteen performers.

A Greek drama was in many ways much simpler than a modern drama. There were fewer characters, and usually only three speaking actors were allowed on the stage at once. There was only one story told and there was nothing to take the attention of the audience away from this. The Chorus, though it no longer told the story, was very important, for it set the atmosphere of the play, and lyrics of haunting loveliness hinted at the tragedy that could not be averted, because of terrible deeds done in the past, or if, indeed, there might be any help, the imagination was carried forward on wings of hope. The Chorus also served another purpose. In a modern drama, when the tragedy of a situation becomes almost too great for the audience to bear, relief is often found in some comic, or partly comic, episode which is introduced to slacken the tension. Shakespeare does this constantly. But comic episodes were felt to be out of place in a Greek drama, and therefore when a tragic scene had taken place, the Chorus followed it by a song of purest poetry. In one play of Euripides, a terrible scene of tragedy was followed by a song in which the Chorus prayed for escape from such sorrows on the wings of a bird to a land where all was peace and beauty. They sang:

> Could I take me to some cavern for mine hiding,
>   In the hill-tops where the Sun scarce hath trod;
> Or a cloud make the home of mine abiding,
>   As a bird among the bird-droves of God.
> And the song goes on to carry the imagination to a spot
> Where a voice of living waters never ceaseth
>   In God's quiet garden by the sea,
> And Earth, the ancient life-giver, increaseth
>   Joy among the meadows, like a tree

**Euripides: *Hippolytus*, translated
by Gilbert Murray**

In the great Greek dramas, the Chorus is a constant reminder that, though they cannot understand or explain them, there are other powers in the world than the wild passions of men.

The great dramatic festival in Athens was held in the spring in the theatre of Dionysus, to the south-east of the Acropolis. The theatre in Athens never became an everyday amusement, as it is today, but was always directly connected with the worship of Dionysus, and the performances were always preceded by a sacrifice. The festival was only held once a year, and whilst it lasted the whole city kept holiday. Originally, admission to the theatre was free, but the crowds became so great and there was such confusion and sometimes fighting in the rush for good seats, that the state decided to charge an admission fee and tickets had to be bought beforehand. But even then there were no reserved seats, except for certain officials who sat in the front row. In the time of Pericles, complaints were made that the poorer citizens could not afford to buy tickets, and so important was the drama then considered, that it was ordered that tickets should be given free to all who applied for them.

An Athenian audience was very critical, and shouts and applause, or groans and hisses showed its approval or disapproval of the play being acted. Several plays were given in one day, and a prize was awarded to the best, so the audience was obliged to start at dawn and would probably remain in the theatre until sunset.

The theatre at Athens was a great semi-circle on the slope of the Acropolis, with rows of stone seats on which about eighteen thousand spectators can sit. The front row consisted of marble chairs, the only seats in the theatre which have backs, and these were reserved for the priests of Dionysus and the chief magistrates. Beyond the front row, was a circular space called the orchestra, where the Chorus sang, and in the centre of which stood the altar of Dionysus. Behind the orchestra, was the stage, at the back of which was a building painted to look like the front of a temple or a palace, to which the actors retire when they were not wanted on the stage or have to change their costumes. The very simplicity of the outward surroundings made the audience give all their attention to the play and the acting.

There were only three actors on the stage at once. They wore very elaborate costumes, and a strange-looking wooden sole called a cothurnus or buskin, about six inches high, on their shoes, to make them look taller and more impressive, and over their faces a curious mask with a wide mouth, so that everyone in that vast audience could hear them. The play was not divided into different acts. When there was a pause in the action, the Chorus filled up the time with their song. If it was tragedy, the audience did not see the final catastrophe on the stage, but a messenger appeared who gave an account of what has happened.

The legends and traditions from which most of the Greek plays took their plots were, of course, well known to the Athenians. They were stories commemorating some great event, or explaining some religious observance, but naturally these legends were differently treated by different dramatists, each of whom brought out a different side of the story to enforce some particular lesson which he wished to bring home to the people, and this is especially true of the legends like that of Iphigenia connected with the Fall of Troy.

IPHIGENIA IN TAURIS

Iphigenia in Tauris was written by in the latter half of the fifth century by Euripides, one of the greatest Athenian dramatists. It is based on the story of Iphigenia, the daughter of Agamemnon, King of Argos, the great leader of the of the host that was bound for Troy. Becalmed at Aulis, he consulted wise men who told him that Artemis demanded the sacrifice of Iphigenia. The sacrifice was offered, but at the supreme moment,

Artemis carried Iphigenia away and placed her in the land of the Tauri, a wild and barbarous tribe, as their priestess.

Iphigenia was exiled in Tauris for ten years, ignorant of the outcome of the Trojan War, or the fate of her father (slain by Clytemnestra, his wife) or her brother Orestes, who had avenged that death by slaughtering his own mother. The play focuses on the moment when Orestes, who has been wandering from place to place pursued by the relentless torment of the Furies, arrives at Tauris, a dangerous fate since Iphigenia, the priestess of Artemis, is required to sacrifice all strangers who were cast on their shores. The Chorus is comprised of Greek women who have been taken captive in war by King Thoas, and so they are friendly to the exiled and lonely Iphigenia, for they are just as homesick as she is.

The play explores the torment of exile and the ravages of guilt. It also speaks eloquently about the love of Greeks for their homeland, and in particular, Athens. It traces Iphigenia's gradual realization that the stranger who arrives in Tauris is in fact her long-lost brother, and follows her intricate plot to extricate him from the life-threatening situation he finds himself in, even if it means sacrificing her own life.

Iphigenia's first speech is a lament to the Chorus about the premonitions of doom she is experiencing about the fate that has befallen her family:

> Alas! O maidens mine,
> I am filled full of tears:
>   My heart filled with the beat
>   Of tears, as of dancing feet,
> A lyreless, joyless line,
> And music meet for the dead.

For a whisper is in mine ears,
By visions borne on the breath
Of the Night that now is fled,
Of a brother gone to death.
Oh sorrow and weeping sore,
 For the house that no more is,
For the dead that were kings of yore
 And the labour of Argolis!

On news that Greeks (Orestes and his companion Pylades) have arrived on the shores of Tauris, the Chorus rejoice in recollections of their homeland, but also lament the fact that the new arrivals have been taken captive and face certain death:

A sail, a sail from Greece,
 Fearless to cross the sea,
With ransom and with peace
 To my sick captivity.
O home, to see thee still,
And the old walls on the hill!
Dreams, dreams, gather to me!
Bear me on wings over the sea;
O joy of the night, to slave and free,
 One good thing that abideth!

Following the encounter between Iphigenia and Orestes, there is a slow and dawning recognition that he is, in fact, her brother. But how can she evade her duty as a priestess of Artemis to sacrifice the stranger?

And now, what end cometh?
Shall Chance yet comfort me,
Finding a way for thee
Back from the Friendless Strand,
  Back from the place of death –
Ere yet the slayers come
And thy blood sink in the sand –
Home unto Argos, home?
Hard heart so swift to slay
Is there to life no way? –
  No ship! – And how by land? –
  A rush of feet
Out to the waste alone.
  Nay: 'twere to meet
Death, amid tribes unknown
And trackless ways of the waste –
Surely the sea were best.
Back by the narrow bar
  To the Dark Blue Gate! –
Ah God, too far, too far! –
  Desolate! Desolate!
What god or man, what unimagined flame,
  Can cleave this road where no road is, and bring
To us last wrecks of Agamemnon's name
  Peace from long suffering?

When Iphigenia learns from Orestes that he has been entrusted with the sacred task of stealing the statue of Artemis and planting it on Attic soil, she faces a true dilemma. She deliberately decides that she will save his life and give him the statue, and then she herself will confront the angry King and give her life for her brother. But Orestes refuses her sacrifice. They must find another means of escape.

What of the Chorus, of these Greek women, companions of the exile and loneliness of Iphigenia? They loyally promise secrecy about all that concerns the plot to escape Tauris. Yet they, too, crave for home and they give voice to their longings. They see in imagination the Greek land. Once again the misery of their capture and enslavement comes before them, but they rise above their sorrow as they sing of what it will mean to Iphigenia to cross the sea, to behold her home once again, and to reach the land of freedom.

Chorus

Bird of the sea rocks, of the bursting spray,
   O halcyon bird,
That wheelest crying, crying, on thy way;
Who knoweth grief can read the tale of thee:
One love long lost, one song for ever heard
   And wings that sweep the sea.
Sister, I too beside the sea complain,
   A bird that hath no wing.
Oh, for a kind Greek market-place again,
For Artemis that healeth woman's pain;
   Here I stand hungering.
Give me the little hill above the sea,
The palm of Delos fringed delicately,
The young sweet laurel and the olive-tree
   Grey-leaved and glimmering...

Iphigenia succeeds in persuading King Thoas that she must perform preparatory rites before sacrificing the two Greeks, and – from the sacred privacy of the temple – she manages to escape, with Orestes, Pylades and the statue of Artemis. King Thoas immediately demands that they are pursued and recaptured:

THOAS

Ho, all ye dwellers of my savage town
Set saddle on your steeds, and gallop down
To watch the heads, and gather what is cast
Alive from this Greek wreck. We shall make fast,
By God's help, the blasphemers. – Send a corps
Out in good boats a furlong from the shore;
So we shall either snare them on the seas
Or ride them down by land, and at our ease
Fling them down gulfs of rock, or pale them high
On stakes in the sun, to feed our birds and die.
Women: you knew this plot. Each one of you
Shall know, before the work I have to do
Is done, what torment is. – Enough! A clear
Task is afoot. I must not linger here.

While Thoas is moving off, his men shouting and running before and behind him, there comes a sudden blasting light and thunder-roll, and Athena is seen in the air confronting them. This sudden appearance of a god to solve a problem at the end of a play is known as the *deus ex machina*, and there was actually some kind of machine by which the god appeared as if suspended in the air.

ATHENA

Ho, whither now, so hot upon the prey,
King Thoas? It is I that bid thee stay,
Athena, child of Zeus. Turn back this flood
Of wrathful men, and get thee temperate blood.
Apollo's word and Fate's ordained path
Have led Orestes here, to escape the wrath
Of Them that hate. To Argos he must bring
His sister's life, and guide that Holy Thing
Which fell from heaven, in mine own land to dwell.
So shall his pain have rest, and all be well.
Thou hast heard my speech, O
King. No death from thee
May snare Orestes between rocks and sea:
Poseidon for my love doth make the sore
Waves gentle, and set free his labouring oar.

And thou, O far away – for, far or near
A goddess speaketh and thy heart must hear –
Go on thy ways, Orestes, bearing home
The Image and thy sister. When ye come
To god-built Athens, lo, a land there is
Half hid on Attica's last boundaries,
A little land, hard by Karystus' Rock,
But sacred. It is called by Attic folk
Halae. Build there a temple, and bestow
Therein thine Image, that the world may know
The tale of Tauris and of thee, cast out
From pole to pole of Greece, a blood-hound rout
Of ill thoughts driving thee. So through the whole

Of time to Artemis the Tauropole
Shall men make hymns at Halae. And withal,
Give them this law. At each high festival,
A sword, in record of thy death undone,
Shall touch a man's throat, and the red blood run —
One drop, for old religion's sake. In this
Shall live that old red rite of Artemis.

And thou, Iphigenia, by the stair
Of Brauron in the rocks, the Key shall bear
Of Artemis. There shalt thou live and die,
And there have burial. [...]

Ye last, O exiled women, true of heart
And faithful found, ye shall in peace depart,
Each to her home: behold Athena's will.

Orestes, long ago on Ares' Hill
I saved thee, when the votes of Death and Life
Lay equal: and henceforth, when men at strife
So stand, mid equal votes of Life and Death,
My law shall hold that Mercy conquereth
Begone. Lead forth thy sister from this shore
In peace; and thou Thoas, be wroth no more.

Euripides: *Iphigenia in Tauris*,
translated by Gilbert Murray

THE PELOPONNESIAN WAR
& ITS AFTERMATH

Athens **was a democracy**, and its freedom, thought and art were not the special possession of a small privileged group but of the whole body of citizens. The greatest Athenian sculpture and architecture were flawless in their simplicity and beauty. They have been copied and imitated, but never surpassed. The Greek stage set certain limitations to the drama, but within these limitations the dramas of the great Athenian dramatists were well-nigh perfect. In their search for truth, the Athenian philosophers went as far as it was possible for them to go, but the very fact that they accepted the institution of slavery as a normal condition of life, made any further advance in political thinking impossible.

Eventually, however, Athens was hated because from being the great deliverer of Greece, it had become a tyrant and an oppressor, and the small states hitherto ruled by Athens were more than ready to transfer their allegiance to Sparta which held out promises of freedom from oppression if they would join her. The Peloponnesian War, which extended over the last three decades of the fifth century BCE, was a bitter struggle between the Greek city-states, which killed tens of thousands and was only resolved with the help of Persia. This assistance came at a price, forcing the abandonment of all the Greek cities that lay within the Persian sphere.

THUCYDIDES' ACCOUNT

This **excerpt** is from Thucydides' *History of the Peloponnesian War*, Chapter IV:

The way in which Athens came to be placed in the circumstances under which her power grew was this. After the Medes had returned from Europe, defeated by sea and land by the Hellenes, and after those of them who had fled with their ships to Mycale had been destroyed, Leotychides, king of the Lacedaemonians, the commander of the Hellenes at Mycale, departed home with the allies from Peloponnese. But the Athenians and the allies from Ionia and Hellespont, who had now revolted from the King, remained and laid siege to Sestos, which was still held by the Medes. After wintering before it, they became masters of the place on its evacuation by the barbarians; and after this they sailed away from Hellespont to their respective cities. Meanwhile the Athenian people, after the departure of the barbarian from their country, at once proceeded to carry over their children and wives, and such property as they had left, from the places where they had deposited them, and prepared to rebuild their city and their walls. For only isolated portions of the circumference had been left standing, and most of the houses were in ruins; though a few remained, in which the Persian grandees had taken up their quarters.

Perceiving what they were going to do, the Lacedaemonians sent an embassy to Athens. They would have themselves preferred to see neither her nor any other city in possession of a wall; though here they acted principally at the instigation of their allies, who were alarmed at the strength of her newly acquired navy and the valour which she had displayed in the war with the Medes. They begged her not only to abstain from building walls for herself, but also to join them in throwing down the walls that still held together of the ultra-Peloponnesian cities. The real meaning of their advice, the suspicion that it contained against the Athenians, was not proclaimed; it was urged that so the barbarian, in the event of a third invasion, would not have any strong place, such as he now had in Thebes, for his base of operations; and that Peloponnese would suffice for all as a base both for retreat and offence. After the Lacedaemonians had thus spoken, they were, on the advice of Themistocles, immediately dismissed by the Athenians, with the answer that ambassadors should be sent to Sparta to discuss the question. Themistocles told the Athenians to send him off with all speed to Lacedaemon, but not to dispatch his colleagues as soon as they had selected them, but to wait until they had raised their wall to the height from which defence was possible. Meanwhile the whole population in the city was to labour at the wall, the Athenians, their wives, and their children, sparing no edifice, private or public, which might be of any use to the work, but throwing all down. After giving these instructions, and adding that he would be responsible for all other matters there, he departed. Arrived at Lacedaemon he did not seek an audience with the authorities, but tried to gain time and made excuses. When any of the government asked him why he did not appear in the assembly, he would say that he was waiting for his colleagues, who had been detained in Athens by some engagement; however, that he expected their speedy arrival, and wondered that they were not yet there. At first the Lacedaemonians trusted the words of Themistocles, through their friendship for him; but when others arrived, all distinctly declaring that the work was going on and already attaining some elevation, they did not know how to disbelieve it. Aware of this, he told them that rumours are deceptive, and should not be trusted; they should send some reputable persons from Sparta to inspect, whose report might be trusted. They dispatched them accordingly. Concerning these Themistocles secretly sent word to the Athenians to detain them as far as possible without putting them under open constraint, and not to let them go until they had themselves returned. For his colleagues had now joined him, Abronichus, son of Lysicles, and Aristides, son of Lysimachus, with the news that the wall was sufficiently advanced; and he feared that when the Lacedaemonians heard the facts, they might refuse to let them go. So the Athenians detained the envoys according to his message, and Themistocles had an audience with the Lacedaemonians, and at last openly told them that Athens was now fortified sufficiently to protect its inhabitants; that any embassy which the Lacedaemonians or their allies might wish to send to them should in future proceed on the assumption that the people to whom they were going was able to distinguish both its own and the general interests. That when the Athenians thought fit to abandon their city and to embark in their ships, they ventured on that perilous step without consulting them; and that on the other hand, wherever they had deliberated with the Lacedaemonians, they had proved themselves to be in judgment second to none. That they now thought it fit that their city should have a wall, and that this would be more for the advantage of both the citizens of Athens and the Hellenic confederacy; for without equal military strength it was impossible to contribute equal or fair counsel to the common interest. It followed, he observed, either that all the members of the confederacy should be without walls, or that the present step should be considered a right one.

The Lacedaemonians did not betray any open signs of anger against the Athenians at what they heard. The embassy, it seems, was prompted not by a desire to obstruct, but to guide the counsels of their government: besides, Spartan feeling was at that time very friendly towards Athens on account of the patriotism which she had displayed in the struggle with the Mede. Still the defeat of their wishes could not but cause them secret annoyance. The envoys of each state departed home without complaint.

In this way the Athenians walled their city in a little while. To this day the building shows signs of the haste of its execution; the foundations are laid of stones of all kinds, and in some places not wrought or fitted, but placed just in the order in which they were brought by the different hands; and many columns, too, from tombs, and sculptured stones were put in with the rest. For the bounds of the city were extended at every point of the circumference; and so they laid hands on everything without exception in their haste. Themistocles also persuaded them to finish the walls of Piraeus, which had been begun before, in his year of office as archon; being influenced alike by the fineness of a locality that has three natural harbours, and by the great start which the Athenians would gain in the acquisition of power by becoming a naval people. For he first ventured to tell them to stick to the sea and forthwith began to lay the foundations of the empire. It was by his advice, too, that they built the walls of that thickness which can still be discerned round Piraeus, the stones being brought up by two wagons meeting each other. Between the walls thus formed there was neither rubble nor mortar, but great stones hewn square and fitted together, cramped to each other on the outside with iron and lead. About half the height that he intended was finished. His idea was by their size and thickness to keep off the attacks of an enemy; he thought that they might be adequately defended by a small garrison of invalids, and the rest be freed for service in the fleet. For the fleet claimed most of his attention. He saw, as I think, that the approach by sea was easier for the king's army than that by land: he also thought Piraeus more valuable than the upper city; indeed, he was always advising the Athenians, if a day should come when they were hard pressed by land, to go down into Piraeus, and defy the world with their fleet. Thus, therefore, the Athenians completed their wall, and commenced their other buildings immediately after the retreat of the Mede.

THE RIVALRY BETWEEN ATHENS AND SPARTA

Pericles had many opponents in Athens. Some disapproved of his imperial policy, and others accused him of extravagance in spending so much of the public money on temples. The most serious accusation brought against him was that in beautifying Athens he was spending not only money from the Athenian treasury, but also using that which belonged to the Delian League. This latter accusation was true, and the people called for an ostracism. But it resulted in the support of Pericles by the majority of the Athenians, and in the banishment of his opponent.

Pericles knew what he was doing when he used the money from the treasury of the Delian League. To Athens had been committed the trust of defending the allied islands and cities from Persian aggression and it was the money contributed by the allies for the cost of this defence that was kept in the treasury of the League. Pericles maintained that the beautifying of Athens was a symbol of her might and power, that the great buildings employed labour and encouraged commerce, both of which added to her prosperity, and that these outward signs of her wealth and might added to her ability to protect her allies. He had won for Athens the foremost position in Greece, and he was determined that Athens should keep it. To this end he argued that Athens was justified in using the money of the League, because the way in which it was being spent added not only to the glory but also to the security of all.

Pericles was also a great lover of all that was beautiful, and he was honestly desirous that the youth of Athens should grow up in a city that should be a joy for ever, that would make them good and useful citizens, and inspire them with an abiding love for and pride in her. But there is a flaw in the character of a man who holds that the end, even if it is a great and glorious one, justifies any means.

Now Attica was very small, and in the days of her prosperity the population of Athens had increased so much that the state could no longer produce enough food to support the people. The far-seeing policy of Themistocles had made Athens stronger on sea than on land, and by the time of Pericles, the salvation of Athens lay in its navy. As Athens increased its sea-power in all directions it established dominance over the Aegean and on the shores of the Euxine. This policy was not only dictated by the greed of power, but by the absolute necessity that if Athens were to live, it should control all the trade routes by which corn reached Greece. Without the corn from the shores of the Euxine, Athens would starve.

Sparta was a great land power, and at first this increasing sea-power of Athens did not touch it very closely, but it did affect Corinth, the next sea-power in Greece after Athens. As long as Athens confined its interests to the Aegean and the East, Corinth was not alarmed, but when the Athenians turned to the West and showed their intention of establishing their power there, the Corinthians became seriously alarmed, for this threatened their interests in Sicily and the south of Italy. Corinth had always been hostile to Athens, and now appealed to Sparta, asking for help to crush Athens. Corinthian envoys went to Sparta, and in a powerful speech one of them set forth the grievances of the Greek world against Athens, representing her power, and entreating the Spartans to lay aside their policy of inaction and to join with them in crushing the Tyrant state.

"Time after time we have warned you of the mischief which the Athenians would do to us, but instead of taking our words to heart, you chose to suspect that we only spoke from interested motives. If the crimes which the Athenians are committing against Hellas were being done in a corner, then you might be ignorant, and we should have to inform you of them: but now, what need of many words? Some of us, as you see, have been already enslaved; they are at this moment intriguing against others, notably against allies of ours; and long ago they had made all their preparations in expectation of war… And you have never considered what manner of men are these Athenians with whom you will have to fight, and how utterly unlike yourselves. They

are revolutionary, equally quick in the conception and in the execution of every new plan; while you are conservative, careful only to keep what you have, originating nothing, and not acting even when action is most necessary. They are bold beyond their strength; they run risks which prudence would condemn; and in the midst of misfortune they are full of hope. Whereas it is your nature, though strong, to act feebly; when your plans are most prudent, to distrust them; and when calamities come upon you, to think that you will never be delivered from them. They are impetuous, and you are dilatory; they are always abroad, and you are always at home. For they hope to gain something by leaving their homes; but you are afraid that any new enterprise may imperil what you have already. When conquerors, they pursue their victory to the utmost; when defeated, they fall back the least. Their bodies they devote to their country as though they belonged to other men; their true self is their mind, which is most truly their own when employed in her service. When they do not carry out an intention which they have formed, they seem to have sustained a personal bereavement; when an enterprise succeeds, they have gained a mere instalment of what is to come; but if they fail, they at once conceive new hopes and so fill up the void. With them alone to hope is to have, for they lose not a moment in the execution of an idea. This is the life-long task, full of danger and toil, which they are always imposing upon themselves. None enjoy their good things less, because they are always seeking for more. To do their duty is their only holiday, and they deem the quiet of inaction to be as disagreeable as the most tiresome business. If a man should say of them, in a word, that they were born neither to have peace themselves nor to allow peace to other men, he would simply speak the truth.

"In the face of such an enemy, Lacedaemonians, you persist in doing nothing. But let your procrastination end. Do not allow friends and kindred to fall into the hands of their worst enemies; or drive us in

*despair to seek the alliance of others; in taking such a course we should
be doing nothing wrong either before the Gods who are the witnesses of
our oaths, or before men whose eyes are upon us. For the true breakers
of treaties are not those who, when forsaken, turn to others, but those
who forsake allies whom they have sworn to defend. We will remain
your friends if you choose to bestir yourselves; for we should be guilty
of an impiety if we deserted you without cause; and we shall not easily
find allies equally congenial to us. Take heed then; you have inherited
from your fathers the leadership of Peloponnesus; see that her greatness
suffers no diminution at your hands."*

*Thus spake the Corinthians. Now there happened to be staying at
Lacedaemon an Athenian embassy which had come on other business,
and when the envoys had heard what the Corinthians had said, they
felt bound to go before the Lacedaemonian assembly, not with the view
of answering the accusations brought against them by the cities, but
they wanted to put before the Lacedaemonians the whole question,
and make them understand that they should take time to deliberate
and not be rash. They also desired to set forth the greatness of their
city, reminding the elder men of what they knew, and informing the
younger of what lay beyond their experience. They thought that their
words would sway the Lacedaemonians in the direction of peace. So
they came and said that, if they might be allowed, they too would like
to address the people.*

Thucydides, I

The Athenians were invited to speak, and they reminded the
Spartans of how Athens had done more than any other State to
save Greece from the Persian invader, and that Sparta herself
owed its liberty to the undismayed courage of Athens. The
Athenians then attempted to justify their imperial policy and to

point out that, had the situation been reversed, and had it been the Lacedaemonians who had acquired an empire, they would have found it just as necessary as had Athens to rule with a strong hand, and that they would have been even worse hated than was Athens. They concluded with a passionate appeal for peace:

Do not then be hasty in deciding a question which is serious; and do not, by listening to the misrepresentations and complaints of others, bring trouble upon yourselves. Realize, while yet there is time, the inscrutable nature of war; and how when protracted it generally ends in becoming a mere matter of chance, over which neither of us can have any control, the event being equally unknown and equally hazardous to both. The misfortune is that in their hurry to go to war, men begin with blows, and when a reverse comes upon them, then have recourse to words. But neither you, nor we, have as yet committed this mistake; and therefore while both of us can still choose the prudent part, we tell you not to break the peace or violate your oaths. Let our differences be determined by arbitration according to the treaty. If you refuse, we call to witness the Gods, by whom you have sworn, that you are the authors of the war; and we will do our best to strike in return.

Thucydides, I

The Spartans did not heed the plea for peace, and in 431 BCE the long dreary war, known in history as the Peloponnesian War, began and dragged itself out for nearly thirty years. Compared to modern warfare the actual fighting was not on a very large scale, and we seem to be reading of battles between what were, after all, only rather small states. But though scale and method of warfare has changed, the effect of war on the minds and lives of men and women living at the time has changed very little.

When the Peloponnesian War broke out, almost fifty years had gone by since the Persians had been driven out of Greece, and the heroes of Marathon, of Thermopylae and of Salamis had already passed into history. That war had been between the Greek and the Persian, this war was between Greek and Greek, and it rapidly spread over almost the whole Greek world. The real cause was the rivalry between Athens and Sparta, and it was fought to determine which should be supreme in Greece. Athens was a great sea-power, Sparta a great land-power; Athens was a freedom-loving democracy, Sparta was still governed by an oligarchy; Athens was dependent for its life on the corn that came from afar, Sparta was practically self-sufficing. When the war began, each side was confident and sure of victory. How was it to end?

ATHENS DURING THE WAR

During the first part of the war Athens was supreme at sea, strengthening its hold on all the trade routes. But the Athenians not dare meet Sparta in a great open pitched battle on land, for the military power of the latter was no legend, but a most formidable fact.

Everything, however, did not go well with Athens during those first few years. Every year the Spartans had invaded Attica and burnt and plundered the land surrounding Athens. This had driven all the country people into the city, where conditions became very congested and intolerable. And then it was that a scourge fell upon Athens from which it never recovered. For two long summers and two long winters the city was beset by plague, and one out of every four citizens died. The whole dreadful story can be read in the pages of Thucydides: how it began in the Peiraeus and then spread to Athens; of the sufferings of those who were seized with it, the rapidity with which it spread and the impossibility of caring for the sick or burying the dead; of the lawlessness in the disorganized terror-stricken city; and of all the misery which came from seeing the inhabitants of the city dying in such numbers and from knowing that without the walls the country was being ravaged.

When the horror had passed the city was no longer the Athens of old. The Athenians' spirit was not only broken but changed. The war and the plague together lay heavy upon the Athenians, and they blamed Pericles because he had persuaded them to go to war, declaring that he was the author of all their troubles. Once again he made a great speech to them, reminding them that Athens had never yet yielded to misfortune, and that the greatest states and the greatest men are those who, when misfortunes come, are the least depressed in spirit and the most resolute in action. But Pericles did not live to guide Athens through the troubled waters which lay ahead. He had experienced the same misfortunes as his fellow citizens. His sister, his sons, and the friends who were nearest to him had died of the plague, and he himself was ill. As he lay dying, some of his friends were sitting near him, and they spoke together of his greatness, his power and the number of his victories. They did not think he was conscious, but he heard all that they said, and when they had finished, asked them why they did not speak or make mention of that which was the most excellent and greatest thing of all. "For," said he, "no Athenian, through my means, ever wore mourning." (Plutarch: *Life of Pericles*)

Pericles had been a good general; he had added to the power of Athens both at home and abroad; and he had made her defences more secure by completing the Long Walls which had been begun by Themistocles. As a statesman, Pericles was an imperialist, and he believed that the Athenian Empire, which had grown naturally out of the position of Athens as Liberator of the Ionian Greeks, embodied the right relationship between Athens and her allies. Like Themistocles, he had a deep distrust of Sparta, and believing that sooner or later war was inevitable, he did all that lay in his power to make Athens ready when that day should come.

Though of noble birth, Pericles had always been on the side of the people in Athens, and during his rule the powers of the people were very much extended. Every office in the state was filled by popular election each year, so that there was constant change amongst those in authority and Athens could never be sure of any settled policy in her affairs either at home or abroad. The supreme and final authority lay in the Assembly, but like all popular assemblies, it could be swayed and, at several critical moments in the history of Athens, was swayed, by sudden bursts of passion, or by the fiery eloquence of an unwise or an ambitious and self-seeking speaker. But as long as Pericles lived, the dangers of the democracy he had developed were not very apparent, for he was trusted absolutely, and he kept a wise, firm and restraining hand on the passions of the people.

Pericles died in the year 429 BCE, and in the years following his death the results of a long war began to be felt. Food became scarce and prices were high; it was difficult to get servants, for in the general disorganization of life that had come with the plague, slaves had escaped in large numbers; the young men of Athens were no longer to be seen in the Agora and other public places, for all men capable of bearing arms were with the army.

Four years after the death of Pericles, Sparta made offers of peace, but feeling ran very high in Athens and it was believed that a peace then would not be lasting, so the offer was rejected and it was determined to carry on the war to the bitter end.

There is nothing that so well describes conditions in Athens during these war years as the comedies of Aristophanes. They carry us back to those exciting days and it is amazing to see how much freedom of speech was allowed. *The Knights*, *The Clouds*, and *The Wasps* were all written in these years, and they are full of the excitement of the time, and often of outspoken criticism of those responsible for the carrying on of the war. But the war brought a lowering of ideals, and even where there was victory, there was also sorrow and loss and the ruin of homes. Euripides, one of the great dramatists of the time, in *The Trojan Women*, a play written during the war, stripped war of all its glamour and showed the misery that comes to the conquered:

And they whom Ares took,
Had never seen their children: no wife came
With gentle arms to shroud the limbs of them
For burial, in a strange and angry earth
Laid dead. And there, at home, the same long dearth
Women that lonely died, and aged men
Waiting for sons that ne'er should turn again,
Nor know their graves, nor pour drink-offerings,
To still the unslaked dust. These be the things
The conquering Greek hath won!
[...]

Would ye be wise, ye Cities, fly from war!
Yet if war come, there is a crown in death
For her that striveth well and perisheth
Unstained: to die in evil were the stain!
Euripides: *The Trojan Women*,
translated by Gilbert Murray

Pericles was dead, and Cleon who had succeeded him as leader of the people had no power to inspire the Athenians to be true to their highest ideals, and as conditions grew more and more difficult, Athens was forced at length to give herself up to a fight for her life. Anger, suspicion and hatred took the place of the old ideals, and it seemed as if her strength had turned to weakness and despair. And then Athens sealed its own doom; the amount of the tribute paid to Athens by its allies every year was doubled to save its citizens from heavy taxation. The Charter once made in good faith between the allies was broken.

But the end had not yet come. For a time success lay with the Athenians, and they forced a Spartan garrison to surrender to them at Sphacteria on the west coast of the Peloponnese, a victory which greatly encouraged them. But the years dragged on and the war continued and there seemed no end in sight. Then it was that Brasidas, a Spartan general, marched north from the Peloponnese through Boeotia and Thessaly until he reached Amphipolis, an Athenian colony on the borders of Thrace and Macedonia, which he besieged. Cleon had gone to Amphipolis to help the Athenians and he was expecting assistance from an Athenian general who was marching to the relief of the city. But he did not arrive in time, and Amphipolis was taken by the Spartans. Both Cleon and Brasidas were killed, and Athens exiled the general who had failed to arrive in time. He devoted the period of his exile to gathering materials for a history of the war, and though he may have been unsuccessful as a general, he became one of the greatest historians, not only of Greece, but of the world. His name was Thucydides.

The surrender of Amphipolis brought a lull in the war, and owing to the efforts of the Athenian general, Nicias, in 421 BCE a peace was made, which was to last for fifty years.

ALCIBIADES

The Peace of Nicias did not last very long, however. Athens and Sparta were both too jealous of each other to be really reconciled, and neither kept to the terms of peace. There was a party in Athens which favoured peace, but it was not so powerful nor so popular as the war party, and its leader, Nicias, did not possess the qualities of leadership which characterized the leader of the other side. This leader was Alcibiades, a young man who had recently risen to power and who was very popular. He was of noble birth, rich, very good-looking and of great personal charm. He lisped when he spoke, but it was said that this "became him well and gave a grace and persuasiveness to his rapid speech." When he began to study, he obeyed all his other masters fairly well, but refused to learn to play the flute, because he said it disfigured the face, and also because it was not possible to speak or sing whilst playing it. Alcibiades was a leader of fashion amongst the Athenian youths and as soon as it became known that he despised the flute, playing on it went out of fashion and became generally neglected.

Alcibiades was sought out by many people who liked to be in his company chiefly because of his great personal beauty, but it is evident that at this time he must have shown many noble qualities and a good disposition, for Socrates, the great philosopher, showed much affection for him. Socrates saw that his wealth and position caused him to be flattered and made so much of by all kinds of people that he feared he would be corrupted by it, and he resolved, if possible, that his good qualities should be preserved. On his side, Alcibiades recognized the great worth of Socrates and listened willingly to his teaching.

Both Socrates and Alcibiades took part in one of the early campaigns of the Peloponnesian War. They shared the same tent and stood next to each other in battle, and in one sharp fight both behaved with special bravery. This was the occasion on which Alcibiades was wounded, but Socrates threw himself before him and protected him and beyond any question saved his life.

Alcibiades had great advantages for entering public life; his noble birth, his riches, the personal courage he had shown in many battles and the multitude of his friends and dependents threw open the doors for him. His popularity had also increased because of his success at the Olympic Games. He had spent great sums of money on horses and chariots, and never did anyone else send so many as seven chariots to the Games. And they were so well equipped that in one race he carried off the first, second and fourth prizes, which far outdid any distinction that ever was known or thought of in that kind.

But Alcibiades did not follow the wise teaching of Socrates, and he grew luxurious, dissipated and lawless in his way of living; he wore long purple robes like a woman, which dragged after him as he went through the market place; and he had a soft and luxurious bed prepared for him on his galley. All this made him disliked by a great number of Athenians and gradually raised up enemies for him; yet such was his personal charm, his eloquence, his courage and his beauty that the Athenians made excuses for his excesses, indulged him in many things and gave soft names to his faults, attributing them to his youth and good nature.

Such was the man, unstable, ambitious and unscrupulous to whom was entrusted the guidance of affairs at Athens at this most critical hour in its fortunes.

Up to this time the relations of Athens with the Greeks beyond the sea had been chiefly confined to those in Ionia, but there were rich lands dwelt in by Greeks to the west, especially in Sicily and the south of Italy. Even in the life-time of Pericles the Athenians had cast a longing eye upon Sicily, but they did not attempt anything there till after his death. An opportunity for interference in Sicilian affairs was given them in 415 BCE when the Peace of Nicias had brought a period of truce in the war with Sparta. The Greeks in one of the cities in Sicily appealed to Athens for help against Syracuse which was oppressing them, and Alcibiades seized upon this as the first step in an Athenian conquest of Sicily. This was but the beginning of his ambitious plan, for he dreamed not only of the mastery of Sicily, but of nothing less than the conquest of Carthage and of Athenian rule over the whole Mediterranean world.

Alcibiades roused Athens to enthusiasm for an expedition to Sicily and the young men, in particular, shared his hopes and ambitions and listened to him when he talked of the wonders of the countries to which they were going, so that great numbers of them might be seen sitting in the wrestling grounds and public places, drawing on the ground maps of Sicily and the situation of Carthage. Nicias, conservative, experienced and loyal, saw that it was not the welfare of Athens but his own personal ambition and love of glory that was moving Alcibiades, and did everything in his power to dissuade the people from following such a rash and ambitious policy. He told them that even if they conquered Sicily they could not hope to keep it, and that the course they were in favour of pursuing would only add to the hatred already felt for them by Sparta, and could only end in disaster.

But the Athenians were deaf to the pleas of Nicias, and it was voted that the expedition should take place.

Then the preparations began. Lists for service were made up at home and orders given to the allies. The city had newly recovered from the plague and from the constant pressure of war; a new population had grown up; there had been time for the accumulation of money during the peace; so that there was abundance of everything at command.

While they were in the midst of their preparations, the Hermae or square stone figures carved after the ancient Athenian fashion, and standing everywhere at the doorways both of temples and private houses, in one night had nearly all of them throughout the city their faces mutilated. The offenders were not known, but great rewards were publicly offered for their detection, and a decree was passed that anyone, whether citizen, stranger, or slave, might without fear of punishment disclose this or any other profanation of which he was cognizant. The Athenians took the matter greatly to heart; it seemed to them ominous of the fate of the expedition; and they ascribed it to conspirators who wanted to effect a revolution and to overthrow the democracy.

Certain metics and servants gave information, not indeed about the Hermae, but about the mutilation of other statues which had shortly before been perpetrated by some young men in a drunken frolic; and of this impiety they accused, among others, Alcibiades. A party who were jealous of his influence over the people took up and exaggerated the charges against him, clamorously insisting that he was at the bottom of the whole affair. In proof they alleged the excesses of his ordinary life, which were unbecoming in the citizen of a free state.

He strove then and there to clear himself of the charges, and also offered to be tried before he sailed (for all was now ready), in order that, if he were guilty, he might be punished, and if acquitted, might retain his command. But his enemies feared that if the trial took place at once he would have the support of the army, and that the people would be lenient. They therefore exerted themselves to postpone the trial. To this end they proposed that he should sail now and not delay the expedition, but should return and stand his trial within a certain number of days. Their intention was that he should be recalled and tried when they had stirred up a stronger feeling against him, which they could better do in his absence. So it was decided that Alcibiades should sail.

About the middle of summer the expedition started for Sicily. Early in the morning of the day appointed for their departure, the Athenians and such of their allies as had already joined them went down to the Peiraeus and began to man the ships. The entire population of Athens accompanied them, citizens and strangers alike. The citizens came to take farewell, one of an acquaintance, another of a kinsman, another of a son; the crowd as they passed along were full of hope and full of tears; hope of conquering Sicily, tears because they doubted whether they would ever see their friends again, when they thought of the long voyage on which they were *sending them. At the moment of parting the danger was nearer; and terrors which had never occurred to them when they were voting the expedition now entered into their souls. Nevertheless their spirits revived at the sight of the armament in all its strength and of the abundant provisions which they had made. The strangers and the rest of the multitude came out of curiosity, desiring to witness an enterprise of which the greatness exceeded belief.*

No armament so magnificent or costly had ever been sent out by any single Hellenic power. Never had a greater expedition been sent to a foreign land; never was there an enterprise in which the hope of future success seemed to be better justified by actual power.

When the ships were manned and everything required for the voyage had been placed on board, silence was proclaimed by the sound of the trumpet, and all with one voice before setting sail offered up the customary prayers; these were recited, not in each ship, but by a single herald, the whole fleet accompanying him. On every deck both officers and men, mingling wine in bowls, made libations from vessels of gold and silver. The multitude of citizens and other well-wishers who were looking on from the land joined in the prayer. The crews raised the Paean, and when the libations were completed, put to sea.

Thucydides, VI

In due time they reached Sicily, where the generals in command held a conference as to the best way of beginning the attack.

In the meantime the enemies of Alcibiades in Athens took up the charges of impiety which had been made against him and did not rest until an order had been sent to Sicily ordering his return that he might be brought to trial. So Alcibiades and those who were accused with him left Sicily. They sailed in their own ship, but were escorted by the Athenian galley sent for them. Before reaching Greece, both ships put in at a port in Italy, and here Alcibiades and his companions left their ship and disappeared, "fearing to return and stand their trial when the prejudice against them was so violent. They were sought for, but the crew of the galley could not find them and so they gave up the search and returned home."

Before making plans for a further escape, Alcibiades lay concealed for a short time in Italy. It seemed strange to one who was with him that he had not enough faith in Athenian justice to return home and face a trial, but when asked if he did not trust his own native country, Alcibiades replied that, when it came to a matter of life or death, he would not trust even his own mother. As Alcibiades did not appear in Athens to answer the charges against him, the Assembly convicted him and his companions of impiety, confiscated their property, sentenced them to death, and pronounced a solemn curse on their names.

Alcibiades crossed to the Peloponnese and went first to Argos. When he found there was no hope of his returning to Athens, he sent a message to Sparta, asking for a safe-conduct to that city, and assuring the Spartans that he would make them amends by his future services for all the mischief he had done them while he was their enemy. The Spartans gave him the security for which he asked, and he went to them eagerly, and was well received. In return for this, he betrayed the weak points of his native city to its enemies and gave them valuable advice as to the best means of conquering Athens.

One characteristic of Alcibiades was the extraordinary ease with which he could adapt himself to his surroundings.

Whenever he saw that it was to his own interest to adopt the habits and ways of those with whom he came in contact, he did so with no hesitation. At Sparta, he gave himself up to athletic exercises, he cut his hair short, bathed in cold water and dined on black broth; in Ionia, he was luxurious and indolent; in Thrace, always drinking; in Thessaly, ever on horseback; and when later he lived with the Persian satrap, he exceeded the Persians themselves in magnificence and pomp

But though in Sparta Alcibiades lived as a Spartan and appeared devoted to their interests, he was, nevertheless, an Athenian, and the Spartans did not trust him. The Greeks never wholly trusted each other, and lack of sincerity in their political relations was one of the weak points in their character. When Alcibiades found that he was looked upon with suspicion in Sparta and that his life was actually in danger, he fled to Ionia and took refuge with the Persian satrap with whom he soon became a great favourite. And, indeed, the charm of daily intercourse with this extraordinarily fascinating and dangerous man was more than any one could resist. Even those who feared and envied him could not but take delight, and feel a friendliness towards him, when they saw him and were in his company. It was only in his absence that his real character was recognized.

And now followed a period of disloyal intrigue with the Persians. Alcibiades advised them to interfere in the war between Athens and Sparta, and sometimes to help one side and sometimes the other, until both should be so exhausted that the Persian King could easily overcome them. Thus, not content with betraying Greek to Greek, Alcibiades descended to the shameful depths of betraying Greece to the Barbarian.

THE DOWNFALL OF ATHENS AND SUPREMACY OF SPARTA

Alcibiades had been summoned back to Athens at the very beginning of the expedition to Sicily. It was in the summer of 415 BCE that the Athenian fleet had set out with such magnificence and with such high hopes. Two years later, news was brought to Athens which at first the Athenians would not believe, it was so appalling. There had been a fearful battle in the harbour at Syracuse, the Athenians had been utterly vanquished, and great numbers had been imprisoned in the quarries which were deep and narrow, where they were exposed to the scorching sun and suffocating heat in the daytime, and the cold autumnal nights. They were only allowed half a pint of water a day. The Athenians were utterly and comprehensively defeated, and few returned home.

The Athenians were at first in utter despair. They had lost the best of their young fighters, they had insufficient ships in their docks and no crews to man them, and the treasury was running short of funds. During the following winter, all Hellas was stirred up by the news of the overthrow of the Athenians in Sicily and many hitherto neutral states felt the time had come to rise up against the Athenians. Athenian subjects everywhere were ready to revolt.

Yet Sparta was at this very time bargaining with the Persian King and promising that it would recognize his right to rule over all that the Great Kings had formerly ruled, even the Greeks who lived in Asia Minor, in return for money with which Sparta could pay its sailors. Never had Athens sunk so low as that. The end was not far off, but Athens, having recovered from the first overwhelming despair, regained some of the old courage. Every sort of economy was made, so that new ships could be built, and the Athenians were on constant alert, lest they should be taken unawares by some surprise attack.

It was at this moment that Alcibiades began to intrigue and plot for a return to Athens. Gradually his friends gained the upper hand, the government of Athens had not been successful and it was overthrown. It had been said that the feeling of the Athenians towards Alcibiades was that "they love, they hate, but cannot do without him," and they proved the truth of the saying by recalling him. As of old, when once they came under the charm of his personality, the Athenians yielded to their enthusiasm for him. Yet there was bitterness mixed with this rejoicing, for the Athenians remembered that it was by following the advice of this man that some of their greatest disasters had fallen upon them.

The story of all that followed may be read in the pages of Thucydides and Xenophon. For a time Athens seemed to regain told power and won so great a victory over the Spartans that they proposed a peace, but it was to be a peace as between equals, and Athens would hear of no peace, unless it was able to dictate the terms. So the war continued, until the ill-success of some ships in an engagement with the Spartans caused the people to turn once more against Alcibiades, and again he was exiled. After that the end came quickly. In 405 BCE one last great battle was fought in which the Athenians were utterly defeated. The news of this disaster was taken to Athens, and it was night when the messenger arrived. When the tale was told

a bitter wail of woe broke forth. From Piraeus, following the line of the Long Walls up to the heart of the city, it swept and swelled, as each man to his neighbour passed on the news. On that night no man slept. There was mourning and sorrow for those that were lost, but the lamentation was merged in even greater sorrow for themselves, as they pictured the evils they were about to suffer. On the following day the public assembly met, and, after debate, it was resolved to block up all the harbours save one, to put the walls in a state of defence, to post guards at various points, and to make all other necessary preparations for a siege.

Xenophon: *Hellenica*, II

The Spartans came and closed in upon Athens. A hundred and fifty ships were moored off the Peiraeus, and a strict blockade was established against all merchant ships entering the harbour. The Athenians were trapped, besieged by land and sea, without ships, allies or provisions. At last, starved into submission, they surrendered, and terms were made with Sparta. They were bitter and humiliating terms:

That the Long Walls and fortifications of Peiraeus should be destroyed; that the Athenian fleet, with the exception of twelve vessels, should be surrendered; that the exiles should be restored; and lastly, that the Athenians should acknowledge the headship of Sparta in peace and war, leaving to her the choice of friends and foes, and following her lead by land and sea.

Xenophon: *Hellenica*, II

The Athenians themselves were made to help in the destruction of the walls, and as they did so, their enemies rejoiced to the music of the flute, believing that with the fall of Athens would dawn a day of liberty for Greece.

For over thirty years Sparta ruled in Greece. At the beginning of the Peloponnesian War, Sparta had demanded of Athens that it should restore the liberties of all the Greeks who were its allies. Athens had refused, and now the Greek world waited anxiously to see what use Sparta would make of its great victory.

It soon became evident that the rule of Sparta was not to be a light one. Military governors were placed in every city of the old Delian League, and the citizens were forced to pay a heavy tribute to Sparta. Thirty men were set to rule in Athens, and for the eight months that these Thirty were in power, Athens endured cruelty, tyranny and lawlessness. The Spartan domination soon became so unendurable that one by one a number of Athenians fled from the city and took refuge in Thebes: in Thebes, which had hitherto been one of the bitterest enemies of Athens, but which now realized that freedom and justice were not to be found in the Spartan ideal of empire, for it was nothing less than empire at which Sparta was aiming. At last a sufficient number of exiles had gathered at Thebes for them to make an attempt to drive out the Thirty from Athens. They were successful, and the old Athenian form of government was restored.

But there was no real peace, and for a few years fighting went on in different places. Sometimes Sparta was successful, sometimes Athens, but nothing decisive happened. At last Sparta began to intrigue with Persia, and in 386 BCE, Artaxerxes the King interfered in the affairs of Greece, and proposed terms of peace, known as the King's Peace, which were accepted. The Greek cities in Asia Minor were to belong once more to the Persians, and all the other Greek city-states were to be independent, and the treaty concluded with the words: "Should any refuse to accept this peace, I, Artaxerxes, will make war upon them, with the help of those who are of my mind, both by land and sea, with ships and with money."

It was a betrayal of Greece to the ancient foe. The Greek states had never been able to unite for long at a time. Had they been able to hold together, and especially had Athens and Sparta done so, they could have prevailed against the Persian in Asia Minor and maintained the independence of their kinsmen in Ionia. But their jealous fears of anything that might limit their freedom as independent states made any permanent alliance impossible, and the long years of the Peloponnesian War, of all wars in history one of the most humiliating, because so unnecessary and unjustifiable, had bred hatreds and suspicion, greed and jealousy, from which Greece never recovered. But though politically Greek power was gone, its work for the world was not finished.

THE MARCH OF THE TEN THOUSAND

Artaxerxes, the King of Persia, had a younger brother, Cyrus, who was accused to him of plotting against his life. He had Cyrus seized and would have put him to death, but his mother made intercession for him and so his life was spared. This set Cyrus to thinking, not only how he might avoid ever again being in his brother's power, but how, if possible, he might become King in his stead. Now Cyrus was a man who was much beloved. He was honourable, upright and chivalrous, and marvellously skilled in horsemanship. He understood, not only how to make friends, but also how to keep them, and any man who did him willing service was sure to win his reward. For this reason, Cyrus was always able to command men who were willing to follow him in any undertaking, no matter how dangerous it might be.

In order to possess himself of the throne of his brother, it was necessary for Cyrus to raise an army, and he sent trusted agents to various places to collect as many men as would be willing to follow him on a hazardous expedition. Amongst other men who joined his army were a great many Greeks. Though the King's Peace was not made for some years after this, the great battles of the Peloponnesian War were over, and there were large numbers of men, who had spent so many years in fighting that they were restless and unwilling to return to their old settled life. About ten thousand Greeks joined the army of Cyrus, and in 401 BCE they set out. These Greeks had not been told the real object of the expedition; they thought they were to fight against some hill-tribes in Asia Minor, and they joined the rest of the army in Sardis, not knowing the long march they were about to begin.

At first all seemed to be going well, but when they had gone for some distance, the Greeks began to suspect that they were going further than they had expected, and some of them wanted to turn back. But Cyrus promised to give them more pay, and they continued their march. On they went, until they reached the Euphrates. They crossed the river, and for some days they continued their march along the opposite bank until they reached Cunaxa, not far from Babylon. Here at length Cyrus met the Persian army, which came against him under the King, his brother. A fierce battle followed, in which the Greeks were victorious, but Cyrus was killed, and so the victory availed them nothing. The Persians entrapped the Greek generals and murdered them, and there was nothing left for the Greeks to do, but in some way or other to return to Greece. But Greece was more than a thousand miles off, and they did not know the way;

they had no leaders, they were in a strange land and surrounded by enemies, and they had no means of procuring supplies by the way. Nevertheless, they decided in spite of all these difficulties, to choose new generals and to start.

Chief of the new generals was a young Athenian called Xenophon, and he advised the Greeks, there were ten thousand of them, to burn all the baggage that they did not need and to set out and find their way back as best they could to Greece. They followed his advice, and Xenophon himself has given us the account of that March of the Ten Thousand back to Greece. He called his story the *Anabasis* or the *March Up Country* and he tells us how they went through strange and unknown lands, and how they suffered from enemies, from the cold and from hunger. They followed the Tigris for a time and passed the ruins of Nineveh, but so complete had been the destruction of that proud city that the retreating Greeks did not know that they were treading her beneath their feet.

Winter came on, and the cold was terrible. In one place they marched through deep snow, with the north wind blowing in their teeth, benumbing the men. They suffered from snow-blindness and frostbite, and some of them in despair refused to go on. But in spite of all these hardships, the greater number went on, until at length they reached a city where they were given a friendly reception. The governor of the city gave them a guide, who promised that within five days he would lead them to a place from which they would see the sea, "and," he added, "if I fail of my word, you are free to take my life." He kept his promise, and on the fifth day they reached a mountain which the men in front immediately climbed. From the top they caught sight of the sea, a symbol to the Greeks of home and safety. A great cry arose and the shout grew louder and louder, so that Xenophon feared that something extraordinary had happened and he mounted his horse and galloped to the rescue. But as he drew nearer, he heard the soldiers shouting and passing on to each other the joyful cry: "Thalatta! Thalatta!" "The Sea! The Sea!" When all had reached the summit, they fell to embracing one another, generals and officers and all, and the tears flowed down their cheeks.

The sea was the Euxine, and without very great difficulty the Greeks found ships which took them home. But before they left the spot from whence they had first seen the sea, they erected a great pile of stones, on which they laid all that was left to them of their scanty possessions, some skins, and wicker shields and staves, and these they dedicated to the Gods of Greece for having granted them so great a deliverance.

THE GREAT DAYS OF THEBES

Up to the end of the Peloponnesian War, the history of Greece had been dominated by the history of Athens and Sparta. The end of the war left Sparta supreme, but it was a stern and harsh regime, that cared little for literature, and disliked changes, and did not know how to wield its power. Sparta's rulers did not the have the imagination to put themselves in the place of Athens and to understand how they should rule such independent, seafaring, intellectually alert and artistic people. The short period of Spartan supremacy ended in failure, and then Sparta was, in turn, overthrown by another Greek state. This state was Thebes, a state which had not hitherto played a very honourable part in Greek history. Always jealous of Athens, Thebes had taken every opportunity to side against it. The sturdy, independent little city of Plataea had been treated with great cruelty by the Thebans; they had sided with the invaders during the Persian Wars and with Sparta during the Peloponnesian War, and it was only when the Spartan rule became intolerable to friends and enemies alike, that Thebes offered a refuge to the Athenian exiles.

The city of Thebes lay in the rich plains of Boeotia, where meat and corn and wine were to be had abundantly. The nearby hills provided excellent hunting, and the Thebans were a people known to their neighbours as loving pleasure and all the good things of the world, as well as being good fighters.

LEGENDS AND EARLY HISTORY OF THEBES

The Thebans had a reputation as being intellectually dull but there were some exceptions, for Thebes produced two men of genius: Pindar, the poet, and Epaminondas, the mighty general.

Pindar was born in the sixth century BCE but he lived to be an old man, and the Persians had been driven out of Greece before he died. He was a noble, and his poems are the last lyrics that sing of an order of society that was about to give way to the rule of the people. Many of Pindar's lyrics were written in honour of the winners at the Olympic Games, and in reading them one can almost see the chariot racing along the course, and hear the people shouting, and feel the joy of the victor as he receives his prize. Pindar was very conservative; he belonged to a generation which had not yet begun to question the existence of the gods, and all his poems are filled with unquestioning faith in them and in their righteousness. Especially did he delight to honour Apollo, and long after his death it was believed that he was particularly dear to the god, for it was said that every night at Delphi he was honoured by the summons: "Let Pindar the poet come in to the supper of the god."

But if Thebes had had no honoured past in history, it was rich in legend and story. Thebes had been founded by Cadmus in obedience to the word of Apollo. On the spot where the city was to be built, he had slain a fearful dragon, and taking the dragon's teeth he had sown them in the ground as a sower sows his seed, and immediately a host of armed men had sprung up from the ground, who became the first citizens of the new city. With their help, Cadmus built a citadel which was known through all the days of Theban history as the Cadmeia.

Thebes was surrounded by strong walls and the city was entered by seven gates. Another story told how the foundations of these walls and gateways had been laid by Amphion, who then took his lyre and played such divine music on it that the walls rose by magic as he played, until they stood in such strength that they completely protected the city, and later were able to endure a great siege.

But the gods had not always smiled upon Thebes. Pindar tells us that "for every good a mortal receives from the gods, he must likewise receive two evils," and this seemed to be true of the royal house of Thebes. The tales of the fate of these ancient rulers are dark and tragic. It was Oedipus, who having first guessed the answer to the riddle of the Sphinx, then in ignorance killed his own father and became King, only to learn in later years of what he had done, and to be driven forth from his kingdom, blind and helpless. Other legends tell of Antigone, the faithful daughter of Oedipus, who accompanied him in his wanderings and tended him until his death.

EPAMINONDAS

Epaminondas was born in Thebes late in the fifth century BCE. He belonged to a very old family, one of the few which claimed to be descended from the dragon's teeth sown by Cadmus. Though an ancient family, he was poor, but he was among the best educated among the Thebans; he had been taught to play the harp and to sing to its accompaniment, to play the flute and to dance. A wise philosopher was his instructor, to whom he was so attached that, young as he was, he preferred the society of the grave and stern old man to that of companions of his own age. After he grew up and began to practise gymnastics, he studied not so much to increase the strength as the agility of his body; for he thought that strength suited the purposes of wrestlers, but that agility made a man a better soldier, so he spent most of his time in war-like exercises.

Epaminondas, we are told, was modest, prudent, brave and skilled in war. He was a truthful man, who never told a falsehood, a master of his passions, and gentle in disposition. A discreet man, he was also an eloquent speaker.

Amongst the statesmen who helped to make Greece great, none were more honourable or of greater integrity than Epaminondas. It was not possible to corrupt or bribe him and he was entirely free from covetousness. This was shown when the envoy of King Artaxerxes the Persian came to Thebes to bribe Epaminondas with a large sum of gold (to get the Thebans to help the King), but Epaminondas replied that money was not necessary; if the King desired something that was good for the Thebans, Epaminondas was ready and willing to do it for nothing; if not, no amount of gold or silver would move him to do something that was not good for his country.

Under Epaminondas, Thebes became the ruling power in Greece, but only for a very short time. The Thebans were good soldiers only as long as they had inspiring leaders, without a great leader they were unable to hold what they had gained. One of the characteristics of a great man is that he knows how to use his opportunities, and Epaminondas had this gift. The story of his life is the story of a great general. At his side was his friend Pelopidas, a man of extraordinary courage, of great enthusiasm, and of utter devotion to his leader.

Epaminondas made the Theban army a very formidable fighting force, and with this powerful army he set himself to break the power of Sparta and to put that of Thebes in its place. In 371 BCE the Spartans were defeated by the Thebans under Epaminondas in a great battle at Leuctra, not far from Thebes, and this victory made Thebes for the time the chief military power in Greece. For nine years Thebes remained power, though fighting continued. Epaminondas wanted to capture Sparta itself, and he marched four times down into the Peloponnese. In spite of the long marches his men were obliged to make, they were in splendid condition and impeccably disciplined. They had implicit faith in their general and would follow him anywhere.

The Thebans had marched for the fourth time to the Peloponnese, and they were at Mantinea, and here in 362 BCE Epaminondas fought his last great battle against Sparta. Thebes was victorious, but bought the victory dearly, for Epaminondas was mortally wounded. As he was carried from the field, he asked for the two captains who stood nearest to him and would take his place. But he was told that both had been killed. "Then make peace with the enemy," he murmured, and drawing out the spear which had wounded him, he fell back dead.

Epaminondas was dead, and there was no one to take his place. He had broken the power of Sparta, and the Peloponnesus was now divided into a number of camps, each at war with the other, and confusion reigned everywhere in Greece. Thebes had been no more able to unite Greece than Sparta had been, but under Epaminondas the art of war had been so developed and changed that in the hands of a commander of genius, an army had become a more formidable weapon than had ever before been deemed possible.

Six years before the battle of Mantinea, a half-barbarian boy of fifteen had been brought from Macedonia to Thebes as a hostage. This boy was Philip of Macedon, and he spent three years in Thebes, learning all that the greatest military state then in Greece could teach him. He was destined himself to be a great commander, and the father of one yet greater. There was now no Greek state powerful enough to uphold Greek freedom. As a statesman, Epaminondas had failed, for he left nothing but confusion behind him, but as a general of genius, he was the teacher of Philip and Alexander of Macedon, whose growing power was now to menace the freedom, not only of Greece, but of the world.

THE APOGEE OF CLASSICAL
GREEK CIVILIZATION

The Greeks showed the world the way to freedom. They won their own national freedom against almost overwhelming odds, for never before had a small country maintained its independence in the face of a great empire, and been victorious. They also maintained a political freedom, which they carried too far, for the inability of Greek states to form alliances and to unite was one of the sources of weakness which finally led to their downfall. Nevertheless the spirit of sturdy independence is one that has endured. The Greeks carried their vision of freedom further than the political independence of each state, and one of their chief characteristics was their personal freedom. In a speech to the Athenian army before the battle in the harbour at Syracuse, Nicias "reminded them that they were the inhabitants of the freest country in the world, and how in Athens there was no interference with the daily life of any man." Modern times are apt to pride themselves on the freedom of speech allowed to all, but no modern state permits greater liberty of speech (and some would not tolerate as much) than was allowed in Athens in the fifth century BCE when Aristophanes wrote his satirical comedies.

The history of a nation is an enquiry into how that nation expresses itself in stone and marble, as well as into what it thinks and does; and its architects, artists and sculptors stand beside its historians, philosophers, dramatists and statesmen as the men who have made its history.

EARLY GREEK PHILOSOPHY

The word *philosophy* means the love of wisdom, and to the Greeks this wisdom was the serious effort made to understand both the world and man. To us *philosophy* generally means a wise understanding of the right way of living, but with the Greeks it included a great deal of what we to-day call *science*. Greek philosophy was concerned with finding out the origins of things, and from that knowledge to build up a right way of life. We do not to-day go to the Greeks to learn science: their answers to the questions asked were, some of them, wrong, and some of them inadequate. But modern science has been made possible by the qualities of mind which the Greeks brought to their enquiries: their passionate desire to know the truth about things, their power of going behind old superstitions, and of seeing things as they really are, their open-mindedness and willingness to accept new truths, their powers of patient study and observation and of reaching the unknown from the known.

The earliest Greek philosophers lived in Ionia in the sixth century BCE, and the greatest of them were Thales of Miletus and Pythagoras of Samos. Thales went further than the

Egyptians and Babylonians had done, not so much because of the new discoveries he made, but because he brought to those discoveries not only the desire to know that they were facts, but the desire to go behind the facts and find out the reason for their existence.

Pythagoras of Samos lived later in the sixth century than Thales. He was a great traveller and seems to have visited not only the mainland of Greece, but also Egypt and Crete, where he had many rare experiences going into the innermost parts of temples where as a rule no strangers were admitted. He also went to Italy where he founded a school, and gathered about three hundred pupils round him.

Though it was not believed by the world at large until nearly two thousand years later, Pythagoras taught that the world was round, and, as far as is known, he was the first thinker who made this discovery. It was Pythagoras who laid the foundations for later mathematical knowledge, especially in geometry and arithmetic, and who taught that there was a science of numbers apart from their use as a practical means of calculation.

SOCRATES

During the last years of the Peloponnesian War, a strange figure might have been seen in Athens: a short, ugly, odd-looking man, poorly-clad and utterly indifferent to criticism of his habits or appearance, but a man to whom every one listened when he began to speak. This was Socrates, the Greek philosopher.

His father was a stone-cutter and a poor man, but he seems to have given to his son the best education that was to be had in Athens, for Socrates often quoted from Greek literature, especially from Homer, and he speaks of having studied with his friends "the treasures which the wise men of old have left us in their books."

Very little is known of the early life of Socrates, but he passed his youth and early manhood during the greatest years of Athenian history. He was born ten years after the Persian had been defeated at Plataea and driven out of Greece; as a boy, he had seen the Long Walls being built; he had grown up in the Athens of Pericles, a contemporary of Sophocles, and Euripides, of Pheidias and of Thucydides. When the clouds gathered over Athens and war came, he served in the army as a common soldier; he had lived through the short-lived triumphs and the tragic disasters which befell the city; he had been hungry when food was scarce, he had seen Athens besieged and taken; he had watched the Long Walls destroyed, and he had lived through the Terror when the Thirty ruled Athens. It was a life lived in very stirring times, and Socrates had taken his share in the happenings. During the war, he served in one of the northern campaigns, and he amazed everyone by his extraordinary power of enduring hunger and thirst, and all the hardships of a cold Thracian winter.

At the close of the war Socrates was in Athens, a man now of over sixty years of age. He held one or two offices of state, when he was known for his fearless refusal to do what he thought was wrong. On one occasion he refused to obey orders that were given him, because he believed that obedience would involve him in doing what he thought to be wrong. "I showed," he said, "not by mere words but by my actions, that I did not care a straw for death: but that I did care very much indeed about doing wrong."

Socrates was very poor and as he would take no money for his teaching, his means of livelihood were very scanty. He went about barefoot and had only one cloak which he wore until it was so old that it became a matter of joke amongst his friends. He not only had no luxuries of any kind, but hardly the bare necessities of life, yet he was quite content and used to say: "How many things there are which I do not want." Socrates married Xanthippe, a woman of a most violent temper.

The Athenians had always been intellectually very alert and had tried to solve all kinds of problems. They asked how it was that things came into being, how they continued to exist, of what they were made and similar questions. But when Athens had become an empire and ruled over many men and states, the questions began to change. People were less interested in how things originated, than in questions arising from their daily experience. They asked, what is a state, what is a citizen, what is justice, what is temperance, courage, cowardice and so on. In order to answer these questions, a body of teachers had arisen in Athens who were called Sophists, or *Wise Men*. They taught every kind of subject and established a number of schools. The older Greek teachers did not like these Sophists, partly because they took money for their teaching, and hitherto, though Athenian philosophers had accepted presents, they had never charged definite fees; partly because they taught so many subjects that it was thought they could teach nothing thoroughly; partly because they seemed to aim at teaching young men to argue in order to get the better of their opponents rather than to seek for truth; and above all, because they were often sceptical as to the existence of the gods. There were some very good teachers amongst the Sophists, and they opened up a great many new fields of thought to the Athenians, but a weak side to their teaching was that they only stated general principles, and often asserted as absolute facts things that never had been definitely proved one way or the other. They used words carelessly without stopping to think of their real meaning, and they never suggested that there was anything they did not know.

Socrates saw that though the teaching of the Sophists might increase *information* it was fatal to real thinking, and he began to teach in Athens in order to show what real thinking was. He taught in no school, had no classes and took no pay. He was willing to talk to any and everyone who would listen to him and tried to show people what real knowledge was. He was filled with a passionate belief in the importance of truth above all things. He said that to make inaccurate statements and to use words with a wrong or careless meaning was "not only a fault in itself, it also created an evil in the soul." He showed those who listened to him the evil that came from pretending to know what one did not know, and the first step in his teaching was to make them realize their ignorance. To this end he questioned and cross-examined them, until they contradicted themselves, or found no answer and generally ended in hopeless difficulties, simply because they would not acknowledge at the beginning that they did not know what he had asked.

Socrates believed that virtue was knowledge, that if a man knew a thing was wrong, he would not do it, and that those who knew what was right would always do it. In this Socrates was not wholly right; he only saw a part of the truth, but his greatness lies in that he was the first to teach the importance of having a reason for what we believe, of learning accurate habits of mind, and that the search for knowledge is one rich in imagination and beauty.

Socrates was always arguing, talking, questioning, but he was never rude or discourteous to those who disagreed with him, he never brought his own personal feelings into his arguments, and he never descended to expressions of wounded pride or irritation.

The teaching of Socrates opened the minds of those who listened to him to the possibilities to which knowing the truth might lead them, and he had great influence over numbers of young Athenians. It was all new to them, they had never heard anything like it before. But if Socrates gained friends, his method of exposing the ignorance of others also gained him enemies. No one before had ever thought such thoughts, and to ordinary Athenians his questioning was wicked. But Xenophon, one of his friends, tells us that "no one ever heard him say or saw him do anything impious or irreverent, and he was so piously and devoutly religious that he would take no step apart from the will of heaven." Yet his enemies maintained that he disbelieved in the gods. His teaching was all the more disturbing because Athens, having been defeated by Sparta, had just lived through the terrible months of the rule of the Thirty, and though these had been driven out (this was in the year 399 BCE), Athens was in a state of unrest, of fear and of suspicion. Anyone who taught anything new was looked upon as a possible enemy to the state, and the enemies of Socrates seized this opportunity to bring definite accusations against him. They accused him of not believeing in the gods worshipped by the city, and corrupting young men – the penalty was death.

A trial followed. In an Athenian trial, first the accusers made their speeches, and then the accused was allowed to defend himself. Plato, the great pupil of Socrates, has given us the speech made by his master at his trial, a speech known as the *Apology of Socrates*. In it, the philosopher, an old man now of over seventy, set forth the principles which had guided him in his teaching.

He began by saying that he had never taught men to disbelieve in the gods, and that the accusation of impiety against him was false, but he did say that it was fair to ask him just what he had been trying to do which had given rise to these reports. He then told them the story of how a friend of his had gone to Delphi, and had asked the oracle if there were any man wiser than he, and that the oracle had answered that there was no man.

Now see why I tell you this. I am going to explain to you the origin of my unpopularity. When I heard of the Oracle I began to reflect. What can God mean by this dark saying? I know very well that I am not wise, even in the smallest degree. Then what can he mean by saying that I am the wisest of men? It cannot be that he is speaking falsely, for he is a god and cannot lie. And for a long time I was at a loss to understand his meaning: then, very reluctantly, I turned to seek for it in this manner. I went to a man who was reputed to be wise, thinking that there, if anywhere, I should prove the answer wrong, and meaning to point out to the Oracle its mistake, and to say, "You said that I was the wisest of men, but this man is wiser than I am."

But Socrates went on to say that after talking to this man, who was a politician, he found that he was not wise because he thought he knew things that he did not know, and because he would not acknowledge his ignorance. He tried to prove to him that he was not wise, but only succeeded in making him his enemy.

By reason of this examination, Athenians, I have made many enemies of a very fierce and bitter kind, who have spread abroad a great number of calumnies about me, and people say that I am a "wise man." For the bystanders always think that I am wise myself in any matter wherein I convict another man of ignorance. But, my friends, I believe that only God is really wise: and that by this oracle he meant that men's wisdom is worth little or nothing. I do not think that he meant that Socrates was wise. He only made use of my name, and took me as an example, as though he would say to men: "He among you is the wisest, who, like Socrates, knows that in very truth his wisdom is worth nothing at all." And therefore I still go about testing and examining every man whom I think wise, whether he be a citizen or a stranger, as God has commanded me: and whenever I find that he is not wise, I point out to him on the part of God that he is not wise. And I am so busy in this pursuit that I have never had leisure to take any part worth mentioning in public matters, or to look after my private affairs. I am in very great poverty by reason of my service to God.

Plato: *Apology*, translated by F.J. Church

Socrates then went on to prove that nothing in his teaching could corrupt the young men, as his enemies declared he was doing, and to prove his belief in the gods. He knew that he was on trial for his life, but no fear of death stopped him from speaking that which he believed to be the truth.

My friends, [he said], if you think that a man of any worth at all ought to reckon the chances of life and death when he acts, or that he ought to think of anything but whether he is acting rightly or wrongly, and as a good or bad man would act, you are grievously mistaken. It would be very strange conduct on my part if I were to desert my post now from fear of death or of any other thing, when God has commanded me, as I am persuaded that he has done, to spend my life in searching for wisdom, and in examining myself and others. That would indeed be a very strange thing: and then certainly I might with justice be brought to trial for not believing in the gods; for I should be disobeying the Oracle, and fearing death, and thinking myself wise when I was not wise. For to fear death, my friends, is only to think ourselves wise, without being wise: for it is to think that we know what we do not know. For anything that man can tell, death may be the greatest good that can happen to them: but they fear it as if they knew quite well that it was the greatest of evils. And what is this but that shameful ignorance of thinking that we know what we do not know?

Athenians, if you put me to death, you will not easily find another man to fill my place. God has sent me to attack the city, as if it were a great and noble horse, to use a quaint simile, which was rather sluggish for its size, and which needed to be roused by a gadfly: and I think that I am that gadfly that God has sent to the city to attack it; for I never cease from settling upon you as it were

*at every point, and rousing and exhorting, and reproaching each
man of you all day long.*
Plato: *Apology*, translated by F.J. Church

Socrates then referred to the custom in Athens that when
a man was on trial for his life, his wife and children sometimes
appeared in court in order to appeal to the pity of the judges
and so obtain a favourable sentence, but he refused to do that,
for knowing that the judges had taken an oath to administer
justice justly, he believed that such an act on his part would be
an attempt to make them break their oaths.

Socrates was found guilty by 281 votes to 220, and the
penalty to be inflicted was death. He accepted the sentence
calmly, "and with infinite gentleness and manliness. No one
within the memory of man, it is said, ever bowed his head to
death more nobly." But death offered no terrors to Socrates.

*But now the time has come, and we must go hence; I to die,
and you to live. Whether life or death is better is known to God,
and to God only.*
Plato: *Apology*, translated by F.J. Church

Socrates was taken to prison where he spent a month
before his sentence was carried out. The delay was caused
by the voyage of the sacred ship, said to be that of Theseus,
which had only just set out on its annual voyage to Delos,
and no Athenian could be put to death during its absence. He
spent this month talking to his friends, especially to Crito,
who was very devoted to him, and who entreated him to
escape from prison, an escape for which he could very easily
have arranged. But the brave old man, loyal to his principles

to the end, refused, and he reminded Crito how all his life he had taught that the greatest misfortune that could befall a man was to do wrong, and the greatest crime a man could commit against his state was to break her laws.

The last day arrived. Once more Socrates and his friends conversed, and once more he expressed his joy at "going to the place where he hoped to gain the wisdom that he had passionately longed for all his life." They talked together until later in the day, and then he rose and went into another room to bathe himself, bade farewell to his wife and children and calmly drank down a cup of poison and expired, surrounded by his friends.

Such was the end [said the friend who was with him to the last] of a man who, I think, was the wisest and justest, and the best man that I have ever known. But I did not pity him, for he seemed to me happy, both in his bearing and in his words, so fearlessly and nobly did he die. I could not help thinking that the gods would watch over him still on his journey to the other world, and that when he arrived there it would be well with him, if it was ever well with any man.
Plato: *Phaedo*, translated by F.J. Church

PLATO AND ARISTOTLE

This **great teacher** did not write anything himself because he believed that it was a greater thing for a man to live well than to write well, and that his particular way of teaching and constant intercourse with his fellow men was the best way of teaching those truths in which he believed.

The account of his life and teaching, however, was written down and given to the world by his pupil Plato, who carried on his master's work. Plato was about twenty-eight years old when Socrates was put to death, and for twelve years after that time he travelled. Then he returned to Athens, bought a house and garden (unlike Socrates he was well-off), and spent the next forty years of his life teaching in the Academy.

Plato was an idealist, and in addition to his writings about Socrates, he has left us the *Republic*, the picture of what he thought an ideal state should be, and some other works in which he discusses at great length what things it is most worthwhile that men should pursue in life, and why they should pursue them. He taught that goodness was worth being sought after for its own sake and not for any material reward that comes from pursuing it. In all his teaching he emphasizes the fact that the greatest things in life and those which are eternal are not always the things that can be seen, and that the soul of man does not live on material things but on wisdom, beauty, truth and love. The importance of Plato in this teaching was that he was the forerunner of the great Christian writers who believed with St. Paul that "the things which are seen are temporal, but the things which are not seen are eternal."

As a young man, Plato had seen in Athens under the rule of the Thirty, the lawlessness and confusion that arose from a tyrannously ordered state, and the *Republic* was an attempt to show what he thought life in an ideal state might be. His vision is not a very practical one, but Plato was not a practical statesman. The great value of the *Republic* to the world to-day is that just because its ideals could never be wholly carried out, the questions which all statesmen in all ages have had to settle, could be and were fearlessly discussed, unhampered by the compromises and conventions which beset modern politics.

Plato could write of other things besides politics and ideals. He had a gift for poetry which comes out in many a fairy-tale that he introduces here and there into his writings, knowing that sometimes a great truth can be more easily driven home in such a form. Socrates and a friend were once walking by the stream Ilissus. It was a hot summer's day, and as they were barefoot, they cooled their feet in the water and then sat down under the shade of a plane-tree to rest and talk. And as they rested, Socrates told his friend the legend of the grasshoppers. They were said to have been

human beings in an age before the Muses. And when the Muses came and song appeared they were ravished with delight; and singing always, never thought of eating and drinking, until at last in their forgetfulness they died. And now they live again in the grasshoppers; and this is the return which the Muses make to them: they neither hunger nor thirst, but from the hour of their birth they are always singing, and never eating or drinking; and when they die they go and inform the Muses in heaven who honour them on earth.

Plato: *Phaedrus*, translated by Jowett

When Philip of Macedon wanted the best Greek teacher known as a tutor for his son Alexander, he sent for Aristotle. We know very little about the life of Aristotle. He had been a pupil of Plato at the Academy for twenty years and had learnt the best of all that great philosopher could teach him. On his return from Macedonia, he founded a school of his own at Athens, the Lyceum, where he spent the rest of his life teaching and studying. He died in 322 BCE, one year after his pupil Alexander. But if little is known of the details of his life, we know something of his character from things that Alexander said about him, and the esteem in which he held him, and something of the kindliness of his nature from his will which has been preserved. He made provision for all who had faithfully served him and gave many of his slaves their freedom. He had been twice married, and his second wife "who behaved so well towards me," was so provided for that she could marry again, and he made arrangements for the marriage of his daughter. In reading of the life of the Athenian man and the Athenian woman, their ways seem to lie far apart and the wife to have had very little share in the interests of her husband. In his will Aristotle gives us a glimpse of the place which the wife sometimes, at least, held. He left directions that the bones of his first wife, the wife of his youth, were to be taken from their resting-place and buried with his, and this was to be done "as she herself charged."

The work of Aristotle is amazing, for he not only wrote on every conceivable subject, but wrote as a master. For more than a thousand years after his death, the books he wrote were studied in schools and universities, and formed the foundation of all education. He wrote on astronomy, mathematics, biology, botany and many other subjects, and he has not only been called the *Father of Natural Science*, but his writings remained the standard authority on many scientific subjects for centuries after his death. Aristotle was more practical than Plato, though less inspiring as a writer. As we have already seen, he, too, wrote about an ideal state in his *Politics*. Aristotle believed that the life of a state was like that of an individual; that the aim of both should be noble living, and that peace and justice between states was just as important as between individuals. But he did more than describe an ideal state; he described the education which such a state should give to its youth, the result of which should be not that a man should boast that his state was great and glorious, but that, being the citizen of such a state, in all that he did he should strive to be worthy of her.

Greek philosophy and science had begun in Ionia and then passed to Athens. To the thinkers of the fourth century BCE the fall of Athens must have seemed a great disaster, but in reality it was of the utmost service to the world. The Greek spirit was one of those imperishable things that cannot die, and it was to go out from Athens and spread over a wider world than it had hitherto known. It spread first to Alexandria where, in the Hellenistic Age, the next great group of philosophers and men of science were to be found.

THE HISTORIANS

The word *history* is a Greek word and means an *enquiry*. The Greeks were not the first people in the world who wrote history, but they wrote it as it had never been written before, and some of the greatest history in the world is that which was written by Greeks. These writers were not content with merely narrating events that had taken place, they made what the word history means, an enquiry. They possessed the imagination, not only to describe events and scenes vividly, but to feel as the people about whom they were writing felt, and to understand the passions that moved them at great crises of their history. They were the first historians who took the trouble to find out why nations and individuals acted as they did, and to sift their evidence, finding out what was true and what was false.

The oldest of the Greek historians was Herodotus, the *Father of History*, an Ionian born in Halicarnassus in 484 BCE. He spent a good part of his life travelling, during which time he collected materials which he afterwards used in his history. He was a man who was intensely interested in everything he saw, a very credulous traveller, for he seems to have believed almost everything that was told him: old traditions, all kinds of miraculous occurrences, and many things that it is evident could never have happened. Though he undoubtedly believed a great deal that was not true, he did not swallow all that was told him, for after narrating some marvel he will say: "I am bound to report all that is said, but I am not bound to believe it."

Herodotus was a deeply religious man, and he lived before the disturbing days when men began to question the existence of the gods. To him history was a great drama, the plot of which was the triumph of the Greek over the Barbarian, which he saw as the will of the gods, and to him, as to all devout Greeks of his day, all wrong-doing, all disobedience to the will of the gods brought its own punishment, its retribution, what the Greeks called its Nemesis.

As a story-teller, Herodotus is unrivalled. He wrote his history in order that "the great and wonderful deeds done by the Greeks and Persians should not lack renown," and the earlier books which give an account of all he had learnt in his travels in the East, of Egypt and Babylonia, of Lydia and Persia, lead up to the great climax, the invasion of Greece by the Persians. In the pages of Herodotus we live again, as we live nowhere else, through all the excitement and thrill of the days when Greece fought the Barbarian and drove him out of the land.

The greatest of the Greek historians was Thucydides, great not only among the Greek writers, but among the historians of the world. He was born about 471 BCE, and he wrote the history of the Peloponnesian War. Thucydides was an Athenian, a man of wealth and good position, and was one of the few who had the plague and recovered from it. As the war went on, he was anxious to fight and help to bring it to a victorious close, but a far greater career was in store for him. He was elected a general and sent at the head of an army to relieve Amphipolis and prevent its surrender to the Spartans. But he arrived too late, the city had been taken, and he was exiled in consequence. To this exile we owe his history.

Thucydides is one of the most accurate and impartial of historians. He was filled with an abiding love for Athens, but, unlike some Athenians, he felt no bitterness towards her for exiling him. The only remark he makes about his banishment is that it gave him the opportunity to write his history. He was scrupulously fair to both sides, and he tells us himself of the care he took to be accurate and to accept nothing on the evidence of mere tradition.

Men do not discriminate, and are too ready to receive ancient traditions about their own as well as about other countries; and so little trouble do they take in the search after truth; so readily do they accept whatever comes first to hand. Of the events of the war I have not ventured to speak from any chance information, nor according to any notion of my own; I have described nothing but what I either saw myself, or learned from others of whom I made the most careful and particular enquiry. The task was a laborious one, because eye-witnesses of the same occurrences gave different accounts of them, as they remembered or were interested in the actions of one side or the other. If he who desires to have before his eyes a true picture of the events which have happened, and of the like events which may be expected to happen hereafter in the order of human things, shall pronounce what I have written to be useful, then I shall be satisfied. My history is an everlasting possession, not a prize composition which is heard and forgotten.

Thucydides, I

Unlike Herodotus, Thucydides did not trace events to the will of the gods, but he held that the deeds of men and the use or misuse they made of their opportunities were responsible for them. He never moralizes, but in the clear and reasoned order in which he narrates events the story is carried down from the beginning to its inevitable conclusion.

Thucydides has preserved for all time the memory of what Athens was in her greatest days, and the ideals of one of her great statesmen. But the claim of his book to be an "everlasting possession" is justified not because of the actual history he recorded, but because of the critical and scientific way in which he made his enquiry which has become a model for all later historians.

Thucydides left the story of the Peloponnesian War unfinished; he never even finished the last sentence. The story was completed by Xenophon. He was not a great historian like his predecessors, but he has left us valuable information about the later events of the war in the *Hellenica*, the romantic tale of adventure which tells how a band of Ten Thousand Greeks found their way home from the heart of Mesopotamia, and the *Economist*, a delightful picture of a Greek household.

There is one other Greek writer, who, though he did not write history, has left us much valuable historical information. This was Plutarch (46–120 CE) who lived long after the great days of Greece had passed. He was a Greek from Boeotia, a well-educated man who had many friends with whom he was wont to discuss all kinds of subjects: Philosophy, history, literature, or politics, and he was also a writer. The great work for which his name is remembered is the *Parallel Lives of the Greeks and Romans*. These are the biographies, arranged in pairs of a Greek and a Roman, each pair followed by a comparison between the two. Plutarch never imagined that he was writing history, and in these *Lives* there is no wide view over a whole period, but in each life there is a vivid picture of a personality and a character. Plutarch knew how to choose picturesque details and anecdotes, and he was attracted by simple, upright, honourable, patriotic characters, which makes his book a storehouse of stories about such men. Few biographies in the world have been read so widely or have achieved such immortality as have the *Lives* of Plutarch, and probably none have done more to encourage manliness and the spirit of good sportsmanship.

GREEK LITERATURE: THE DRAMATISTS

A **classic is a work** of art or of literature that never dies, a book that will be read for ever, no matter when or by whom it was written. We have said that when the history of a nation is recorded in language we call it literature, but by such literature is meant not only historical writing, but whatever takes the form of letters. The history of a nation is an enquiry into how that nation *thinks* as well as into what it *does*, and its philosophers, historians and dramatists are as much a part of its history as its statesmen and men of action. The great Greek dramatists were men living the life of their time, and it was a time when stirring things were happening. The dramas of Aeschylus, Sophocles and Euripides were written during the period which began with the repulse of the Persians, which included the golden days of Pericles, and which saw the tragic changes which came over Athens during the long-drawn-out misery of the Peloponnesian War.

Now the great Greek dramas are among the classics of the world. There are various reasons for this, but one, and not the least, is that they are the outward expression of that love of beauty and of self-control that is one of the priceless gifts of Greece to the world. To the Greek, beauty meant perfection in all that he did, the association of beautiful words and forms with beautiful deeds and scenes. To him *beauty* was the same as *goodness*, and ugliness was evil. And beauty meant self-control, the absence of all excess and exaggeration. The Greek dramatists had no models to guide them, yet they produced works that almost perfectly attained this Greek ideal of beauty.

The oldest of these dramatists was Aeschylus. He took an active part in the Persian Wars, and he thought this of so much greater importance than any literary success he had achieved, that his epitaph, said to have been written by himself, saying nothing about his poetry, states only that he fought the Persians. His name and birthplace were inscribed and then that "the grove of Marathon can bear witness to his good soldierhood, and the long-haired Mede who felt it." One of the few Greek plays of which the plot was not taken from ancient Greek legend was the *Persians* of Aeschylus, interesting because it is the first historical play written by a poet who took part himself in the events of which it tells.

The greatest work of Aeschylus was a Trilogy, (i.e., three consecutive plays bearing on the same subject): the *Agamemnon*, the greatest of all his plays; the *Libation-Bearers*, and the *Furies*. These tell the tale, so often told in the Greek drama, of the murder by his wife of Agamemnon on his return from Troy, of Orestes who avenged his father's death, of the Furies who followed him as a result of his deed, and of how in the end he found release. These plays are haunted throughout by the belief that over certain families hangs a curse, that the sins of their fathers are visited on their children, and that from this punishment there is no escape. Aeschylus was filled with the realization of the power of the great unseen forces that move the world, but he believed that if on one side there were the Furies demanding blood for blood, on the other were Apollo and Athena, symbols of the self-control that could overcome the heritage of anger and of passion.

Sophocles lived through the great years of Athens. Only sixteen years old when the battle of Salamis was fought, he must have been filled with all the enthusiasm of youth over the victory. It was said of Sophocles that he had "such charm of character that he was loved by everybody wherever he went." Life seems to have been happy and prosperous for him from the beginning. He won the first prize at the festival with his first play, and when he was only twenty-eight he won a prize over Aeschylus who was then nearly sixty.

The greatest plays of Sophocles are those which tell of the ancient legends of Thebes: of Oedipus as King, and then as outcast, and of Antigone, who in one play – *Oedipus at Colonus* – goes forth with her exiled father, and in another, the great play that bears her name, was faced with the terrible problem of having to break either the laws of God or those of the state, and of deciding which she would do. By all who understand the real greatness of the Greek drama, Sophocles is accounted the greatest of the dramatists. He represents in literature the spirit that Athena Parthenos represented on the Acropolis: a spirit of reverence, of the serenity that comes when the conflict is over and the victory won, and of triumphant belief in all that is good and beautiful and true.

Very different from either Aeschylus or Sophocles was Euripides. According to tradition, he was born in the island of Salamis on the very day of the battle. As he grew up, he became a friend of Socrates, but for the most part he lived a solitary life, not very much liked, and taking as little part in public life as he could. He was essentially a student, and was one of the first Athenians to collect a library. Euripides lived in Athens during the Peloponnesian War, a period of restless questioning, of breaking away from old traditions and beliefs, of lowering of the old ideals. The war had brought a new spirit and Euripides represented it. He criticized customs and beliefs which he thought were unworthy of the best spirit in Athens, he questioned belief in the gods, and in one great play, *The Trojan Women*, he showed the misery brought by war. He was the first poet to strip war of its glamour and to show it as it affected the conquered. In the *Electra* and in *Iphigenia in Tauris*, Euripides deals with the familiar tragedy of Orestes, pursued by the Furies after the murder of his mother, and in the *Alcestis* he tells the old tale of how a noble woman was willing to sacrifice her life for that of a selfish husband, and of how she was brought back from the gates of Hades by Heracles.

The strength of Euripides lies in his wonderful portrayal of character. He judges his characters by the standards of the men and women of his own day and not by those of the gods and heroes, and he is a merciless critic. This makes his dramas most extraordinarily vivid and human, but it also accounts for some of the criticism and dislike he met with in his own day.

Aristophanes wrote comedies. His plays are based on the daily life of his time, and, to understand them, one must know what were the political questions of his day, who were the leaders, who were the writers, the gossip of the Agora and the barber's shop, the likes and dislikes of the men amongst whom he lived. But to those who know enough of these things to follow his allusions, the plays of Aristophanes are full of interest, and we learn a great deal about life in Athens from them.

Aristophanes was younger than Euripides, but, unlike the older man, he was very conservative, and he disliked the new ways by which the Sophists were teaching the youths, for he believed that the new methods would make them irreverent, good at idle talk but at nothing else, shallow and effeminate. He constantly compared the young men of his own day with those of the generation that had fought at Marathon, and in comparing them he found them wanting, for to him the heroes of the age of Marathon represented all that was best in Athenian manhood.

GREEK ART

The Greeks loved beauty, especially the Athenians of the fifth century BCE, but they did not spend all their time in a conscious search for it. They were very busy about and interested in a great many other things: the administration of the city, relations with other states, often fighting, trading and travelling, building ships and sending out colonies.

A great mistake has been made in modern times in that art has too often been looked upon as a luxury, as something that the rich can have but not the poor, something that has not very much to do with a practical every-day life. But to believe that is to misunderstand altogether what art is, for art is something that is *done*, not something that is merely *looked at*. All humans have within them a vision of what kind of world they would make, if it was left to them to order, and in its widest meaning art is the outward and concrete expression of that vision. To confine art to architecture, sculpture and painting, is to rob it of half its meaning. The forms of art are as many and varied as are the interests of every-day life, and this belief is one of the great gifts of Greece to the world. It was not given to every Greek to be a great artist. Not every one could be an Aeschylus and write the *Agamemnon*, a Sophocles and write the *Antigone*, a Pheidias and create the *Parthenon*, or a Praxiteles and model the *Hermes*, but every one could work in the spirit of which these great works are the supreme examples.

In its narrower, modern sense, art is the outward sign of the spirit of a nation as it is expressed in painting and in stone and marble. Except for the vase-paintings, Greek painting has almost entirely disappeared, but the achievements of the Greeks in architecture and sculpture are amongst the greatest that the world has ever seen. Something has already been said about Greek architecture; the same spirit expressed itself in Greek sculpture. To know the Greeks and the real worth of what they have given to the world, it is not enough to read *about* them; one must learn to know them at first-hand. To do that one must read what they wrote (if not in Greek, then in translations), and look at what they built and at their sculpture (if not at the originals, then by means of casts and photographs), and when one does that, one begins to know a little of what the spirit was that produced such things. The Greeks considered that the human form was the most fitting subject for representation in sculpture, yet they were not great portrait makers; that was left for a later race to achieve. What they aimed at doing was to give outward expression to those qualities of the mind and spirit which they, as a people, prized so highly: beauty, self-control, harmony, restraint. The greatest Greek sculpture was, as it were, the answer, wrought in marble, to the prayer of Socrates to Pan: "Beloved Pan, and all ye other gods who haunt this place, give me beauty in the inward soul; and may the outward and the inward man be at one."

The Greeks lived at a time when so much was being done for the first time, and to all their art they brought a spirit of youth and of joy in creation, yet also a spirit of patience in achieving results, for they were never in a hurry, and they knew that there were no short cuts to the perfection which was to them so important a part of beauty. Their statues are very idealistic, but their idealism was practical, and though, as we know, they did not always fulfil their ideals, they knew that fulfilment was possible. Though the sculpture of the Greeks represented man, not as he always was, but as they believed he might be, did he but follow where his best instincts led, it did sometimes result in something that to them was not only an ideal, but something so real and life-like that they could say of a sculptured figure of a Sleeping Ariadne:

Strangers, touch not the marble Ariadne, lest she
even start up on the quest of Theseus.
Anonymous Epigram

THE RISE OF MACEDONIA

THE RISE OF MACEDONIA

Not very much is known about the early Macedonians. They were partly barbarian, and partly Greek, and when they first appear in history were very disunited. In the plains dwelt a number of tribes, who were said to be of Greek origin. They were closely bound to the King and the chief of them were known as his Companions. Scattered about the hills were numerous tribes, more barbarian than Greek, who looked on the King of Macedonia as their overlord, but who were a constant source of danger to him, as they were frequently struggling for independence. When a weak king ruled, the story of Macedonia became that of petty warfare with these hill-tribes, but strong kings were always trying to unite these warring elements into a nation.

Philip was a rugged soldier king who united Greece under his rule. He died young and at the age of twenty, his son Alexander succeeded to Philip's throne. He is one of the personalities in history who have most appealed to the imagination, not only of his contemporaries, but of all ages. He had the beauty of a young Greek god, a brilliant mind and personal charm which endeared him to his companions. From his father he had inherited great military genius, extraordinary powers of organization, tireless energy and inordinate ambition; and from his mother, a wild, half-barbarian princess, a passionate nature, given to outbursts of fierce and uncontrolled anger, and a romantic imagination.

PHILIP OF MACEDON

Greece was living through one of these periods of change when Philip became King of Macedon in 359 BCE. He had spent three years in Thebes, where he had seen the transformation that the military genius of Epaminondas had effected in the Theban army, and now at the age of twenty-four, he found himself ruler of Macedonia. But his inheritance was one that might have daunted the stoutest heart. He had no allies and no money; enemies surrounded him on all sides, and there was no unity in his kingdom. But he had youth, a few faithful friends, unbounded ambition, and a body fit to endure any hardships. Philip never asked anything of his soldiers that he was not ready to do himself, yet he was not a man whom they loved, and he inspired fear rather than affection.

Philip had three definite aims in his policy: to create a standing army, one that would be ready to march and fight at all times, in winter as well as summer; to unite all Macedonia into a real kingdom, and then to unite all Greece under his rule. Having done that, he intended to march into Asia against the Persian King.

Philip created his army, he subdued and united Macedonia, and then he was ready to turn to Greece. Athens, Sparta and Thebes were now all weak. The power of the city-state was passing away and was to yield in time to the new idea of national unity, but it was not to yield without a conflict. The struggle between Philip and the Greek states was more than a struggle between a strong state and several weak ones; it was a conflict of ideas. On the one side was Athens and allied states, the last representatives of the independent city-state who still jealously guarded their political freedom; on the other side was Philip, who represented this new idea of national unity. He determined to subdue most of Greece by force, but he would have liked Athens to yield to him of her own free will. The power of the Athenian fleet and armies had been broken, but Athenian thought, he art and her culture remained. Could Philip have been received by Athens with good-will, and been recognized by her as the leader of all Greece; he would have held it of greater importance than any military victory.

He wrote letters to her statesmen, sent special envoys to Athens to plead his cause, he tried to prove to her that fears of him were groundless, and he treated the very soil of Attica as if it were sacred. It is a striking picture: Philip, the warrior, at the head of a powerful army, lowering his sword before the politically weak little state, because of the might of her spirit. And that spirit was not dead. One more flash of the old Athenian independence flamed out in the defiance hurled at Philip.

Philip advanced. He seized and held Thermopylae, the gateway into Greece; he upheld the rights of Delphi against a neighbouring state and was recognized by the oracle as the defender of Apollo. Then he marched into Boeotia, where Athens and Thebes made a last tremendous stand against him. In 338 BCE one of the decisive battles of the world was fought at Chaeronea. On one side was an army of the last representatives of the old city-state, a confused array of men, some of them citizen-soldiers serving without pay, some of them hired mercenaries; and on the other side, the first great army of one united nation. The battle was fought on a hot summer's day, and it was fierce and long, but at length the Greeks gave way and Philip was victorious. He had little mercy for Thebes; some Theban leaders were banished, others were put to death, a Macedonian garrison was placed in the city and all Theban lands were confiscated.

Athens was treated with greater mercy. On the day of his victory, Philip did not engage in triumphal celebrations, and he chose not to call himself the King, but instead general of Greece. He sent back Athenian prisoners without ransoms and restored the bodies of those that had been slain in battle.

Underlying all his ambition, all his reliance on military power, was yet the feeling, partly unconscious yet there, that, after all, the things of the spirit were greater than those of pomp and power, and he longed for recognition from Athens. But Athens, though forced to recognize his supremacy, never accepted him willingly.

Philip's next move was to organize an expedition into Asia, in order to crush the power of Persia, and as such an expedition would take Philip out of Greece, most of the Greek states agreed to join it. But first he returned to Macedonia, where enemies were always to be found stirring up hostility to him. A royal marriage gave a good excuse for a great public festivity, and a procession was planned, in which Philip, robed in white, was to walk in state. It must have been a moment of great triumph. His ambitions were fulfilled. The Macedonian army was the greatest in the world, he had united the hostile elements in his kingdom and made of them a nation, he had conquered Greece and been recognized as the chief general of all the Greek armies, and now he was about to set forth to conquer Persia. He was still young, and there seemed nothing to prevent the fulfilment of every further ambition. But suddenly, as the stately procession moved forward, a man darted out from the crowd of spectators, buried his dagger deep in the heart of the King, and Philip fell dead.

He was succeeded by his son Alexander, who in a speech to the Macedonians summed up the achievements of his father. He said to them:

My father found you, vagabond and poor, most of you clad only in skins, tending a few sheep on the mountain sides, and to protect them you had to fight against the border tribes, often with small success. Instead of the skins, my father gave you cloaks to wear and he led you down from the hills into the plains and made you the equal in battle of the neighbouring barbarians, so that your safety depended no longer on the inaccessibility of your mountain strongholds, but on your own valour. He taught you to live in cities, and he gave you good laws and customs, and instead of being the slaves and subjects of those barbarians by whom you and your possessions had long been harried, he made you lords over them. He also added the greater part of Thrace to Macedonia, and by seizing the most conveniently situated places on the sea-coast, he threw open your country to commerce. He made it possible for you to work your mines in safety. He made you rulers over the Thessalonians, of whom you had formerly been in mortal fear, and by humbling the Phocians he gave you, instead of a narrow and difficult road into Greece, a broad and easy one. To such a degree did he humble the Athenians and Thebans, who had ever been ready to fall upon Macedonia, that instead of your paying tribute to the former and being vassals to the latter, both states turned to us for protection. He marched into the Peloponnesus and after setting affairs there in order, he was publicly declared commander-in-chief of the whole of Greece in the expedition against the Persian. And he considered this great distinction not as personal honour to himself, but as a glory for Macedonia.

Arrian: *Anabasis of Alexander*

The new King was only twenty years old. It seemed as if his father had been cut off at the height of his career, and that his death could mean nothing but disaster to the power of Macedonia. But what seems like a tragedy and the failure of human hopes, is sometimes the door through which an individual or a nation passes to greater things. Philip had done his work. He was a great soldier and had made great conquests, but he inspired no love and he lacked the imagination which would have made him see with the eyes of the conquered, and so rule them that they would have become real parts of a mighty whole. His son was young, but he had this gift, and so the tragedy of his father's death was the beginning of new and greater opportunities for him, and the door through which Greece was to pass from the old order into the new.

DEMOSTHENES

Though **forced** to acknowledge the political supremacy of Philip, Athens had never given him the real homage he so greatly desired, that of the spirit. This persistent refusal was largely due to the orator Demosthenes.

Politically, Athens was now weak, and her constant wars were a great strain on resources. But at this time, most of her fighting was done at a distance from Athens and by hired mercenaries. A great change had come over Athens since the days of Marathon and Salamis. No longer was it the pride of the Athenians that the citizens themselves had come to the city's defence, and though the young men liked to boast that their forefathers had fought at Marathon, they preferred a more pleasure-loving life than was possible in a camp, and so they paid other men to go out and fight for them.

Demosthenes fought against this spirit, and when Philip made advances to Athens and tried to conclude an alliance with her, Demosthenes made speech after speech against such a policy, imploring the people not to make terms with the stranger, but to make ready for war, and to give their own lives on the battle-field instead of paying others to die for them.

Demosthenes had been a delicate child, very shy and with a stammer in his speech. He grew up, however, with a passion for oratory, and he would go to hear the noted orators of his time and listen to every word they said, going home afterwards to practise the art of speaking himself. The first time he spoke in public, he met with discouragement, for his style was awkward, his voice weak and he stammered. He determined, however, that he would overcome all these obstacles.

It was known that Demosthenes worked very hard over his speeches, and that he never spoke in the Assembly unless he had thought over the subject and prepared what he intended to say. It became a matter of joke in Athens that instead of depending on inspiration, his speeches "smelt of the lamp." In his old age, Demosthenes told some of his friends how he had overcome his defects of speech: he had conquered his tendency to stammer and stutter by s peaking with pebbles in his mouth; he disciplined his voice by declaiming and reciting when he out of breath; he exercised in front of a large mirror. To cure a habit he had of raising his left shoulder while speaking, he suspended a naked sword over it whenever he practised, and he would stand on the sea-shore during a storm to declaim, so that he might accustom himself to the uproar in a public assembly.

Demosthenes has been called the greatest of orators. Opinions have differed since, as to whether his policy was the wisest for Athens to follow at that moment, but every word he uttered was inspired by a passionate love for Athens, and he at all times entreated the Athenians to be true to their own great spirit and their ancient patriotism.

The speeches of Demosthenes against the policy of making friends with Philip are known as the *Philippics*, a word which has become part of later language, and in the greatest of these, he shows the Athenians how their lowered ideals have permitted political corruption and were leading them to destruction.

What is the cause of these things? [he asked], for as it was not without reason that the Hellenes in old days were so prompt for freedom, so it is not without reason or cause that they are now so prompt to be slaves. There was a spirit, men of Athens, a spirit in the mind of the People in those days which is absent today, the spirit which vanquished the wealth of Persia, which led Hellas in the path of freedom, and never gave way in face of battle by sea or land; a spirit whose extinction today has brought universal ruin and turned Hellas upside down. What was this spirit? It was nothing subtle or clever. It meant that those who took money from those who aimed at dominion or at the ruin of Hellas were execrated by all. Where are such sentiments now? They have been sold in the market and are gone.

Third Philippic

Demosthenes possessed the power of appealing to both the reason and the emotions of his hearers, and in the end Athens followed his advice. But it resulted in disaster. Those who had opposed Demosthenes, especially the statesman Aeschines, turned upon him in anger, and accused him of sacrificing the lives of the young men, and of spending their treasure for nothing. Athens had followed his advice and had been beaten, and now Philip was her master. As Aeschines and his opponents had been laying such stress on the consequences of his policy, Demosthenes defended himself in what was, perhaps, the greatest of his speeches. In one part of it he warned the Athenians that what he had to say might startle them, but

let no one, [he said], in the name of Heaven, be amazed at the length to which I go, but give a kindly consideration to what I say. Even if what was to come was plain to all beforehand; even if all foreknew it; even if you, Aeschines, had been crying with a loud voice in warning and protestation, you who uttered not so much as a sound; even then, I say, it was not right for the city to abandon her course, if she had any regard for her fame, or for our forefathers, or for the ages to come. As it is, she is thought, no doubt, to have failed to secure her object, as happens to all alike, whenever God wills it: but then, by abandoning in favour of Philip her claim to take the lead of others, she must have incurred the blame of having betrayed them all. Had she surrendered without a struggle those claims in defence of which our forefathers faced every imaginable peril, who would not have cast scorn upon you, Aeschines – upon you, I say; not, I trust, upon Athens nor upon me? In God's name, with what faces should we have looked upon those who came to visit the city, if events had come round to the same conclusion as they now have, if Philip had been chosen as commander and lord of all, and we had stood apart, while others carried on the struggle to prevent these things; and that, although the city had never yet in time past preferred an inglorious security to the hazardous vindication of a noble cause? What Hellene, what foreigner, does not know that the Thebans, and the Spartans who were powerful still earlier, and the Persian King would all gratefully and gladly have allowed Athens to take and keep all that was her own, if she would do the bidding of another, and let another take the first place in Hellas? But this was not, it appears, the tradition of the Athenians; it was not tolerable; it was not in their nature. From the beginning of time no one had ever yet succeeded in persuading the city to throw in her lot with those who were strong, but unrighteous in their dealings, and to enjoy the security of servitude. Throughout all time she has maintained her perilous struggle for pre-eminence, honour and glory. And this policy you look upon as so lofty, so proper to your own national character that, of your forefathers also, it is those who have acted thus that you praise most highly. And naturally, for who would not admire the courage of those men, who did not fear to leave their land and their city, and to embark upon their ships that they might not do the bidding of another; who chose for their general Themistocles (who had counselled them thus), and stoned Cyrsilus to death, when he gave his voice for submission to a master's orders – and not him alone, for your wives stoned his wife also to death. For the Athenians of that day did not look for an orator or a general who would enable them to live in happy servitude; they cared not to live at all, unless they might live in freedom. For everyone of them felt that he had come into being, not for his father and his mother alone, but also for his country. And wherein lies the difference? He who thinks he was born for his parents alone awaits the death which destiny assigns him in the course of nature: but he who thinks that he was born for his country also will be willing to die, that he may not see her in bondage, and will look upon the outrages and the indignities that he must needs bear in a city that is in bondage as more to be dreaded than death.

Now were I attempting to argue that I had induced you to show a spirit worthy of your forefathers, there is not a man who might not

rebuke me with good reason. But, in fact, I am declaring that such
principles as these are your own; I am showing that before my time
the city displayed this spirit, though I claim that I, too, have had some
share, as your servant, in carrying out your policy in detail. But in
denouncing the policy as a whole, in bidding you be harsh with me, as
one who has brought terrors and dangers upon the city, the prosecutor,
in his eagerness to deprive me of my distinction at the present moment,
is trying to rob you of praises that will last throughout all time. For if
you condemn the defendant on the ground that my policy was not for
the best, men will think that your own judgment has been wrong, and
that it was not through the unkindness of fortune that you suffered
what befell you. But it cannot, it cannot be that you were wrong,
men of Athens, when you took upon you the struggle for freedom and
deliverance. No! by those who at Marathon bore the brunt of the peril
– our forefathers. No! by those who at Plataea drew up their battle-
line, by those who at Salamis, by those who off Artemisium fought the
fight at sea, by the many who lie in the sepulchres where the People laid
them, brave men, all alike deemed worthy by their country, Aeschines,
of the same honour and the same obsequies – not the successful or the
victorious alone! And she acted justly. For all these have done that
which it was the duty of brave men to do; but their fortune has been
that which Heaven assigned to each.

Second Olynthiac Oration

ALEXANDER THE GREAT

At the age of twenty, Alexander succeeded to Philip's throne.
During his boyhood, his father was constantly away at war,
but he saw to it that his son was well educated. His first teachers

accustomed him to a Spartan discipline, and so trained his body that in later years he was able to undergo fatigue and endure hardships that astonished all who were with him.

When Alexander was twelve years old, an episode occurred which convinced his father that he needed the best guidance that could be found for him. A horse, Bucephalus by name, was offered to Philip for the sum of thirteen talents, and the King, with the Prince and many others,

went into the field to try him. But they found him so very vicious and unmanageable that he reared up when they endeavoured to mount him, and would not so much as endure the voice of any of Philip's attendants. Upon which as they were leading him away as wholly useless and untractable, Alexander, who stood by, said: "What an excellent horse do they lose for want of address and boldness to manage him!" Philip at first took no notice of what he said; but when he heard him repeat the same thing several times, and saw he was much vexed to see the horse sent away, "Do you reproach," said he to him, "those who are older than yourself, as if you knew more, and were better able to manage him than they?" "I could manage this horse," said he, "better than others do." "And if you do not," said Philip, "what will you forfeit for your rashness?" "I will pay," answered Alexander, "the whole price of the horse." At this the whole company fell a-laughing; and as soon as the wager was settled amongst them, he immediately ran to the horse, and taking hold of the bridle, turned him directly towards the sun, having, it seems, observed that he was disturbed at and afraid of the motion of his own shadow; then letting him go forward a little, still keeping the reins in his hands and stroking him gently, when he found him begin to grow eager and fiery, with one nimble leap he securely mounted him, and when he was seated, by little and little drew in the bridle, and curbed him without either striking or spurring him. Presently, when he found him free from all rebelliousness he let him go at full speed. Philip and his friends looked on at first in silence and anxiety for the result; till seeing him turn and come back rejoicing and triumphing for what he had performed, they all burst out into acclamations of applause; and his father, shedding tears, it is said, for joy, kissed him as he came down from his horse, and in his transport said: "O my son look thee out a kingdom equal to and worthy of thyself, for Macedonia is too little for thee!"

Plutarch: *Life of Alexander*

It was evident that Alexander would not submit to be controlled in what he did, but that a steady guiding hand was needed to develop his best nature, and so Philip sent for the philosopher Aristotle, who was his tutor for four years. Aristotle taught him the best that Greece could offer in literature, philosophy and natural science. Alexander had no small opinion of his own powers, and considered himself quite the equal, if not the superior, of the best minds of his time, and he wanted to be recognized as such. Later, when Aristotle had published some of his writings, Alexander, according to Plutarch, wrote to him: "You have not done well to publish your books of oral doctrine; for what is there now that we excel others in, if those things which we have been particularly instructed in be laid open to all?" Alexander had been born with a love for study, and his education gave him a real appreciation of all that was best in Greek thought. He used to sleep with a copy of Homer under his pillow, and he told Aristotle that he would "rather excel others in the knowledge of what is excellent than in the extent of his power and dominion." Alexander grew to love his tutor greatly, and in after years he would say that as from his father he had received life, so from Aristotle had he learned to lead a good life.

Such a personality soon made Alexander the idol of Macedonia, but, as in the case of his father, that was not enough; Macedonian, and therefore in the eyes of Greece a half-barbarian, he wanted to be accepted by the Greeks as a Greek and to receive their hero-worship. Like Philip, he was determined to march into Asia, subdue the Persian King and become a world ruler, but it was necessary that he should subdue Greece first. He did this very quickly, and in 335 BCE, one year after he became King, he marched against Thebes, which had organized a revolt against him. He came upon the city with almost magical swiftness, for in thirteen days he had transported his army two hundred and fifty miles. A rumour had spread in Greece that he was dead, but suddenly, there he was before the walls of Thebes. In two days all was over. The city was razed to the ground, and the inhabitants either slain or sold into slavery. Yet in the midst of all the horror, Alexander gave an order which seized upon the Greek imagination: the house of Pindar was to be left untouched for no war was being waged against Greek civilization.

Alexander went to Corinth, where he was elected General of the army that was to invade Persia. The time had now come when at the head of a mighty army, Alexander could start for Asia. This army was made up of Macedonians and of men from all the most warlike states of Greece. It had been thoroughly trained and disciplined, and it served under a general only twenty-two years of age, it is true, but who had already shown himself a military genius and who was adored by every soldier from the highest to the lowest. It was an army that was never to know defeat.

Alexander did not hide his purpose from the Persian King, for he sent him word that he considered himself lord of Asia: "I, Alexander, consider the whole of thy treasure, and the whole of thy land to be mine." To the Greeks this did not represent any over-weening pride, for Alexander was but expressing the belief that was held by Aristotle, the greatest Greek thinker of the age, that Greeks were justified in enslaving the Barbarian.

No story of conquest is more romantic than that of Alexander. On first reaching Asia Minor he went to Ilium, where he dedicated his armour to Athena, and took in its place some weapons which tradition said had been used in the Trojan War, and he laid a wreath on the tomb of Achilles. Then he started on his march. He came, whilst passing through Asia Minor, to Gordium, where he saw the celebrated Gordian knot, by which the yoke was fastened to the pole of an ancient chariot. An old prophecy had been made that the man who untied this knot would rule the world. Alexander tried to loosen it, but losing patience, he took his sword and cut it. He meant to rule the world, and he knew that his empire would only be won by the sword.

Alexander marched through Syria into Egypt, and when he was in Egypt, he made a journey through the desert of Libya to consult the oracle, Zeus Ammon.

Few men would have started upon so long and dangerous a journey without misgivings, for there was likely to be scarcity of water, and violent winds that would blow about the poisonous sand of the desert and cause the death of those who inhaled it. But Alexander was not to be turned from anything he was bent upon; for hitherto fortune had helped him in all his plans, and the boldness of his temper gave him a passion for overcoming difficulties. In this journey the gods seemed to favour him as usual, for plentiful rains fell, which not only relieved the soldiers from fear of dying of thirst, but made the sand moist and firm to travel on and purified the air. Besides, some ravens kept up with them in their march, flying before them and waiting for them if they fell behind; but the greatest miracle of all was that if any of the company went astray in the night, the ravens never ceased croaking until they were guided to the right path again.

Having passed through the wilderness, they came to the place where the high-priest of Ammon bade Alexander welcome in the name of the god, and called him son of Zeus. And being asked by the King whether any of his father's murderers had escaped punishment, the priest charged him to speak with more respect, since his was not a mortal father. Then Alexander desired to know of the oracle if any of those who murdered Philip were yet unpunished, and further concerning dominion, whether the empire of the world should be his? This, the god answered, he should obtain, and that Philip's death was fully revenged, which gave him so much satisfaction that he made splendid offerings to Zeus, and gave the priests very rich presents.

Plutarch: *Life of Alexander*

Before leaving Egypt, Alexander founded the city of Alexandria, on the Nile delta. He marked out the boundaries of the city himself, pointing out where the market-place and temples were to be constructed, what Greek gods were to be dedications, and marking a spot for the temple of Egyptian Isis.

Before his death, Alexander went on to many cities called by his name, but the Alexandria of Egypt was the greatest, and the one that was to survive even to the present day. For more than two thousand years it has held its position as one of the chief ports in the eastern part of the Mediterranean. Alexander did not intend that it should become the capital of Egypt, but he did intend that it should take the place of Tyre, so that the trade coming from the East should be in the hands of Greeks and not of Phoenicians.

The army worshipped Alexander, and he knew how to appeal to the imagination of his followers and to gain their devotion. On one occasion

he had made a long and painful march of eleven days, during which his soldiers suffered so much from want of water that they were ready to give up. While they were in this distress it happened that some Macedonians who had fetched water in skins upon their mules from a river they had found out came about noon to the place where Alexander was, and seeing him almost choked with thirst, presently filled a helmet and offered it to him. He asked them to whom they were carrying the water; they told him to their children, adding that if his life were but saved, it was no matter for them though they all perished. Then he took the helmet into his hands, and looking round about, when he saw all those who were with him stretching their heads out and looking earnestly after the drink, he returned it again with thanks without taking a drop of it. "For," said he, "if I alone should drink, the rest will be out of heart." When the soldiers heard him speak in this way, they one and all cried out to him to lead them forward boldly, and began whipping on their horses. For whilst they had such a King they said they defied both weariness and thirst, and looked upon themselves to be little less than immortal.

Plutarch: *Life of Alexander*

On another occasion the hardships endured by the army were so great that the men were almost ready to refuse to follow

Alexander any further. But he called them together, and spoke to them, reminding them that he asked no one to suffer what he himself did not suffer. And the magic of his personality silenced all their murmuring and banished all their discontent.

Followed by this devoted army, Alexander started on a marvellous campaign which led him to the uttermost limit of the then known world, even beyond the Indus into India. In battle after battle he met those who opposed his path and conquered them. Alexander did not know the meaning of the word *impossible*. He was told once that a certain mountain pass was impracticable. For other men, it would have been, but Alexander gave orders that his spearmen should cut steps in the steep rock, and where before only the surest-footed goats had climbed, Alexander and his men passed in safety. His men followed him over snowy mountains in winter, and across thirsty deserts in summer, up and down the lower ranges of the Himalaya Mountains, where the best European armies of today can only go with difficulty. They crossed the plains of India in the rainy season, and even went through that country so unfit for human habitation that Mohammedan conquerors of a later age declared it was a place fit only to be dwelt in by the souls of the lost.

Nothing stopped Alexander, not the mountain barrier, nor the deep river, nor the burning sands. On he went, until he reached what he believed to be the River Ocean that girdled the earth.

Everywhere Alexander had been victorious, until even the Great King of Persia himself was utterly defeated and Alexander was seated upon his throne. He burnt the Persian palace at Persepolis in order to take vengeance on the Persians for their invasion of Greece and to punish them for the injuries they had done the Greeks.

When the news of the victories of Alexander over the Persians reached Greece, great was the amazement. For centuries, the name of the Great King had stood for all that was powerful and invincible. Though he had been driven out of Greece, he was still believed to be omnipotent in Asia. The general feeling was voiced by one of the orators, speaking of what was happening in the Athenian Assembly:

What is there strange and unexpected that has not happened in our time? We have not lived the life of ordinary men, and the things we have seen will become a tale of wonder to posterity. Is not the King of the Persians, he who channelled Athos, he who bridged the Hellespont, he who demanded earth and water of the Greeks, he who dared to write in his letters that he was lord of all men from the rising of the sun unto its setting, is he not struggling now, no longer for lordship over others, but already for his life?

Aeschines, Against Ctesiphon

Alexander had conquered the Great King and seated himself on the royal throne of Persia under the canopy of gold. But now that he had reached the summit of his ambition and was master of the greatest empire in the world, a change came over him, and he began to indulge his passions and to give himself up to all kinds of dissipation. He dressed like a Persian, which deeply offended the Greeks, who became jealous of the increasing favour the King showed to the Barbarian.

Slowly the leaders of Alexander's army began to realize the change that was taking place in their general, and though he gained in popularity with the Persians, he began to lose some of the devotion hitherto felt for him by the Greeks and Macedonians, and he was becoming estranged from his old followers. At length they realized that it was not a Greek conquest that would enslave Asia of which he dreamed, but of a world empire, in which the Barbarian would live on equal terms with the Greek. Alexander was far-seeing beyond his age, and he had learned that men whose customs are alien to those in which he had been brought up were not always to be despised, and that if he dreamed of holding the world empire he had conquered, he could only do so by treating all parts of it alike, and by encouraging intercourse between the different races which composed it.

However wise this may have been, it is not difficult to understand the feeling of the older Greeks who had been educated to feel a gulf between them and the Barbarian that nothing could ever bridge. The climax of the estrangement between Alexander and his old companions came in a tragic scene at a banquet. Alexander and his friends had been drinking fast and furiously, then songs had been sung, some of which ridiculed the Macedonian officers who had recently been unfortunate in a skirmish. The older men present were offended, but Alexander laughed and had the song repeated. Clitus, who had been an old and trusted friend of the King, said angrily: "It is not well to make a jest of Macedonians among their enemies, for, though they have met with misfortunes, they are better men than those who laugh at them." Angry words passed between him and the King, until, unable to control his rage, Alexander snatched a spear from one of his guards and ran it through the body of Clitus, who fell dead to the ground. Dead silence followed this mad deed, and Alexander was sobered by the sight of the man he had loved lying dead at his feet, slain by his own hand. He drew the spear out of the body and would have killed himself with it, had the guards not interfered and led him by force to his chamber. All that night and the next day he wept bitterly and would speak to no one. At length one of his friends entered the room where he lay and said to him in a loud voice:

Is this the Alexander whom the whole world looks to, lying here weeping like a slave for fear of what men will say? It is Alexander himself who, by the right of his conquests, should be the law to decide what is right and wrong. Do you not know, Alexander, that Zeus is represented with Justice and Law on either side of him, to show that all the deeds of a conqueror are lawful and just?

Plutarch: *Life of Alexander*

The King was soothed by these words, for he was only too ready to believe, as his friend had said, that whatever he might choose to do was right. But he was spoiled by such flattery which only increased his arrogance and made him yield more to his passions than before.

Having conquered and established an empire which extended from Greece and Macedonia in Europe across Asia to India, and which included Egypt and Libya, Alexander prepared to set out on yet another expedition to the West and to enter Arabia. He was in Babylon, and spent a long day attending to military duties. Towards evening, he left his chair of state to take a little relaxation. During his absence, a half-crazy man appeared, who, without any warning, sat himself down on the King's seat. The attendants looked on in horror at such an act, which seemed to them great impiety, but they did not dare turn him out, for suddenly superstitious fears took hold of them, and in frightened voices they whispered to each other that this could foretell nothing but some great calamity.

It was in the early summer of 323 BCE that Alexander was ready to start on his march, but the night before he was to leave Babylon, he became ill of a fever. For a few days he was still able to attend to some business from his bed, but he grew rapidly worse. Suddenly the army realized that he was dying, and his old friends, forgetting whatever estrangement had come between them, entreated to be allowed to see him once more. They were admitted to the chamber where he lay, and passed in silence before him. He was so weak that he "could not speak, and only touched the right hand of each, and raised his head a little, and signed with his eyes." The next day Alexander was dead. Deep and awe-struck silence fell upon the city and camp for four days, and then, his generals having found amongst his papers plans for the western campaign, they endeavoured to carry them out. But they were not successful, and never again did the great army fight under one leader. Having lost the almost magical inspiration of Alexander's leadership, his successors were unable to keep the empire which he had conquered.

Almost from the moment of his death, Alexander was worshipped as a god. He was the great hero of his age, and even in his life-time, it was believed that he was half-divine. Dying so young, he was only thirty-three, possessed of great strength and god-like beauty, capable of rare generosity, brave almost to recklessness, planning conquests so far-reaching that they appealed to the imagination of everyone, given to outbursts of savage anger and vindictive rage, all these characteristics were looked upon as more than human. For more than two thousand years, the name of Alexander has been immortal in the East. There is hardly an ancient city from Babylon almost to the borders of China that does not claim Alexander as its founder; his name still clings to old traditions and legends; to this very day the Parsees curse him for having caused the destruction of the ancient sacred Persian writings when he captured Persepolis and burnt it. Later generations of men have differed as to the lasting value of some of his work, but the name of Alexander, and the story of his hero-deeds have become a permanent possession of the imagination of mankind.

THE HELLENISTIC AGE

THE HELLENISTIC AGE

The results of the twenty years' war were disastrous to Greece and Macedonia, not only by the exhausting expenditure of blood and treasure, but by the introduction of Oriental habits of luxury and servility, in place of the free and simple manners of former times. Though the minds of the Greeks were enlarged by a knowledge of the history and philosophy of the Eastern nations, and by observation of the natural world and its productions in new climates and circumstances, yet most of the influences which had kept alive the free spirit of the people had ceased to work. Patriotism was dead; learning took the place of genius; and imitation, the place of art.

At the same time, Asia had gained many splendid cities, its commerce had vastly increased, and the Greek military discipline and forms of civil government gave new strength to her armies and states. From the Indus to the Adriatic, and from the Crimea to the southern bounds of Egypt, the Greek language prevailed, at least among the educated and ruling classes. In Asia Minor, Syria and Egypt, the influence of Hellenic thought continued a thousand years in full force, until Mahomet and his successors set up their new Semitic empire. The wide diffusion of the Greek language in western Asia was among the most important preparations for the spread of Christianity. If Alexander had lived to complete his great scheme of interfusing the eastern and western races, Asia would have gained and Europe lost in still greater measure.

THE LEGACY OF ALEXANDER

Alexander named no successor, but shortly before his death he gave his ring to Perdiccas. This general, as prime minister, kept the empire united for two years in the royal family. An infant prince, Alexander IV, born after his father's death, was associated on the throne with Philip Arrhidaeus, half-brother of the great Alexander. Four regents or guardians of the empire were appointed – two in Europe and two in Asia. One of these was murdered by Perdiccas, who thus acquired for himself the sole administration of Asia, Antipater and Craterus ruling west of the Bosphorus.

The provinces not already bestowed by the conqueror were divided among ten of his generals, who were expected to govern in the name and for the benefit of the two kings. Finding it impossible, however, either by management or force, to keep these lieutenants in subjection to the mere name of royalty, Perdiccas formed a plan to seize the sovereignty for himself. Eumenes was on his side, while his colleagues in the regency, and the two great provincial governors, Ptolemy and Antigonus, were his most powerful opponents.

In a campaign against Ptolemy, in Egypt, Perdiccas was slain by his own mutinous soldiers. Craterus fell in a battle with Eumenes, in Cappadocia, and the sole regency devolved upon Antipater. This general defeated the schemes of Eurydice – niece of Alexander the Great, and wife of the imbecile king, Philip

Arrhidaeus – who even harangued the army at Triparadisus, in Syria, demanding to be admitted to a share in the government. A fresh division and assignment of the provinces was now made. Antigonus was charged with the prosecution of the war against Eumenes, in which he made himself master of the greater part of Asia Minor.

Antipater died in Macedon, 319 BCE, leaving the regency, not to his son Cassander, but to his friend Polysperchon. Cassander, in disgust, fled to Antigonus; and in the war which followed, these two, with Ptolemy, sought the disruption of the empire, while Eumenes and Polysperchon fought for its unity. Eumenes collected a force in Cilicia, with which he meant to conquer Syria and Phœnicia, and thus gain command of the sea. Antigonus first defeated a royal fleet near Byzantium, and then marched across the country to the borders of Syria, and pursued Eumenes inland beyond the Tigris. A number of the eastern satraps here joined Eumenes, but after two indecisive battles he was seized by his own troops and given up to Antigonus, who put him to death, 316 BCE.

In Macedonia, the mock king, Philip Arrhidaeus, and his wife were executed, by order of Olympias, the mother of Alexander the Great. But this imperious princess was captured, in her turn, at Pydna; and, in violation of the terms of her surrender, was murdered by her enemies. Cassander became master of Macedonia and Greece. He married Thessalonica, half-sister of the Conqueror, and founded in her honour the city which bears her name, 316 BCE.

The ambition of Antigonus now began to alarm his colleagues, for he was evidently not to be satisfied with less than the entire dominion of Alexander. He gave away the eastern satrapies according to his pleasure. From Babylonia he drove Seleucus, who took refuge with Ptolemy in Egypt, and formed a league with Cassander, Lysimachus, and Asander. A war of four years followed (315–311 BCE), which resulted in the re-establishment of Seleucus in Babylon and the East, while Antigonus gained power in Greece, Syria and Asia Minor. The peace of 311 BCE provided for the independence of the Greek cities, but allowed each general to keep what he had gained, and left Cassander regent of Macedonia until Alexander IV should be of age. It was probably understood between the contracting parties that this last event was never to occur. The young king and his mother were murdered, by order of Cassander.

At the end of a year, Ptolemy broke the peace, on the pretense that Antigonus had not liberated the Greek cities of Asia Minor. He was opposed in Cilicia by Demetrius, son of Antigonus, who gained in this war the title of *Poliorcetes*, the Besieger. Ptolemy, entering Greece, seized Sicyon and Corinth, and aimed to marry Cleopatra, the last survivor of the royal house of Macedon; but the princess was assassinated, by order of Cassander, in 308 BCE. Demetrius now arriving with a fleet to the relief of Athens, Ptolemy withdrew to Cyprus, and gained possession of the island. A great battle followed off Salamis, one of the most severe in the world's history. Ptolemy was defeated, with the loss of all but eight of his ships, leaving 17,000 prisoners in the hands of the enemy.

The five principal generals now assumed the kingly title. Demetrius spent a year in the siege of Rhodes, which, by its brave and memorable defence, secured the privileges of a neutral in the remaining years of the war. Returning to Greece, he assembled a congress at Corinth, which conferred upon him the titles formerly bestowed on Philip and Alexander, and then marched northward against the regent, or, rather, King of Macedon. Alarmed at his endangered position, Cassander stirred up his allies to invade Asia Minor.

The decisive battle took place, at Ipsus 301 BCE, in Phrygia. Demetrius had arrived from Europe to the assistance of his father; but Seleucus, with the forces of the East, including 480 Indian elephants, increased the army of Lysimachus. Antigonus, in his eighty-first year, was slain; Demetrius, completely defeated, took refuge in Greece, but was not permitted to enter Athens. The two conquerors, Seleucus and Lysimachus, divided the dominions of Alexander, with due regard to their own interests. Seleucus received the Euphrates Valley, Upper Syria, Cappadocia, and part of Phrygia. Lysimachus added the rest of Asia Minor to his Thracian dominion, which extended along the western shores of the Euxine as far as the mouths of the Danube; Ptolemy retained Egypt, and Cassander continued to reign in Macedonia until his death.

THE SYRIAN KINGDOM OF SELEUCUS

After the restoration of Seleucus to the government of Babylonia, he extended his power over all the provinces between the Euphrates and the Indus. He even made war against an Indian kingdom upon the western headwaters of the Ganges, gaining thereby a great extension of commerce, and the addition of five hundred elephants to his army. The battle of Ipsus added to his dominions the country as far west as the Mediterranean and the center of Phrygia, making his kingdom by far the greatest that had been formed from the fragments of Alexander's empire.

This vast dominion was organized by Seleucus with great skill and energy. In each of the seventy-two provinces new cities sprang up, as monuments of his power and centres of Greek civilization. Sixteen of these were named Antioch, in honor of his father; five Laodicea, for his mother, Laodice; seven for himself, Seleucia; and several for his two wives, Apamea and Stratonice. To watch more effectually the movements of his rivals, Ptolemy and Lysimachus, he removed the seat of government from the Euphrates to his new capital, Antioch, on the Orontes, which continued for nearly a thousand years to be one of the richest and most populous cities in the world.

In 293 BCE, Seleucus divided his empire with his son Antiochus, giving the younger prince all the provinces east of the Euphrates. Demetrius Poliorcetes, after gaining and then losing Macedonia, sought to make for himself a new kingdom in Asia, out of the possessions of Lysimachus and Seleucus. He was defeated by the latter, and remained a prisoner the rest of his life.

Lysimachus, king of Thrace, under the influence of his Egyptian wife and her brother, Ptolemy Ceraunus, had alienated the hearts of his subjects by the murder of his son. The widow of the murdered prince fled for protection to the court of Seleucus, who undertook her cause and invaded the territories of Lysimachus. The two aged kings were now the only survivors of the companions and generals of Alexander. In the battle of Corupedion, 281 BCE, Lysimachus was slain, and all his Asiatic dominions were transferred to Seleucus.

The empire of Alexander seemed about to be united in the hands of one man. Before crossing the Hellespont to seize the European provinces, the Syrian king committed the government of his present dominion to his son, Antiochus. Then passing the strait, he advanced to Lysimachia, the capital of his late enemy; but here he was killed by the hand of Ptolemy Ceraunus, 280 BCE. Thrace and Macedonia became the prize of the murderer.

Antiochus I. (Soter) inherited the Asiatic dominions of his father, and made war in Asia Minor against the native kings of Bithynia. One of these, Nicomedes, called to his assistance the Gauls, who were ravaging eastern Europe, and rewarded their services with a large territory in northern Phrygia, which was thence called Galatia. North-western Lydia was also wrested from Antiochus, and formed the kingdom of Pergamus. From his only important victory over the Gauls, 275 BCE, the Syrian king derived his title *Soter* (the Deliverer); but his operations were usually unsuccessful, and his kingdom was much reduced both in wealth and power during his reign. He was defeated and slain near Ephesus, in a battle with the Gauls, 261 BCE.

Antiochus II bore the blasphemous title of *Theos* (the God), but he showed himself less than a man by the weakness and licentiousness of his reign. He abandoned all affairs to worthless favourites, who were neither feared nor respected in the distant provinces, and two independent kingdoms sprang up unchecked in Parthia and Bactria, 255 BCE. The influence of his wife, Laodice, involved him in a war with Egypt. It was ended by the divorce of Laodice, and the marriage of Antiochus with Berenice, daughter of Ptolemy Philadelphus (260–252 BCE). On the death of Philadelphus, Antiochus sent away Berenice and took back Laodice; but she, doubting his constancy, murdered him to secure the kingdom for her son, Seleucus. Berenice and her infant son were also put to death.

Seleucus II (Callinicus) was first engaged in war with the king of Egypt, Ptolemy Euergetes, who came to avenge the deaths of his sister and nephew. With the exception of part of Lydia and Phrygia, all Asia west of the Tigris, and even Susiana, Media and Persia, submitted to the invader; but the severity of his exactions excited discontent, and a revolt in Egypt called him home, whereupon Callinicus regained his territories. Antiochus Hierax (the Hawk), a younger brother of the king, revolted at fourteen years of age, with the assistance of his uncle and a troop of Gauls. At the same time, Arsaces II, the Parthian king, gained great advantages in Upper Asia, and signally defeated Callinicus (237 BCE), who led an expedition in person against him. The war between the brothers ended, 229 BCE, in the defeat of the rebellious prince. Seleucus died by a fall from his horse, 226 BCE.

Seleucus III (Ceraunus) reigned only three years. In the midst of an expedition against Attalus, king of Pergamus, he was killed in a mutiny by some of his own officers.

Antiochus III, the Great, had an eventful reign of thirty-six years. Molo, his general, first revolted, and made himself master, one by one, of the countries east of the Euphrates, destroying all the armies sent against him. Antiochus at length defeated him, 220 BCE, and then made war upon Egypt for the recovery of Syria and Palestine, which had hitherto been held by Ptolemy. He was successful at first, but his defeat at Rapia robbed him of all his conquests, except Seleucia in Syria. Achus, his cousin, and hitherto a faithful servant of Antiochus and his father, had meanwhile been driven into revolt by the false accusations of Hermas, the prime minister. He subjected to his control all the countries west of the Taurus. As soon as peace had been made with Egypt, the King of Syria marched against him, deprived him of all his possessions in one campaign, besieged him two years in Sardis, and finally captured and put him to death.

The Parthian king, Arsaces III, had taken up arms against Media. Antiochus led an army across the desert to Hecatompylos, the Parthian capital, which he captured; but the battle which followed was indecisive, and Arsaces remained independent, with the possession of Parthia and Hyrcania. The war against the Bactrian monarch had a similar result, Euthydmus retaining Bactria and Sogdiana. Antiochus penetrated India, and renewed the old alliance of Seleucus Nicator with the king of the upper Ganges. Wintering in Kermnia, the Syrian king made a naval expedition, the next year, against the piratical Arabs of the western shores of the Persian Gulf. On his return from his seven years' absence in the East, Antiochus received the title of "Great," by which he is known in history.

The same year, 205 BCE, Ptolemy Epiphanes, a child of five years, succeeded his father in Egypt. Tempted by the unprotected state of the kingdom, Antiochus made a treaty with Philip of Macedon to divide the dominions of Ptolemy between them. Philip's designs were interrupted by a war with Rome, the now powerful republic of the West. Antiochus carried on the contest with great energy, but with varying success, in Cœle-Syria and Palestine. By the decisive battle of Paneas, 198 BCE, he gained complete possession of those provinces; but desiring to prosecute his wars in another direction, he married his daughter Cleopatra to the young King of Egypt, and promised the conquered country as her dower.

He then overran Asia Minor, and crossing the Hellespont, seized the Thracian Chersonesus. The Romans, who had conquered Philip and were guardians of Ptolemy, now sent an embassy to Antiochus, requiring him to surrender all his conquests of territory belonging to either prince, 196 BCE. Antiochus indignantly rejected their interference, and prepared for war, with the aid of their great enemy, Hannibal, who had taken refuge at his court. In 192 BCE, he crossed into Greece and captured Chalcis; but he was signally defeated soon after by the Romans, at Thermopylae, and compelled to withdraw from Europe. They followed him across the sea, and by two naval victories gained the western coast of Asia Minor. The two Scipios crossed the Hellespont and defeated Antiochus a fourth time, near Magnesia, in Lydia.

He obtained peace only by surrendering all Asia Minor except Cilicia, with his navy and all his elephants, and by paying an enormous war indemnity. Twenty hostages were given for the payment, among whom was Antiochus Epiphanes, the king's son. The king of Pergamus received the ceded provinces, and became a most formidable rival to Syria. To meet his engagements with the Romans, Antiochus plundered the temples of Asia, and in a commoti]on excited by this means in Elymais, he lost his life.

Seleucus IV (Philopator) had a reign of eleven years, unmarked by important events. The kingdom was exhausted, and the Romans were ready to seize any exposed province at the least hostile movement of the Syrians. Heliodorus, the treasurer, at length murdered his master and assumed the crown; but his usurpation was cut short by the arrival of Antiochus Epiphanes, brother of the late king, who with the aid of Eumenes, King of Pergamus, established himself upon the throne.

Antiochus IV had been thirteen years a hostage at Rome, and surprised his people by the Roman customs which he introduced. He made a four years' war against Egypt, and had nearly conquered the country when the Romans interfered, and commanded him to give up all his conquests. He was forced to obey, but he vented his rage upon the Jews, whose temple he plundered and desecrated. They sprang to arms, under the leadership of Mattathias, the priest, and his brave son, Judas Maccabaeus, and defeated the army sent to subdue them. Antiochus, who was now in the East, set forth in person to avenge this insult to his authority. On his way, he attempted to plunder the temple at Elymais, and was seized with a furious insanity, in which he died. Both Jews and Greeks believed his madness to be a judgment for his sacrilege.

Antiochus V (Eupator), a boy of twelve years, came to the throne under the control of Lysias, the regent. But his father, when dying, had appointed him another guardian in the person of Philip, who returned to Antioch bearing the royal signet, while the young king and his minister were absent in Judaea. Lysias, on hearing this, hastened to make peace with Judas Maccabaeus, and turned back to fight with Philip, whom he defeated and put to death. The Parthians, meanwhile, were overrunning the kingdom on the east; and the Romans, on the west, were harshly enforcing the terms of the treaty made by Antiochus the Great. Demetrius, the son of Seleucus Philopator, now escaped from Rome, and gained possession of the kingdom, after ordering the execution of both Eupator and his guardian.

Demetrius I spent some years in vain attempts to put down the Jewish rebellion. His armies were defeated by Judas Maccabaeus, and the Romans entered into alliance with Judaea, which they now declared an independent kingdom. The Syrian king was no more successful in Cappadocia; and in Babylon, the satrap whom he had deposed set up an impostor, Alexander Balas, who claimed to be a son of Antiochus Epiphanes. Aided by the forces of Rome, Pergamus, Cappadocia, Egypt and Judaea, this man conquered Demetrius and kept the kingdom five years.

Alexander Balas proved unworthy of a crown, by leaving public affairs in the weak and incompetent hands of his favourite, Ammonius, while he abandoned himself to indolence and luxury. Demetrius Nicator, eldest son of the former king, encouraged by the contempt of the Syrians for the licentiousness of Alexander, landed in Cilicia and made war for the recovery of his kingdom. Ptolemy of Egypt, who had entered Syria with an army for the aid of his son-in-law, Alexander, became disgusted by his ingratitude and came over to the side of Demetrius. A battle near Antioch was decided in favour of the allies. Alexander fled into Arabia, where he was assassinated by some of his own officers.

Demetrius II (Nicator) ruled with such wanton cruelty as to alienate his subjects. One of them, Diootus Tryphon, set up a rival king in the person of Antiochus VI, a child two years of age, the son of Alexander Balas. After three or four years he removed this infant monarch and made himself king, with the aid of Judas Maccabaeus. Demetrius, after fighting ineffectually seven years against his rivals in the west, left the regency of Syria to his wife, Cleopatra, while he turned against the Parthians, who had nearly conquered his eastern provinces. He was defeated and made prisoner by Arsaces VI, and remained ten years a captive, though he was treated with all the honours of royalty, and received a Parthian princess for his second wife.

Cleopatra, unable to wage war alone against Tryphon, called in Antiochus Sidetes, her husband's brother, who conquered the usurper and seated himself on the vacant throne. He made war against the Jews, and captured Jerusalem by a siege of nearly a year. He afterward turned against the Parthians and gained some advantages, but he was finally defeated and lost his life after a reign of nine years. Demetrius Nicator had been released by the Parthian king, and now re-established himself in Syria. But Ptolemy Physcon, of Egypt, raised up a new pretender, Zabinas, who defeated Demetrius at Damascus. Attempting to enter Tyre, the Syrian king was captured and put to death.

Seleucus V, his eldest son, assumed the crown without the permission of his mother, who thereupon caused him to be executed, and associated with herself her second son, Antiochus VIII (Grypus). Zabinas, the pretender, reigned at the same time in part of Syria, until he was defeated by Antiochus, and put to death by poison, 122 BCE. The same year Cleopatra was detected in a plot against the life of her son, and was herself executed.

Exhausted by long wars, and greatly reduced both in power and extent, Syria now enjoyed eight years of peace. Judaea and the provinces east of the Euphrates were wholly independent. The few Syrians who possessed wealth were enfeebled by luxury, while the mass of the people were crushed by want. In 114 BCE, Antiochus Cyzicenus, a half-brother of the king, revolted against him, and involved the country in another bloody war of three years. The territory was then divided between them; but war broke out afresh in 105 BCE, and continued nine years, resulting in no gain to either party, but great loss and misery to the nation. Tyre, Sidon, Seleucia and the whole province of Cilicia became independent. The Arabs on one side, and the Egyptians on the other, ravaged the country at pleasure. At length the reign of Antiochus VIII was ended with his life, by Hercleon, an officer of his court, 96 BCE.

The murderer did not receive the reward of his crime, for Seleucus VI (Epiphanes), the eldest son of Grypus, gained possession of the kingdom. In two years he conquered Cyzicenus, who committed suicide to avoid capture; but the claims of the rival house were still maintained by Antiochus X (Eusebes), his eldest son. Seleucus was now driven into Cilicia. Here he came to a miserable end, for he was burnt alive by the people of a town from which he had demanded a subsidy. Philip, the brother of Seleucus, and second son of Antiochus Grypus, became king, and with the aid of his younger brothers continued the war against Eusebes. This prince was defeated and driven to take refuge in Parthia. But no peace came to the country, for Philip and his brothers, Antiochus XI, Demetrius, and Antiochus XII, made war with each other, until the unhappy Syrians called upon Tigranes, King of Armenia, to end their miseries.

Tigranes governed, wisely and well, fourteen years (83–69 BCE); but having at length incurred the vengeance of the Romans, by rendering aid to his father-in-law, Mithridates of Pontus, he was forced to give up all except his hereditary kingdom. Four years longer (69–65 BCE), Syria continued its separate existence, under Antiochus XIII (Asiaticus), the son of Eusebes. At the end of that time the kingdom was subdued by Pompey the Great, and became a Roman province.

EGYPT UNDER THE PTOLEMIES 323–30 BCE

The Macedonian Kingdom in Egypt presented a marked and brilliant contrast to the native empires and the Persian satrapy. By removing the capital to Alexandria, the conqueror had provided for free intercourse with foreign countries, and the old exclusiveness of the Egyptians was for ever broken down.

While Palestine was attached to this kingdom, especial favour was shown to the Jews; and in the Greek conquerors, the native Egyptians, and the Jewish merchants, the three families of Shem, Ham and Japhet were reunited as they had never been since the dispersion at Babel. The Egyptians, who had abhorred the Persian dominion, hailed the Macedonians as deliverers; the common people engaged with zeal in the new industries that promised wealth as the reward of enterprise, and the learned class found their delight in the intellectual society, as well as the rare treasures of literature and art, that filled the court of the Ptolemies.

Ptolemy I (Soter) received the Egyptian province immediately upon the death of Alexander, and proceeded to organize it with great energy and wisdom. Desiring to make Egypt a maritime power, he sought at once to conquer Palestine, Phœnicia and Cyprus, whose forests were as needful to him for ship-building as their sea-faring people for sailors. The two countries on the mainland were occupied by Ptolemy in 320 BCE and remained six years in his possession. They were lost in the war with Antigonus, and only fully regained after the battle of Ipsus, 301 BCE. Cyprus was the scene of many conflicts, of which the great naval battle off Salamis, 306 BCE, was the most severe and decisive. It was then lost to Egypt, but in 294 or 293 BCE it was regained, and continued her most valuable foreign possession as long as the kingdom existed. Cyrene and all the Libyan tribes between it and Egypt were also annexed by Ptolemy.

Few changes were made in the internal government of Egypt. The country, as before, was divided into nomes, each having its own ruler, who was usually a native Egyptian. The old laws and worship prevailed. The Ptolemies rebuilt the temples, paid especial honours to the Apis, and made the most of all points of resemblance between the Greek and Egyptian religions. A magnificent temple to Serapis was erected at Alexandria. The priests retained their privileges and honours, being exempt from all taxation. The army was chiefly, and its officers wholly, Greek or Macedonian, and all civil dignities of any importance were also filled by the conquering people. The Greek inhabitants of the cities alone possessed entire freedom in the management of their affairs.

Ptolemy followed the liberal policy of Alexander toward men of genius and learning. He collected a vast and precious library, which he placed in a building connected with the palace; and he founded the "Museum," which drew students and professors from all parts of the world. No spot ever witnessed more literary and intellectual activity than Alexandria, the University of the East. There Euclid first unfolded the "Elements of Geometry"; Eratosthenes discoursed of Geography; Hipparchus, of Astronomy; Aristophanes and Aristarchus, of Criticism; Manetho, of History; while Apelles and Antiphilus added their paintings, and Philetas, Callimachus and Apollonius their poems, for the delight of a court whose monarch was himself an author, and in which talent constituted rank. Alexandria during this reign was adorned with many costly and magnificent works. The royal palace; the Museum; the great light-house on the island of Pharos, which has given its name to many similar constructions in modern times; the mole or causeway which connected this island with the mainland; the Hippodrome, and the Mausoleum, containing the tomb of Alexander, were among the chief. Ptolemy Soter was distinguished by his truth and magnanimity from most of the princes and generals of his age. His unlimited power never led him to cruelty or self-indulgence. He died at the age of eighty-four, 283 BCE.

Ptolemy II (Philadelphus), through the influence of his mother, had been raised to the throne two years before his father's death, instead of his elder brother, Ceraunus. He had been carefully educated by several of the learned men whom the patronage of his father had drawn to the court; and he continued, on a still more liberal scale, that encouragement of science and literature which had already made Alexandria a successful rival of Athens. He so greatly increased the Alexandrian Library that he is often mentioned as its founder. Agents were appointed to search Europe and Asia for every literary work of value, and to secure it at any cost. An embassy was sent to the high priest at Jerusalem to bring a copy of the Holy Scriptures, together with a company of learned men who could translate them into Greek. The translators were entertained by the king with the greatest honour. The first five books were completed in the reign of Philadelphus, the rest were translated by order of the later Ptolemies and the entire version – still an invaluable treasure to Biblical scholars – is known as the Septuagint, either from the seventy translators, or because it was authorized by the Sanhedrim of Alexandria, which consisted of the same number.

Ptolemy II was engaged in various wars; first for the furtherance of the Achaean League, and the protection of the Greeks against Macedonian aggressions; afterward against his half-brother, Magas, King of Cyrene, and the kings of Syria, with whom Magas was allied. He gained possession of the whole coast of Asia Minor, with many of the Cyclades. By the wisdom of his internal policy, Egypt was meanwhile raised to her highest pitch of wealth and prosperity. He re-opened the canal made by Rameses the Great and built the port of Arsinoë, on the site of the modern Suez. To avoid the dangers of Red Sea navigation, he founded two cities, named Berenice, farther to the southward, and connected one of them by a highway with Coptos on the Nile. Egypt thus reaped the full commercial advantage of her position midway between the East and the West. For centuries the rich productions of India, Arabia and Ethiopia were conveyed along these various highways to Alexandria, whence they were distributed to Syria, Greece and Rome. The revenues of Egypt were equal to those which Darius had derived from the vast empire of Persia.

The personal character of Philadelphus was less admirable than that of his father. He killed two of his brothers, banished a most faithful counsellor, and by marrying his own sister, Arsinoë, introduced a custom which caused untold misery and mischief in the kingdom. He died 247 BCE, having reigned thirty-eight years, or thirty-six from the death of his father.

Ptolemy III (Euergetes) was the most enterprising monarch of his race, and pushed the boundaries of his kingdom to their greatest extent. He gained the Cyrenaica by marriage with the daughter of Magas, and annexed portions of Ethiopia and Arabia. In his war against Syria to avenge his sister, he even passed the Euphrates and conquered all the country to the borders of Bactria; but he lost all this by his sudden recall to Egypt. His conquests on the sea-board, which could be defended by his fleet, remained permanently in his possession. All the shores of the Mediterranean, from Cyrene to the Hellespont, with many important islands, and even a portion of Europe, including Lysimachia in Thrace, belonged to his dominion.

He continued the patronage of art and letters, and enriched the Alexandrian libraries with many rare manuscripts. The

Egyptians were still more gratified by the recovery of some ancient images of their gods, which had been carried away to Assyria by Sargon or Esarhaddon, and were brought back by Ptolemy from his eastern campaign. Euergetes died 222 BCE, after a prosperous reign of twenty-five years; and with him ended the glory of the Macedonian monarchy in Egypt.

Ptolemy IV was suspected of having murdered his father, and therefore took the surname Philopator to allay suspicion. He began his reign, however, by murdering his mother, his brother and his uncle, and marrying his sister Arsinoë. A few years later she, too, was put to death, at the instigation of a worthless favourite of the king. The control of affairs was left to Sosibius, a minister who was equally wicked and incompetent. Through his neglect, the army became weakened by lack of discipline, and the Syrians seized the opportunity to recover their lost possessions. They were defeated, however, at Raphia, and gained only their port of Seleucia. A revolt of the native Egyptians occupied many years of this reign.

Ptolemy V (Epiphanes) was only five years old at his father's death. The kings of Syria and Macedon plotted to divide his dominions between them, and the only resource of the incompetent ministers was to call the Romans to their aid. All the foreign dependencies, except Cyprus and the Cyrenaica, were lost; but by the good management of M. Lepidus, Egypt was saved to the little Ptolemy. Aristomenes, an Acarnanian, succeeded Lepidus as regent, and his energy and justice restored for a time the prosperity of the kingdom. At the age of fourteen, Epiphanes was declared of age, and the government was thenceforth in his name. Few events of his reign are known. He married Cleopatra of Syria, and soon after poisoned his late guardian, Aristomenes.

His plans for a war with Syria were prevented by his own assassination, 181 BCE.

Ptolemy VI (Philometor) became king at the age of seven, under the vigorous regency of his mother, Cleopatra. She died 173 BCE, and the power passed into the hands of two weak and corrupt ministers, who involved the kingdom in war, and almost in ruin, by their rash invasion of Syria. Antiochus IV defeated them at Pelusium, and advancing to Memphis, gained possession of the young king, whom he used as a tool for the reduction of the whole country. The Alexandrians crowned Ptolemy Physcon, a younger brother of the king, and successfully withstood the besieging army of Antiochus. The Romans now interposing, he was obliged to retreat.

The two brothers agreed to reign together, and prepared for war with Antiochus. He captured Cyprus, invaded Egypt a second time, and would doubtless have added the entire dominion of the Ptolemies to his own, if the Romans, who claimed the protectorate of Egypt, had not again interfered and commanded him to withdraw. The Syrian king reluctantly obeyed, and the brothers reigned four years in peace. They then quarrelled, and Philometor went to plead his cause before the Roman Senate. The Romans re-instated him in the possession of Egypt, giving to his brother Physcon Libya and the Cyrenaica. Dissatisfied with his portion, Physcon went to Rome and obtained a further grant of Cyprus; but Philometor refused to give it up, and the brothers were preparing for war, when a revolt in Cyrene engaged the attention of its king. After nine years he renewed his claim, and obtained from Rome a small squadron to aid in the capture of the island. He was defeated and made prisoner by his brother; but his life was spared, and he was restored to his kingdom of

Cyrene. Philometor fell, 146 BCE, in a battle near Antioch, with Alexander Balas, whom he had himself encouraged to assume the crown of Syria.

Ptolemy VII (Eupator) had reigned but a few days when he was murdered by his uncle, Ptolemy Physcon, who, aided by the Romans, united in himself the two kingdoms, Egypt and Cyrene. This monster created such terror by his inhuman cruelties, and such disgust by his excesses, that his capital became half depopulated, and the citizens who remained were almost constantly in revolt. At last he was forced to take refuge in Cyprus, the crown remaining to his sister, Cleopatra. To wound the queen most deeply, he murdered her son, and sent her the head and hands of the victim. The Alexandrians were so enraged by this atrocity, that they fought bravely for Cleopatra; but when she applied for aid to the King of Syria, they became alarmed and recalled Physcon, after an exile of three years. Warned by his punishment, Physcon now desisted from his cruelties, and devoted himself to literary pursuits, even gaining some reputation as an author.

Ptolemy VIII (Lathyrus) succeeded his father in Egypt, while his brother Alexander reigned in Cyprus, and Apion, another son of Physcon, received the Cyrenaica. Cleopatra, the queen mother, had the real power. After ten years, Lathyrus offended his mother by pursuing a policy of his own, and was compelled to change places with Alexander, who reigned eighteen years in Egypt, with the title of Ptolemy IX. Cleopatra was then put to death, Alexander expelled, and Ptolemy Lathyrus recalled. He reigned eight years as sole monarch, defeated Alexander, who attempted to regain Cyprus, and punished a revolt in Thebes by a siege of three years, ending with the destruction of the city, 89–86 BCE.

Berenice, the only legitimate child of Lathyrus, reigned six months alone, and was then married and associated upon the throne with her cousin, Ptolemy X, a son of Alexander, whose claims were supported by the Romans. Within three weeks he put his wife to death, and the Alexandrians, revolting, kiled him in the gymnasium, 80 BCE. Fifteen years of great confusion followed, during which the succession was disputed by at least five claimants, and Cyprus became a separate kingdom.

Ptolemy XI (Auletes, or the Flute-Player) then obtained the crown, and dated his reign from the death of his half-sister, Berenice. In 59 BCE, he was acknowledged by the Romans; but by that time his oppressive and profligate government had so disgusted the people, that they drove him from the kingdom. He took refuge four years in Rome, while his two daughters nominally governed Egypt, first jointly, and then the younger alone, after her sister's death. In 55 BCE Auletes returned, supported by a Roman army, put to death his daughter, who had opposed his restoration, and reigned under Roman protection three and a half years. He died, 51 BCE, leaving four children: the famous Cleopatra, aged seventeen; Ptolemy XII; another Ptolemy, and a daughter Arsinoë, still younger.

The princess Cleopatra received the crown under Roman patronage, in conjunction with the elder Ptolemy. The brother and sister quarrelled, and Cleopatra was driven into Syria. Here she met Julius Caesar, and by her talents and accomplishments gained great ascendency over his mind. By his aid Ptolemy was conquered and slain, and Cleopatra established in the kingdom. She removed her younger brother by poison, and had thenceforth no rival. With consummate ability, mixed with the unscrupulous cruelty of her race, she reigned seventeen years in great prosperity. Caesar was her protector while he lived, and Antony then became her slave, sacrificing all his interests, and his honour as a Roman and a general, to her slightest caprices. In the civil wars of Rome, Antony was at length defeated at Actium; Cleopatra committed suicide, and her kingdom became a Roman province in 30 BCE.

The kingdom of the Ptolemies had continued 293 years, from the death of Alexander to that of Cleopatra. During 101 years, under the first three kings, it was the most flourishing, well organized and prosperous of the Macedonian monarchies; the nearly two centuries which remained were among the most degraded periods in the history of the human race.

MACEDONIA AND GREECE

Upon the death of Alexander, the greater part of Greece revolted against Macedon, Athens, as of old, being the leader. Antipater, the Macedonian regent, was defeated near Thermopylae, and besieged in Lamia, in Thessaly. The confederates were afterward worsted at Cranon, and the good management of Antipater dissolved the league by treating with its members separately, and offering the most lenient terms to all except the leaders. Athens suffered the punishment it had often inflicted on others. Twelve thousand Athenian citizens were forcibly removed to Thrace, Illyria, Italy and Africa, only nine thousand of the wealthier sort being left, who willingly submitted to the Macedonian supremacy. Demosthenes, with the principal members of his party, were executed, and the last remains of Athenian independence destroyed.

Three years after the battle of Ipsus, Cassander died, 298 BCE, leaving the crown to his son, Philip IV. The young king reigned less than a year, and his mother, Thessalonica, then divided Macedonia between her two remaining sons, Antipater and Alexander. The former, being dissatisfied with his portion, murdered his mother and called in his father-in-law, Lysimachus, to aid him in gaining the whole. His brother, at the same time, asked aid of Demetrius, who reigned in Greece, and of Pyrrhus, King of Epirus. With their help he drove Antipater out of Macedonia; but he gained nothing by the victory, for Demetrius had undertaken the war solely with the view of placing himself upon the throne, which he accomplished by the murder of Alexander. Antipater II was put to death the same year by Lysimachus, 294 BCE.

The kingdom now included Thessaly, Attica and the greater part of the Peloponneses, Pyrrhus having received several countries on the western coast of Greece. Demetrius, however, sacrificed all his dominions to his unbounded ambition and conceit. He failed in an attack on Pyrrhus, and being invaded both from the east and west, was compelled to abandon Macedonia, 287 BCE. In a later expedition into Asia, he became the prisoner of Seleucus, and died in the third year of his captivity.

Pyrrhus remained king of the greater part of Macedonia nearly a year, but was then driven back to his hereditary kingdom by Lysimachus, who thus extended his own dominions from the Halys to Mount Pindus, 286 BCE. The capital of this consolidated kingdom was Lysimachia, in the Chersonese, and Macedonia for five years was merely a province. The nobles, becoming discontented, called in Seleucus, who defeated and killed Lysimachus, 281 BCE.

For a few weeks the aged Seleucus governed nearly all the dominions of Alexander, except Egypt. He was then assassinated by Ptolemy Ceraunus, who became king in his stead. The Egyptian prince was soon overwhelmed by a new peril in the invasion of the Gauls. This restless people had been pouring for nearly a century into northern Italy, where they had driven out the Etruscans from the plain of the Po, and given their own name to Gallia Cisalpina. Now turning eastward, they occupied the plain of the Danube, and pressed southward as far as Illyricum, whence they proceeded in three divisions, one falling upon the Thracians, another upon the Paeonians, and a third upon the Macedonians. The last army encountered Ptolemy Ceraunus, who was defeated and slain in battle. For two years they ravaged Macedonia, while Meleager, a brother of Ceraunus, and Antipater, a nephew of Cassander, successively occupied the throne, 279–277 BCE.

Brennus, a Gallic leader, with more than 200,000 men, marched through Thessaly, laying all waste with fire and sword. A furious battle took place at Thermopylae, and the Gauls, at last, only gained the rear of the Greek army by the same mountain path which had admitted the troops of Xerxes two hundred years before. Brennus pushed on to plunder Delphi, but an army of 4,000, well posted upon the heights of Parnassus, withstood him with success; and a violent wintry storm, which confused and benumbed the assailants, convinced devout Greeks that Apollo was once more defending his sanctuary. The Gallic leader was severely wounded, and unwilling to survive his disgrace, put an end to his own life. His army broke up into a multitude of marauding bands, without order or discipline, and the greater part perished from cold, hunger or battle. Their countrymen, however, established a kingdom in Thrace; and another band, invited into Asia Minor by Nicomedes, became possessed of a large tract of country, which received their name as Galatia.

During the disorders in Macedonia, Sosthenes, an officer of noble birth, had been placed at the head of affairs, instead of Antipater, who was deposed for his incapacity. After the Gauls had retired, Antipater regained the throne. But Antigonus Gonatas, who had maintained himself as an independent prince in central and southern Greece, ever since the captivity of his father, Demetrius, now appeared with an army composed mainly of Gallic mercenaries, defeated Antipater, and gained possession of Macedonia. Antiochus Soter made war against him, but was opposed with so much energy that he acknowledged Antigonus as king, and gave him his sister Phila in marriage. But Antigonus was never acceptable to either Greeks or Macedonians, and when Pyrrhus, the most popular prince of his age, returned from Italy, the whole Macedonian army was ready to desert to his side. Antigonus was defeated, and for a year or more was a fugitive, 273–271 BCE.

Pyrrhus was the greatest warrior and one of the best princes of his time – a time from which truth and fidelity seemed almost to have disappeared. He might have become the most powerful monarch in the world, if his perseverance had been equal to his talents and ambition. But instead of organizing the territory he possessed, he was ever thirsting for new conquests. In a war upon southern Greece he was repulsed from Sparta, and in attempting to seize Argos by night, he was killed by a tile thrown by a woman from a house-top.

Antigonus Gonatas now returned and reigned thirty-two years. He extended his power over most of the Peloponnese, and waged war five years against the Athenians, who were aided by

Sparta and Egypt. In the meantime, Antigonus was recalled by the incursion of Alexander, son of Pyrrhus, who was carrying all before him, and had been acknowledged King of Macedon. Demetrius, son of Antigonus, chased him out of Macedonia, and even out of Epirus; and though he was soon restored to his paternal dominion, he remained thenceforth at peace with his neighbours. Athens fell in 263 BCE. Nineteen years later, Antigonus gained possession of Corinth; but this was the last of his successes.

The Achaean League, which had been suppressed by the immediate successors of Alexander, had soon revived, and extended itself beyond the limits of Achaia, receiving cities from all the Peloponnesus. In 243 BCE, Aratus, its head, by a sudden and well-concerted movement captured Corinth, which immediately joined the League. Several important cities followed the example; and Antigonus, who had grown old and cautious, was unable to oppose them, except by stirring up Aetolia to attack the Achaeans. He died 239 BCE, having lived eighty and reigned thirty-seven years.

Demetrius II allied himself with Epirus, and broke friendship with the Aetolians, who were enemies of that kingdom. The consequence was, that the Aetolians made a junction with the Achaean League to oppose him. He was able to defeat them in Thessaly and Bœotia, but south of the isthmus the ascendency of Macedon was at an end. The Romans now for the first time interfered in Grecian affairs, by requiring the Aetolian confederacy to abstain from aggressions upon Acarnania. Corcyra, Apollonia and Epidamnus fell into their hands, 228 BCE, a year after the death of Demetrius II.

Philip V was but eight years old when he inherited his father's dominions, under the guardianship of his kinsman, Antigonus

Doson. During this regency great changes took place in Sparta, which led to a brief return of its old energy. The laws of Lycurgus had continued in force more than five centuries, but the time of their fitness and usefulness had passed away. The rigid separation which they made between the different classes, now limited the number of true Spartans to 700, while the property tests were so severe, that only 100 enjoyed the full rights of citizens. The wealth of the community was concentrated in the hands of a few, who violated the old law by living in great luxury. In this condition, Sparta was unable even to defend itself against Illyrian pirates or Aetolian marauders, still less to exert any influence, as of old, in the general affairs of Greece.

The reforms proposed 230 BCE, by Agis IV, and carried, four years later, by Cleomenes, added 3,800 to the number of citizens, and re-divided the lands of the state between these and 15,000 selected Laconians. Debts were abolished, and the old simple and frugal customs of Lycurgus restored. Sparta was now able to defeat the forces of the Achaean League, and to draw from it, into its own alliance, most of the Peloponnesian towns out of Achaia. But Aratus, the head of the League, violated all its principles by calling in Antigonus, the Macedonian regent, and putting him in possession of Acro-Corinthus. In the battle of Sellasia, 221 BCE, Cleomenes was defeated, and forced to take refuge at the court of Ptolemy Philopator. The League which had been created to defend the liberties of Greece, had betrayed them; and there was no longer any hope either of restoring the glories of Sparta, or of checking the overwhelming power of Macedon and Rome.

Antigonus died in 220 BCE, and Philip, now seventeen years of age, assumed the government. The great advantages gained during the regency were soon lost by his rashness. He hastily allied himself with Hannibal against Rome, and then with Antiochus of Syria against Egypt. His first war, however, was against Aetolia, which had sprung to arms immediately upon his accession, hoping at once to overbalance its rival, Achaia, and to increase its own territories at the expense of Macedon. As early as the time of Alexander the Great, the Aetolian tribes had formed themselves into a federal republic, which occupied a similar position in central Greece to that of the Achaean League in the Peloponnesus. By the subjection or annexation of several states, it was now extended from the Ionian to the Aegean Sea. Philip overran Aetolia with great energy, captured its seat of government, and by his brilliant successes showed a military talent worthy of the early days of Macedonian conquest. But the news of a great victory gained by Hannibal at Lake Thrasymene, recalled his attention to the object of his chief ambition, a war with Rome.

The first movement in the new war was the siege of Apollonia, a Roman colony in Illyricum. Philip hoped to drive the Romans from the western coast of Greece, and thus prepare the way for an invasion of Italy. His camp was surprised at night by Valerius, and he was forced to burn his ships and retreat in all haste. The Aetolians and all their allies – Sparta, Elis, and the kings of Illyricum and Pergamus – took sides with Rome, and carried the war into Macedonia, forcing Philip to ask the aid of Carthage. The Romans captured Zacynthus, Nesos and Œniadae, Anticyra in Locris, and the island of Aegina, and presented all to the Aetolians.

At this crisis, Philopœmen, the greatest Greek of his time, became commander of the Achaean cavalry, and, two years later, the head of the League. He improved the drill and tactics of the army, and infused new spirit into the whole nation. His invasion of Elis, in concert with Philip, was unsuccessful, and the king was defeated by Sulpicius Galba; but, in 207 BCE, the great victory of Mantinea placed the Macedonians and Achaeans on a more equal footing with the Romans. Peace was made on terms honourable to all parties.

Philip, spoiled by ambition, had become unscrupulous and reckless. Instead of securing what he already possessed, he continually grasped after new conquests; and disregarding the storm that was sure to burst upon him sooner or later from the west, he now turned to the east and south. He made a treaty with Antiochus the Great for a partition of the Egyptian dependencies, by which he was to receive Thrace and the western part of Asia Minor. This led at once to war with Attalus of Pergamus, an ally of Rome, as well as with Rhodes, which took the part of Egypt. His fleet was signally defeated off Chios, 201 BCE; and though he afterward gained a victory at Lade, his losses were not retrieved. He captured, however, the important islands of Samos, Thasos, and Chios, with the province of Caria, and several places in Ionia.

The great disaster of the war was the rupture of the treaty with Rome. That power interfered on behalf of its allies, Egypt, Rhodes and Pergamus; and when Philip rejected all reasonable demands, Rome declared the peace at an end. In the second war with Rome, Greece was at first divided into three parties, some states remaining neutral, some siding with Rome, and some with Macedon. But when the consul, Flaminius, proclaimed liberty to all the Greeks, and declared himself their champion against the long detested power of Macedon, nearly every state went over to the Roman side. On the land, Macedonia was attacked by Sulpicius Galba, aided by the Illyrians and Dardanians; while by sea, a Roman fleet, increased by Rhodian and Pergamene vessels, threatened the coast. Several important towns in Euboea were taken, but the great decisive battle was fought (197 BCE) at Cynocephalae, where Philip was defeated and his power utterly prostrated. He was compelled to abandon all the Greek cities which he held, either in Europe or Asia, to surrender his entire navy, and to pay a war indemnity of one thousand talents.

In settling the affairs of Greece, the Romans subdivided the states into still smaller sections than of old, and guaranteed perfect independence to each. The two leagues of Achaia and Aetolia were, however, left to balance each other. The states were generally satisfied with the arrangement, but the Aetolians stirred up a new war in the very year of Flamininus's departure, and called in Antiochus from Asia to their aid. He was defeated at Thermopylae by the Romans, 191 BCE, and the great battle of Magnesia, in the following year, ended all hope of resistance to the power of Rome. The Achaean League, sustained by the wise and able management of Philopœmen, gained in power by the weakening of its rival, and now included the whole Peloponnesus, with Megaris and some other territories beyond the peninsula.

Philip had aided the Romans in the recent war, and had been permitted to extend his dominions over part of Thrace, and southward into Thessaly. But when peace was secured, he was required to give up all except his hereditary kingdom. Demetrius, the second son of Philip, had long been a hostage at Rome, and acted now as his father's ambassador. The Roman Senate conceded many points, for the sake of the warm friendship which it professed for this young prince; but its favour only aroused the suspicions of his father and the jealousy of his elder brother,

Perseus. The latter forged letters to convince his father of the treason of Demetrius, and the innocent youth was put to death by order of the king. But the grief and remorse of Philip exceeded all bounds, when he learned the deception that had been practiced. He believed that he was haunted by the spirit of Demetrius, and it was agony of mind, rather than bodily illness, that soon occasioned his death.

An ancient historian remarked that there were few monarchs of whom more good or more evil could justly be said, than of Philip V. If the promise of his youth had been fulfilled, and the opportunities of his reign improved, he would have done great things for Macedonia and Greece. But his talents became obscured by drunkenness and profligacy, his natural generosity was spoiled by the habit of supreme command, and he became in later years a gloomy, unscrupulous, and suspicious tyrant.

Philip had designed to punish the crime of Perseus by leaving the throne to a distant relative, Antigonus; but the sudden death of the father, while Antigonus was absent from court, enabled the son to make himself king without opposition. He pursued with much diligence the policy of Philip, in preparing Macedonia for a second struggle with Rome. The revenues were increased by a careful working of the mines; the population, wasted by so many wars, was recruited by colonies of Thracians and others; and close alliances were made with the kings of Asia, and with the hardy barbarians of the north, Gauls, Illyrians and Germans, whose aid might be invaluable when the decisive moment should arrive. But Perseus failed to unite the states of Greece, in which a large party already preferred his supremacy to that of Rome; and instead of using his treasures to satisfy and confirm his allies, he hoarded them penuriously, only to enrich his enemies at the end of the war.

In the spring of 171 BCE, the Romans landed in Epirus, and spent some months in winning the Greek states to their side by money and influence. In the autumn they met Perseus in Thessaly, with nearly equal forces, and were defeated. The Macedonian made no use, however, of his victory, and nothing of importance was done for two years. In 168 BCE, L. Aemilius Paulus assumed the command, and forced Perseus to a battle near Pydna. Here the fate of Macedon was finally decided. Perseus was defeated and fled to Samothrace, where he was soon captured with all his treasures. He was taken to Rome, and compelled to walk in chains in the splendid triumph of Aemilius. After several years, the last of the Macedonian kings died in imprisonment at Alba.

Macedonia was not immediately made a Roman province, but was divided into four distinct states, which were forbidden all intercourse with each other. The people were consoled by a great reduction in the taxes, the Romans demanding only half the amount which they had been accustomed to pay their native kings.

In Greece, all confederacies, except the Achaean League, were dissolved. Achaia had been the constant friend of Rome during the war; but to insure its submission, one thousand of the principal citizens were accused of having secretly aided Perseus, and were carried to Italy for trial. They were imprisoned seventeen years without a hearing; and then, when all but three hundred had died, these were sent back, in the certainty that their resentment against Rome would lead them to some rash act of hostility.

All happened as the Romans had foreseen. The three of the exiles who were most embittered by this unprovoked outrage came into power, and their enmity gave to their foes what they most desired, a pretext for an armed invasion of the territories of the League. In 146 BCE, war was declared. One of the Achaean leaders was disastrously defeated and slain near Thermopylae; another, with the remnant of the army, made a last stand at Corinth, but he was defeated and the city was taken, plundered and destroyed. Within a few years Greece was placed under proconsular government, like other provinces of Rome. It remained nearly sixteen centuries a part of that great empire, which, though driven from Italy, maintained its existence in the East, until it was overthrown by the Turks, 1453 CE.

OTHER SUCCESSOR KINGDOMS

Thrace

The several tribes of the Thracian kingdom of Lysimachus wasted much of their time fighting against each other, and thus they were reduced either to subjects or humble allies of nations to the southward. At the same time, their position on the Danube exposed them to the incursions of the northern barbarians; and the history of Thrace under the Romans is only a record of wars and devastations.

Pergamus

Pergamus, on the Caicus in Mysia, possessed a strong fortress, which was used by Lysimachus as a place of safe keeping for his treasures, under the charge of Philetaerus, of Tium, an officer in whom he reposed the greatest confidence. This person, provoked by ill-treatment from the Thracian queen, made himself independent, and by means of the ample treasures of Lysimachus, maintained his principality undisturbed for twenty years, 283–263 BCE.

His nephew, Eumenes, who succeeded him, increased his territories by a victory over Antiochus I, near Sardis. After reigning twenty-two years (263–241 BCE), he was succeeded by his cousin, Attalus I, who gained a great victory over the Gauls, and, first of his family, took the title of king. Ten years later, he defeated Antiochus Hierax and included in his own dominions all the countries west of the Halys and north of the Taurus. In wars with the kings of Syria, he lost these conquests, and was limited for seven years to his own principality of Pergamus; but by the aid of Gallic mercenaries and his own good management, he won back most of the territories.

Eumenes I, his eldest son and successor, aided the Roman operations against the kings of Syria and Macedonia, with so much energy and talent, that he was rewarded with an increase of territory on both sides of the Hellespont, and his kingdom was for a time one of the greatest in Asia. He continued his father's liberal policy in the encouragement of art and literature, founded the great Library of Pergamus, which was second only to that of Alexandria, and beautified his capital with many magnificent buildings. At his death his crown was assumed by his brother, Attalus II (Philadelphus), as the son of Eumenes was still a child. More than half the twenty-one years of Philadelphus's reign were occupied by wars. When Philadelphus died in 138 BCE, he left the kingdom to his nephew, Attalus III (Philometor), the son of Eumenes II This king crowded into the short period of five years more crimes and atrocities than can be found in all the other reigns of his dynasty put together. He murdered all the old friends of his father and uncle, with their families; all who still held any office of trust in the kingdom; and, finally, his own nearest relatives, including his mother. He died of a fever, leaving his kingdom a legacy to the Roman people. Aristonicus, a half-brother of Attalus III, successfully resisted the Roman claims for three years, but was eventually made prisoner, and Pergamus was added to the territories of Rome, 130 BCE.

Bithynia

Bithynia was a tributary province of Persia that regained its independence upon the overthrow of that empire, and resisted all the efforts of Alexander's generals to reduce it. Among its kings were Nicomedes I, who founded Nicomedia on the Propontis; Zeilas, who gained his crown by the aid of the Gauls; and Prusias, his son, who extended his kingdom by constant wars.

The contemptibly wicked Prusias II sent his son Nicomedes to Rome, with secret orders for his assassination. But the plot failed; and Nicomedes II, whose popularity had excited his father's jealousy, now returned with the support of the Romans and the Pergamene king, and gained possession of the throne. He reigned fifty-eight years with the title Epiphanes (Illustrious). His son, Nicomedes III, in alliance with the Romans, made war seven years with Mithridates, King of Pontus, their most able and resolute opponent. He was twice expelled from his dominions; but after the close of the first Mithridatic War, he reigned peacefully ten years, and, having no children, left his kingdom to the Romans, 74 BCE.

Pontus

In Cappadocia in 363 BCE, a son of the satrap Mithridates revolted, and made himself king of that portion of Cappadocia which lay next the sea, and was thence called Pontus by the Greeks, ruling as Mithridates I. The annals of the next two reigns are of no great importance. Mithridates III (245–190 BCE) enlarged and strengthened his dominion by alliances with the Asiatic monarchs, as well as by wars. His son Pharnaces conquered Sinope from the Greeks, and made it his capital. The next king, Mithridates IV (160–120 BCE), aided Rome against Carthage and Pergamus, and was rewarded by the addition of the Greater Phrygia to his dominions.

Mithridates V, the Great, came to the throne at the age of eleven years, his father having been murdered by some officers of the court. The young prince, distrusting his guardians, began in his earliest years to accustom himself to antidotes against poison, and to spend much of his time in hunting, which enabled him to take refuge in the most rough and inaccessible portions of his kingdom. He had, however, received a Greek education at Sinope; and when, at the age of twenty, he assumed the government, he possessed not only a soul and body inured to every sort of peril and hardship, but a mind furnished with all the knowledge needful to a king. He spoke twenty-five languages, and could transact business with every tribe of his dominions, in its own peculiar dialect.

He determined to extend his kingdom to the eastward and northward, thus increasing its power and wealth, so as to make it more nearly a match for an expansionist Rome. In seven years he added to his dominions half the shores of the Black Sea, including the Cimmerian peninsula (Crimea) – and extending westward to the Dniester. He made alliances with the wild and powerful tribes upon the Danube, and with the kings of Armenia, Cappadocia, and Bithynia. From the last two countries he afterward drove out their hereditary king, placing his own son on the throne of Cappadocia, and Socrates, a younger brother of Nicomedes III, on that of Bithynia.

The Roman Senate now interfered, and with their favor Nicomedes invaded Pontus. Mithridates marched into Cappadocia and drove out its newly reinstated king; then into Bithynia, where he routed the army of Nicomedes and defeated the Romans. He speedily made himself master of all Asia Minor, except a few towns in the extreme south and west; and from his headquarters at Pergamus, gave orders for a general massacre of all Romans and Italians in Asia. Eighty thousand persons fell in consequence of this atrocious act, but from that moment the tide turned against Mithridates. Two large armies which he sent into Greece, were defeated by Sulla at Chaeronea. A great battle in Bithynia was lost by the Pontic generals. Pontus itself was invaded, and its king became a fugitive.

Peace was at length made, on terms most humiliating to Mithridates. He surrendered all his conquests, and a fleet of seventy vessels; agreed to pay 2,000 talents; and recognized the kings of Cappadocia and Bithynia, whom he had formerly expelled. The reverses of Mithridates naturally led the subject nations on the Euxine to throw off his yoke. He was preparing to march against them, when a second Roman war was kindled by a sudden and unprovoked aggression of Murena, the general of the Republic in the East. The Romans were defeated on the Halys, and peace was restored, 82 BCE.

Over the next seven years, Mithridates subdued all his revolted subjects, and recruited his forces with the utmost energy. Both the Pontic king and the Romans would willingly have remained some years longer at peace, but, in 74 BCE, the legacy of Bithynia to the latter power, by Nicomedes III, brought them into unavoidable collision. Mithridates first seized the country, and gained a double victory over Cotta, by sea and land. But he failed in the sieges of Chalcedon and Cyzicus, his fleet was first defeated off Tenedos, and then wrecked by a storm. In the third year Mithridates was driven out of his own dominions, and those of his son-in-law, Tigranes. For three years the war was carried on in Armenia, where the two kings were twice defeated by Lucullus.

In 68 BCE, Mithridates returned to his kingdom, and defeated the Romans twice within a few months. But in 66 BCE, Pompey assumed the command, and Mithridates, after the loss of nearly his whole army, abandoned Pontus, and retired into the regions north of the Euxine. With a spirit untamed either by years or misfortunes, he plotted to gather the wild tribes along the Danube, and march upon Italy from the north. But his officers did not share his enthusiasm. A conspiracy against him was headed by his own son; and the old king, deserted by all whom he would have trusted, attempted to end his life by poison. His constitution had been for many years so guarded by antidotes, that the drugs had no effect, and he was finally dispatched by one of his Gallic soldiers. Pontus became a Roman province, only a small portion of its territory continuing, a century or more, under princes of the ancient dynasty.

Cappadocia

The southern part of Cappadocia was conquered by Perdiccas after the death of Alexander, but within six years became independent, and continued under native kings until it was absorbed into the Roman dominions, 17 CE. The history of these monarchs is of little importance, except so far as it is included in that of the neighbouring nations. The fifth king, Ariarathes IV, made, in his later years, a close and friendly alliance with the Romans, which continued unbroken under his successors. The last king, Archelaus (36 BCE–17 CE), was summoned by Tiberius to Rome, where he died, and his kingdom became a Roman province.

Armenia

Armenia was included in the kingdom of the Seleucidae, from the battle of Ipsus to that of Magnesia, 190 BCE. Two generals of Antiochus III then revolted against him, and set up the kingdoms of Armenia Major on the east, and Armenia Minor on the west of the Euphrates. The greatest king of Armenia Major was Tigranes I. (96–55 BCE), who not only gained important victories from the Parthian monarch, but conquered all Syria, and held it fourteen years. He incurred the vengeance of Rome in various ways, but chiefly by sustaining his father-in-law, Mithridates, in his wars against the Republic. He suffered several calamitous defeats, with the loss of his capital, Tigranocerta.

In 67 BCE, the disaffection of the Roman troops gave the two kings the opportunity to recover much of what they had lost. The appearance of the great Pompey upon the scene again turned the tide. The young Tigranes rebelled against his father, with the aid of Parthia and Rome. The king surrendered all his conquests, retaining only his hereditary kingdom of the

Greater Armenia. His son, Artavasdes I (55–34 BCE), aided the expedition of Crassus against the Parthians; but having afterward offended Antony, he was taken prisoner and put to death by order of Cleopatra. Artaxias, his son, ordered a massacre of all the Romans in Armenia. In 19 BCE, he was himself murdered by his own relations. The remaining kings were sovereigns only in name, being set up or displaced alternately by the Romans and Parthians, until Armenia was absorbed by the former, 114 CE. Armenia Minor was usually a dependency of some neighbouring kingdom, from the time of Mithridates to that of Vespasian (69–79 CE), when it, too, became a Roman province.

Bactria

Bactria was a part of the Syrian empire from 305 to 255 BCE Diodotus, the satrap, then made himself independent, and established a new Greek kingdom, the most easterly of all the scattered fragments of Alexander's conquests. Euthydemus, the third king, was a native of Magnesia, and a usurper (222–200 BCE). His son Demetrius made many victorious campaigns, extending over Afghanistan and into India (200–180 BCE). He lost a part of his native dominions to the north to a rebel, Eucratides, who after his death, reigned over the whole country. He, too, carried on Indian wars with great energy and success. Under his son, Heliocles (160–150 BCE), the Bactrian kingdom rapidly declined, being invaded by the Parthian kings on the west, and the Tartar tribes from the north.

The Parthian Empire of the Arsacidae

The Parthians established their independence about 250 BCE, under the lead of the Scythian Arsaces. This warlike people gave the Romans a more troublesome resistance than they encountered in any other portion of Alexander's former empire; and the dominion of the Arsacidae lasted nearly 500 years, until it was overthrown by the new Persian kingdom, 226 CE. The greatness of the Parthian empire dates from Mithridates, who is also called Arsaces VI, 174–136 BCE. The neighbouring kingdom of Bactria, with its Greek monarchs and its higher civilization, had hitherto maintained the ascendency; but while these kings were absorbed in their Indian conquests, Mithridates seized upon several of their provinces, and eventually absorbed their whole dominion.

The Parthian empire, at its greatest extent, comprised all the countries between the Euphrates and the Indus; from the Araxes and the Caspian on the north, to the Persian Gulf and Indian Ocean on the south. Its numerous parts were not consolidated into one government, as were the satrapies of Persia or the provinces of Rome; but each nation, with its own laws and usages, retained its native king, who was tributary to the lord-paramount in the Arsacid family. Hence the Parthian coins, like the Assyrian monuments, commonly bear the title "King of Kings." The wars of Mithridates made the Euphrates the boundary-line between the Parthian and Roman empires. The wealth and power of the Oriental monarchy provoked at once the avarice and the jealousy of the western Republic, and a collision between the two great empires was inevitable.

ACHIEVEMENTS OF THE HELLENISTIC AGE

Alexander was a great conqueror and he won for himself a mighty empire. But that empire did not last, for his successors were unable to hold it together. Alexander, however, did more than create a passing empire; he did more than any other one man to spread the knowledge of Greek civilization over the world. Wherever he passed with his conquering army he founded cities, where he established colonies of Greeks: men who spoke the Greek tongue, who worshipped the Greek gods, who read and loved Greek literature, and who lived according to Greek ideals. Such cities were founded in Egypt, in Asia Minor, in Syria, in Babylonia, in Persia and even in the distant lands till then unknown, further to the mysterious East.

But Alexander did yet more to spread Greek civilization than by the founding of cities. All the great ports of the Eastern Mediterranean were in his hands, which meant that Greek merchants were established there, and that the whole commerce of that region was in the hand of Greeks.

The history of Greek civilization may be divided into two periods. The first lasted until the days of Alexander; it included the early experiments made by Greek states in the art of governing themselves, the repulse of the Barbarian, the great days of Athens, the disastrous Peloponnesian War.

Beginning with Alexander, Greek civilization stepped out into a new age. Greece was the teacher of the world, in science, in art, and in all that was meant by civilized living. This period lasted from the time of Alexander until Greece became part of the Roman Empire in 146 BCE, and is known as the *Hellenistic Age*. The centre of Greek civilization was now no longer in Athens, but in Alexandria, the city in Egypt founded by Alexander, and which from its situation was the natural link between the East and the West.

ALEXANDRIA

Alexandria had not been founded for very many years before it rivalled Carthage, that powerful commercial city founded by the Phoenicians, as the dominant power of the Mediterranean, and in the Eastern Mediterranean, known as the Levant, Alexandria held undisputed sway. From that time to the present day Alexandria has been the door through which the commerce of the East and the West has passed.

In the Hellenistic Age, Alexandria developed into a very beautiful city. Temples and all kinds of public buildings, great palaces and gardens, docks and warehouses were built. At the entrance to the harbour stood a great lighthouse, called the Pharos from the island on which it stood, and which was considered so great a marvel that it was numbered amongst the Seven Wonders of the Ancient World.

This period was in many ways like a more modern one. Greek civilization had stepped out into a new world. The conquering armies of Alexander, going out to the ends of the earth, had made communication possible between places that had hitherto hardly known of each other's existence. Science had made such remarkable strides that man's power over nature had been enormously increased, and the increase of scientific knowledge was affecting the old religious beliefs in the gods. Nothing seemed to be quite the same as it had hitherto been, and then, as at all such times, the minds of men were affected by the changes. Some became more conservative than before and wanted nothing changed, because to them the old was necessarily the best, and there was only evil in what was new. Others went to the other extreme and wanted everything changed, because to them the new must necessarily be better than the old. But quietly in between these two extremes were the thinkers, those who were keeping alive that Greek spirit which knew that the vision of the whole truth had not yet been given to any man, and that the way to progress was not by destroying the old, but by building upon it in order to go on from a firm foundation to a fuller knowledge of the truth. Not to Thales, nor to Socrates, nor to Aristotle, nor yet to the men of the twentieth century has the complete vision of the truth of all things been vouchsafed, but to those who follow the quest in the spirit of the Greeks of old is granted to add a little to the progress of human knowledge.

It was in the Museum at Alexandria that the thinkers worked. This Museum was founded by Ptolemy Soter, one of the rulers of Egypt after the break-up of Alexander's empire, and very much developed by his son, Ptolemy Philadelphus. This Museum, the Temple of the Muses, was what today would be called a university. It had lecture halls where mathematicians, astronomers, poets and philosophers taught; courts and porches where men walked and talked, houses where the men of learning lived. Above all, it had a Library, which contained several thousand books. This library was catalogued by Callimachus, the first librarian of whom there is any record, and there were a hundred and twenty books of his catalogue. Book, however, is a wrong word to use for the collection in the Alexandrian Library, for there were no *books* then, as we know them. Rolls took the place of books, and Callimachus soon found that the big rolls were very inconvenient. It is said that he complained that "a big book is a big nuisance", and that it was when he was librarian that the plan of dividing the large rolls into a number of smaller ones was thought of. These were easier to handle, but one work required a great many of the smaller rolls, and thirty-six were required for the *Iliad* and the *Odyssey*.

As the fame of the Library spread, students from all over the Greek world came to Alexandria, and there was a great demand for additional copies of the works in the Library. For more than three centuries, Alexandria was the great book-producing mart in the world. The Museum possessed a good collection of the best-known copies of the works of the classic writers, and Ptolemy Philadelphus very much enlarged this collection. He bought every copy of all existing Greek works he could find, and as he paid very high prices for them, there was a steady flow of books to Alexandria from all over the civilized world. It is said that he refused to send food to the Athenians at a time of famine unless they agreed to give him certain copies they still possessed of the works of Aeschylus, Sophocles and Euripides. He paid liberally for them, not only in the promised shipment of corn but also in silver.

As more and more copies of the classic writers were wanted, a regular publishing trade arose in Alexandria. Callimachus was not only the Librarian of the Library, but a publisher of the works of classic writers. Large numbers of copyists were employed whose business it was to make careful and accurate copies of the works required. This accounts for the fact that in certain works of ancient literature it is sometimes difficult to know what is the really original form of certain lines or passages, because in spite of their care, the copyists made mistakes, and unfortunately many original copies of the classics were lost in the great fire which destroyed the Library in the last century BCE. The Alexandrian school of copyists was a very famous one, and Alexandrian Editions of the classics were considered the very best to be had.

Not only were Greek works copied, but other literature was translated into Greek and then copied. It was in Alexandria that the oldest manuscript of the Old Testament we possess was transcribed. It was a translation of the whole of the Old Testament from Hebrew into Greek, made, according to tradition, by a group of seventy Jewish scholars, whence comes its name, the Septuagint. These scholars were encouraged to undertake this work by the King, who is said to have provided the means for their support whilst they were engaged on the translation, and who gave them a special quarter of the city in which to live.

SCIENCE IN THE HELLENISTIC AGE

Greek science had been born in Ionia, and during the Hellenic Period of Greek civilization, it had gone hand in hand with philosophy. The earliest days of pure science came in the Hellenistic Age, and its home was in Alexandria. Amongst the many names of men of this time who contributed something of value to science, there are two which must be remembered: those of Euclid and Archimedes.

Euclid lived in Alexandria. He was a mathematician and wrote a great work on geometry. No scientific work in the world has lived in quite the same way as has this book of Euclid, for since the time that the Elements of Euclid were written, it was used as a school text book without interruption until a very few years ago.

Archimedes was probably the greatest of the Greek scientific thinkers of the third century BCE. He did not live in Alexandria; he was a native of Syracuse in Sicily, but he was in close touch with all the scientific work that was being done there. He was a great scientific investigator, the inventor of many practical and ingenious devices and discovered the principle of moving heavy bodies by means of pulleys and levers. An extraordinarily large ship was made for the King of Syracuse, a ship of marvel to that age. It contained a gymnasium, gardens of most wonderful beauty and full of rich plants, a temple to Aphrodite, a drawing-room with its walls and doors of boxwood, having a bookcase in it, a bathroom with three brazen vessels for holding hot water, and a fish-pond. All the furnishings were of the most exquisite craftsmanship, and all the rooms had floors of mosaic, in which the whole story of the *Iliad* was depicted in a most marvellous manner. There were doors of ivory, beautiful couches, and it was full of pictures and statues, goblets and vases of every form and shape imaginable. But the ship was so large that no one could move it. Archimedes, however, we are told, launched it by himself with the aid of only a few people. For having prepared a helix (probably some mechanical contrivance with pulleys), he drew this vessel, enormous as it was, down to the sea. And it was said that Archimedes was the first person who ever invented this helix.

Archimedes believed it possible to move greater bodies even than the ship, and he is said to have boasted: "Give me a place to stand on, and I will move the earth."

This great inventor did other things which struck the imagination of the men amongst whom he lived, for of some of them they had never seen the like before. During the siege of Syracuse by the Romans, in 212 BCE, Archimedes invented marvellous war-engines: strange grappling hooks which, it was said, could seize an enemy's ship and overturn it in the sea, and he showed the Syracusans how to set up a water pump in their ships, so that should water get into the hold, it could be pumped out and the ship saved from sinking. He is also said to have made some arrangement of mirrors and burning glass by means of which the Roman ships were set on fire. But in spite of all these inventions, the Romans took the city, and Archimedes was killed. He was found by a Roman soldier, sitting in his house and paying no heed to any danger, but intent on drawing mathematical diagrams on the ground. Looking up and seeing the enemy, all he said was: "Stand away, fellow, from my diagram." The soldier, not knowing who he was, killed him.

CONCLUSION

The old Greece of history no longer existed. Greek civilization had spread over the Mediterranean world, but the free and independent city-state had disappeared and nothing lasting had taken its place. Alexander himself, and still more his successors, had failed to create an empire which gave to those who belonged to it any sense of citizenship in it. The Hellenistic world was a Greek civilization, but it failed to arouse in men of Greek birth that patriotism which the city-state had inspired.

The creation of a world state of which men were to be proud to call themselves citizens and for which they would gladly die, was to be the work of another great power, which even as the old Greece was passing, was growing strong in the West. Rome was steadily conquering the civilized world and extending its power over the Eastern Mediterranean. Greece became a Roman province in 146 BCE. The citizens of this great state, which was to include, not only Greece and the Levant, but the whole Mediterranean and lands far beyond its shores, were to be proud of the name of Roman. Yet Rome, destined to be the Mistress of the World, and in political power an empire, succeeding where Greece had failed, owed all that was most worthwhile in the things of the higher intellectual life of the mind to Greece. The Greek spirit was never to die.

ANCIENT KINGS & LEADERS

Ancient cultures often traded with and influenced
each other, while others grew independently.
This section provides the key leaders from a
number of regions, to offer comparative insights
into developments across the ancient world.

SUMERIAN KING LIST

This list is based on the *Sumerian King List* or *Chronicle of the One Monarchy*. The lists were often originally carved into clay tablets and several versions have been found, mainly in southern Mesopotamia. Some of these are incomplete and others contradict one another. Dates are based on archaeological evidence as far as possible but are thus approximate. There may also be differences in name spellings between different sources. Nevertheless, the lists remain an invaluable source of information.

As with many civilizations, lists of leaders often begin with mythological and legendary figures before they merge into the more solidly historical, hence why you will see some reigns of seemingly impossible length.

After the kingship descended from heaven, the kingship was in Eridug.

Alulim	28,800 years (8 *sars**)
Alalngar	36,000 years (10 *sars*)

Then Eridug fell and the kingship was taken to Bad-tibira.

En-men-lu-ana	43,200 years (12 *sars*)
En-mel-gal-ana	28,800 years (8 *sars*)
Dumuzid the Shepherd (or Tammuz)	36,000 years (10 *sars*)

Then Bad-tibira fell and the kingship was taken to Larag.
En-sipad-zid-ana   28,800 years (8 *sars*)

Then Larag fell and the kingship was taken to Zimbir.

En-men-dur-ana   21,000 years (5 *sars* and 5 *ners*)

Then Zimbir fell and the kingship was taken to Shuruppag.

Ubara-Tutu   18,600 years (5 *sars* and 1 *ner**)

Then the flood swept over.

*A *sar* is a numerical unit of 3,600; a *ner* is a numerical unit of 600.

FIRST DYNASTY OF KISH

After the flood had swept over, and the kingship had descended from heaven, the kingship was in Kish.

Jushur	1,200 years	Zuqaqip	900 years
Kullassina-bel	960 years	Atab (or A-ba)	600 years
Nangishlisma	1,200 years	Mashda (son of Atab)	840 years
En-tarah-ana	420 years	Arwium (son of	
Babum	300 years	Mashda)	720 years
Puannum	840 years	Etana the Shepherd	1,500 years
Kalibum	960 years	Balih (son of Etana)	400 years
Kalumum	840 years	En-me-nuna	660 years

Melem-Kish (son of
Enme-nuna)   900 years
Barsal-nuna (son of
Enme-nuna)   1,200 years
Zamug (son of
Barsal-nuna)   140 years
Tizqar (son of Zamug)
305 years
Ilku   900 years
Iltasadum   1,200 years

Enmebaragesi   900 years
(earliest proven ruler
based on archaeological
sources; Early Dynastic
Period, 2900–2350 BCE)
Aga of Kish (son of
Enmebaragesi)   625 years
(Early Dynastic Period,
2900–2350 BCE)

Then Kish was defeated and the kingship was taken to E-anna.

FIRST RULERS OF URUK

Mesh-ki-ang-gasher (son of Utu)   324 years (Late Uruk Period,
                                                              4000–3100 BCE)

Enmerkar (son of Mesh-ki-ang-gasher)   420 years (Late Uruk
                                                              Period, 4000–3100 BCE)

Lugal-banda the shepherd   1200 years (Late Uruk
                                                              Period, 4000–3100 BCE)

Dumuzid the fisherman   100 years (Jemdet Nasr Period,
                                                              3100–2900 BCE)

Gilgamesh   126 years (Early Dynastic Period,
                                                              2900–2350 BCE)

Ur-Nungal (son of Gilgamesh)   30 years
Udul-kalama (son of Ur-Nungal)   15 years
La-ba'shum   9 years
En-nun-tarah-ana   8 years

Mesh-he	36 years
Melem-ana	6 years
Lugal-kitun	36 years

Then Unug was defeated and the kingship was taken to Urim (Ur).

FIRST DYNASTY OF UR

Mesh-Ane-pada	80 years
Mesh-ki-ang-Nuna (son of Mesh-Ane-pada)	36 years
Elulu	25 years
Balulu	36 years

Then Urim was defeated and the kingship was taken to Awan.

DYNASTY OF AWAN

Three kings of Awan	356 years

Then Awan was defeated and the kingship was taken to Kish.

SECOND DYNASTY OF KISH

Susuda the fuller	201 years
Dadasig	81 years
Mamagal the boatman	360 years
Kalbum (son of Mamagal)	195 years

Tuge	360 years
Men-nuna (son of Tuge)	180 years
Enbi-Ishtar	290 years
Lugalngu	360 years

Then Kish was defeated and the kingship was taken to Hamazi.

DYNASTY OF HAMAZI

| Hadanish | 360 years |

Then Hamazi was defeated and the kingship was taken to Unug (Uruk).

SECOND DYNASTY OF URUK

En-shag-kush-ana	60 years (*c.* 25th century BCE)
Lugal-kinishe-dudu	120 years
Argandea	7 years

Then Unug was defeated and the kingship was taken to Urim (Ur).

SECOND DYNASTY OF UR

| Nanni | 120 years |
| Mesh-ki-ang-Nanna II (son of Nanni) | 48 years |

Then Urim was defeated and the kingship was taken to Adab.

DYNASTY OF ADAB

Lugal-Ane-mundu   90 years (c. 25th century BCE)

Then Adab was defeated and the kingship was taken to Mari.

DYNASTY OF MARI

Anbu	30 years	Zizi of Mari, the fuller	20 years
Anba (son of Anbu)	17 years	Limer the 'gudug'	
Bazi the		priest	30 years
leatherworker	30 years	Sharrum-iter	9 years

Then Mari was defeated and the kingship was taken to Kish.

THIRD DYNASTY OF KISH

Kug-Bau (Kubaba)   100 years (c. 25th century BCE)

Then Kish was defeated and the kingship was taken to Akshak.

DYNASTY OF AKSHAK

Unzi	30 years	Ishu-Il	24 years
Undalulu	6 years	Shu-Suen (son of	
Urur	6 years	Ishu-Il)	7 years
Puzur-Nirah	20 years		

Then Akshak was defeated and the kingship was taken to Kish.

FOURTH DYNASTY OF KISH

Puzur-Suen (son of Kug-bau)	25 years (*c.* 2350 BCE)
Ur-Zababa (son of Puzur-Suen)	400 years (*c.* 2300 BCE)
Zimudar	30 years
Usi-watar (son of Zimudar)	7 years
Eshtar-muti	11 years
Ishme-Shamash	11 years
Shu-ilishu	15 years
Nanniya the jeweller	7 years

Then Kish was defeated and the kingship was taken to Unug (Uruk).

THIRD DYNASTY OF URUK

Lugal-zage-si	25 years (*c.* 2296–2271 BCE)

Then Unug was defeated and the kingship was taken to Agade (Akkad).

DYNASTY OF AKKAD

Sargon of Akkad	56 years (*c.* 2270–2215 BCE)
Rimush of Akkad (son of Sargon)	9 years (*c.* 2214–2206 BCE)
Manishtushu (son of Sargon)	15 years (*c.* 2205–2191 BCE)

Naram-Sin of Akkad (son of
   Manishtushu)   56 years (c. 2190–2154 BCE)
Shar-kali-sharri (son of Naram-Sin) 24 years (c. 2153–2129 BCE)

Then who was king? Who was not the king?

Irgigi, Nanum, Imi and Ilulu   3 years (four rivals who fought
                                   to be king during a three-year
                                   period; c. 2128–2125 BCE)
Dudu of Akkad   21 years (c. 2125–2104 BCE)
Shu-Durul (son of Duu)   15 years (c. 2104–2083 BCE)

Then Agade was defeated and the kingship was taken to Unug (Uruk).

FOURTH DYNASTY OF URUK

Ur-ningin   7 years (c. 2091?–2061? BCE)
Ur-gigir (son of Ur-ningin)   6 years
Kuda   6 years
Puzur-ili   5 years
Ur-Utu (or Lugal-melem; son of Ur-gigir)   6 years

Unug was defeated and the kingship was taken to the army of Gutium.

GUTIAN RULE

Inkišuš   6 years (c. 2147–2050 BCE)
Sarlagab (or Zarlagab)   6 years

Shulme (or Yarlagash)	6 years
Elulmeš (or Silulumeš or Silulu)	6 years
Inimabakeš (or Duga)	5 years
Igešauš (or Ilu-An)	6 years
Yarlagab	3 years
Ibate of Gutium	3 years
Yarla (or Yarlangab)	3 years
Kurum	1 year
Apilkin	3 years
La-erabum	2 years
Irarum	2 years
Ibranum	1 year
Hablum	2 years
Puzur-Suen (son of Hablum)	7 years
Yarlaganda	7 years
Si'um (or Si-u)	7 years
Tirigan	40 days

Then the army of Gutium was defeated and the kingship taken to Unug (Uruk).

FIFTH DYNASTY OF URUK

Utu-hengal   427 years / 26 years / 7 years
(conflicting dates; c. 2055–2048 BCE)

THIRD DYNASTY OF UR

Ur-Namma (or Ur-Nammu)	18 years (*c.* 2047–2030 BCE)
Shulgi (son of Ur-Namma)	48 years (*c.* 2029–1982 BCE)
Amar-Suena (son of Shulgi)	9 years (*c.* 1981–1973 BCE)
Shu-Suen (son of Amar-Suena)	9 years (*c.* 1972–1964 BCE)
Ibbi-Suen (son of Shu-Suen)	24 years (*c.* 1963–1940 BCE)

*Then Urim was defeated. The very foundation of Sumer was torn out.
The kingship was taken to Isin.*

DYNASTY OF ISIN

Ishbi-Erra	33 years (*c.* 1953–1920 BCE)
Shu-Ilishu (son of Ishbi-Erra)	20 years
Iddin-Dagan (son of Shu-Ilishu)	20 years
Ishme-Dagan (son of Iddin-Dagan)	20 years
Lipit-Eshtar (son of Ishme-Dagan or Iddin Dagan)	11 years
Ur-Ninurta (son of Ishkur)	28 years
Bur-Suen (son of Ur-Ninurta)	21 years
Lipit-Enlil (son of Bur-Suen)	5 years
Erra-imitti	8 years
Enlil-bani	24 years
Zambiya	3 years
Iter-pisha	4 years
Ur-du-kuga	4 years
Suen-magir	11 years
Damiq-ilishu (son of Suen-magir)	23 years

ANCIENT EGYPTIAN PHARAOHS

There is dispute about the dates and position of pharaohs within dynasties due to several historical sources being incomplete or inconsistent. This list aims to provide an overview of the ancient Egyptian dynasties, but is not exhaustive and dates are approximate. There may also be differences in name spellings between different sources. Also please note that the throne name is given first, followed by the personal name – more commonly they are known by the latter.

ANCIENT EGYPTIAN DEITIES

Ancient Egyptian gods and goddesses were worshipped as deities. They were responsible for maat (divine order or stability), and different deities represented different natural forces, such as Ra the Sun God. After the Egyptian state was first founded in around 3100 BCE, pharaohs claimed to be divine representatives of these gods and were thought to be successors of the gods.

While there are many conflicting Egyptian myths, some of the significant gods and goddesses and their significant responsibilities are listed here.

Amun/Amen/Amen-Ra	Creation
Atem/Tem	Creation, the sun

Ra	The sun
Isis	The afterlife, fertility, magic
Osiris	Death and resurrection, agriculture
Hathor	The sky, the sun, motherhood
Horus	Kingship, the sky
Set	Storms, violence, deserts
Maat	Truth and justice, she personifies *maat*
Anubis	The dead, the underworld

PREDYNASTIC AND EARLY DYNASTIC PERIODS (c. 3000–2686 BCE)

First Dynasty (c. 3150–2890 BCE)

The first dynasty begins at the unification of Upper and Lower Egypt.

Narmer (Menes/M'na?)	c. 3150 BCE
Aha (Teti)	c. 3125 BCE
Djer (Itej)	54 years
Djet (Ita)	10 years
Merneith (possibly the first female Egyptian pharaoh)	c. 2950 BCE
Khasti (Den)	42 years
Merybiap (Adjib)	10 years
Semerkhet (Iry)	8.5 years
Qa'a (Qebeh)	34 years
Sneferka	c. 2900 BCE
Horus-Ba (Horus Bird)	c. 2900 BCE

Second Dynasty (c. 2890–2686 BCE)

Little is known about the second dynasty of Egypt.

Hetepsekhemwy (Nebtyhotep)	15 years
Nebra	14 years
Nynetjer (Banetjer)	43–45 years
Ba	unknown
Weneg-Nebty	c. 2740 BCE
Wadjenes (Wadj-sen)	c. 2740 BCE
Nubnefer	unknown
Senedj	c. 47 years
Peribsen (Seth-Peribsen)	unknown
Sekhemib (Sekhemib-Perenmaat)	c. 2720 BCE
Neferkara I	25 years
Neferkasokkar	8 years
Horus Sa	unknown
Hudejefa (real name missing)	11 years
Khasekhemwy (Bebty)	18 years

OLD KINGDOM (c. 2686-2181 BCE)

Third Dynasty (c. 2686-2613 BCE)

The third dynasty was the first dynasty of the Old Kingdom. Its capital was at Memphis.

Djoser (Netjerikhet)	c. 2650 BCE
Sekhemkhet (Djoser-Teti)	2649–2643 BCE
Nebka? (Sanakht)	c. 2650 BCE
Qahedjet (Huni?)	unknown
Khaba (Huni?)	2643–2637 BCE
Huni	2637–2613 BCE

Fourth Dynasty (c. 2613–2498 BCE)

The fourth dynasty is sometimes known as the 'golden age' of Egypt's Old Kingdom.

Snefru (Nebmaat)	2613–2589 BCE
Khufu, or Cheops (Medjedu)	2589–2566 BCE
Djedefre (Kheper)	2566–2558 BCE
Khafre (Userib)	2558–2532 BCE
Menkaure (Kakhet)	2532–2503 BCE
Shepseskaf (Shepeskhet)	2503–2498 BCE

Fifth Dynasty (c. 2498–2345 BCE)

There is some doubt over the succession of pharaohs in the fifth dynasty, especially Shepseskare.

Userkaf	2496/8–2491 BCE
Sahure	2490–2477 BCE
Neferirkare-Kakai	2477–2467 BCE
Neferefre (Izi)	2460–2458 BCE
Shepseskare (Netjeruser)	few months between 2458 and 2445 BCE
Niuserre (Ini)	2445–2422 BCE
Menkauhor (Kaiu)	2422–2414 BCE
Djedkare (Isesi)	2414–2375 BCE
Unis (Wenis)	2375–2345 BCE

Sixth Dynasty (c. 2345–2181 BCE)

Teti	2345–2333 BCE
Userkare	2333–2332 BCE
Meryre (Pepi I)	2332–2283 BCE

Merenre I (Nemtyemsaf I)	2283–2278 BCE
Neferkare (Pepi II)	2278–2183 BCE
Merenre II (Nemtyemsaf II)	2183 or 2184 BCE
Netjerkare (Siptah I) or Nitocris	2182–2179 BCE

FIRST INTERMEDIATE PERIOD (c. 2181-2040 BCE)

Seventh and Eighth Dynasties (c. 2181-2160 BCE)

There is little evidence on this period in ancient Egyptian history, which is why many of the periods of rule are unknown.

Menkare	c. 2181 BCE
Neferkare II	unknown
Neferkare III (Neby)	unknown
Djedkare (Shemai)	unknown
Neferkare IV (Khendu)	unknown
Merenhor	unknown
Sneferka (Neferkamin I)	unknown
Nikare	unknown
Neferkare V (Tereru)	unknown
Neferkahor	unknown
Neferkare VI (Peiseneb)	unknown to 2171 BCE
Neferkamin (Anu)	c. 2170 BCE
Qakare (Ibi)	2175–2171 BCE
Neferkaure	2167–2163 BCE
Neferkauhor (Khuwihapi)	2163–2161 BCE
Neferiirkkare (Pepi)	2161–2160 BCE

Ninth Dynasty (c. 2160–2130 BCE)

There is little evidence on this period in ancient Egyptian history which is why many of the periods of rule are unknown.

Maryibre (Khety I)	2160 BCE to unknown
Name unknown	unknown
Naferkare VII	unknown
Seneh (Setut)	unknown

The following pharaohs and their dates of rule are unknown or widely unconfirmed.

Tenth Dynasty (c. 2130–2040 BCE)

Rulers in the Tenth dynasty were based in Lower Egypt.

Meryhathor	2130 BCE to unknown
Neferkare VIII	2130–2040 BCE
Wahkare (Khety III)	unknown
Merykare	unknown to 2040 BCE
Name unknown	unknown

Eleventh Dynasty (c. 2134–1991 BCE)

Rulers in the eleventh dynasty were based in Upper Egypt.

Intef the Elder	unknown
Tepia (Mentuhotep I)	unknown to 2133 BCE
Sehertawy (Intef I)	2133–2117 BCE
Wahankh (Intef II)	2117–2068 BCE
Nakhtnebtepefer (Intef III)	2068–2060/40 BCE

MIDDLE KINGDOM (c. 2040-1802 BCE)

Eleventh Dynasty Continued (c. 2134-1991 BCE)

This period is usually known as the beginning of the Middle Kingdom.

Nebhepetre (Mentuhotep II)	2060–2040 BCE as king of Upper Egypt, 2040–2009 BCE as King of Upper and Lower Egypt
Sankhkare (Mentuhotep III)	2009–1997 BCE
Nebtawyre (Mentuhotep IV)	1997–1991 BCE

Twelfth Dynasty (c. 1991-1802 BCE)

The twelfth dynasty was one of the most stable prior to the New Kingdom, and is often thought to be the peak of the Middle Kingdom.

Sehetepibre (Amenemhat I)	1991–1962 BCE
Kheperkare (Senusret I / Sesostris I)	1971–1926 BCE
Nubkaure (Amenemhat II)	1929–1895 BCE
Khakheperre (Senusret II / Sesostris II)	1898–1878 BCE
Khakaure (Senusret III / Sesostris III)	1878–1839 BCE
Nimaatre (Amenemhat III)	1860–1815 BCE
Maakherure (Amenemhat IV)	1815–1807 BCE
Sobekkare (Sobekneferu/Nefrusobek)	1807–1802 BCE

SECOND INTERMEDIATE PERIOD (c. 1802-1550 BCE)

Thirteenth Dynasty (c. 1802-c. 1649 BCE)

There is some ambiguity on the periods of rule of the thirteenth dynasty, but it is marked by a period of several short rules.

This dynasty is often combined with the eleventh, twelfth and fourteenth dynasties under the Middle Kingdom.

Sekhemre Khutawy (Sobekhotep I)	1802–1800 BCE
Mehibtawy Sekhemkare (Amenemhat Sonbef)	1800–1796 BCE
Nerikare (Sobek)	1796 BCE
Sekhemkare (Amenemhat V)	1796–1793 BCE
Ameny Qemau	1795–1792 BCE
Hotepibre (Qemau Siharnedjheritef)	1792–1790 BCE
Lufni	1790–1788 BCE
Seankhibre (Amenemhat VI)	1788–1785 BCE
Semenkare (Nebnuni)	1785–1783 BCE
Sehetepibre (Sewesekhtawy)	1783–1781 BCE
Sewadijkare I	1781 BCE
Nedjemibre (Amenemhat V)	1780 BCE
Khaankhre (Sobekhotep)	1780–1777 BCE
Renseneb	1777 BCE
Awybre (Hor)	1777–1775 BCE
Sekhemrekhutawy Khabaw	1775–1772 BCE
Djedkheperew	1772–1770 BCE
Sebkay	unknown
Sedjefakare (Kay Amenemhat)	1769–1766 BCE
Khutawyre (Wegaf)	c. 1767 BCE
Userkare (Khendjer)	c. 1765 BCE
Smenkhkare (Imyremeshaw)	started in 1759 BCE
Sehetepkare (Intef IV)	c. 10 years
Meribre (Seth)	ended in 1749 BCE
Sekhemresewadjtawy (Sobekhotep III)	1755–1751 BCE
Khasekhemre (Neferhotep I)	1751–1740 BCE
Menwadjre (Sihathor)	1739 BCE

Khaneferre (Sobekhotep IV)	1740–1730 BCE
Merhotepre (Sobekhotep V)	1730 BCE
Knahotepre (Sobekhotep VI)	c. 1725 BCE
Wahibre (Ibiau)	1725–1714 BCE
Merneferre (Ay I)	1714–1691 BCE
Merhotepre (Ini)	1691–1689 BCE
Sankhenre (Sewadjtu)	1675–1672 BCE
Mersekhemre (Ined)	1672–1669 BCE
Sewadjkare II (Hori)	c. 5 years
Merkawre (Sobekhotep VII)	1664–1663 BCE
Seven kings (names unknown)	1663–? BCE

Note: the remaining pharaohs of the thirteenth dynasty are not listed here as they are either unknown or there is a lot of ambiguity about when they ruled.

Fourteenth Dynasty (c. 1805/1710–1650 BCE)

Rulers in the fourteenth dynasty were based at Avaris, the capital of this dynasty.

Sekhaenre (Yakbim)	1805–1780 BCE
Nubwoserre (Ya'ammu)	1780–1770 BCE
Khawoserre (Qareh)	1770–1745 BCE
Aahotepre ('Ammu)	1760–1745 BCE
Maaibre (Sheshi)	1745–1705 BCE
Aasehre (Nehesy)	c. 1705 BCE
Khakherewre	unknown
Nebefawre	c. 1704 BCE
Sehebre	1704–1699 BCE
Merdjefare	c. 1699 BCE

Note: the remaining pharaohs of the fourteenth dynasty are not listed here as they are either unknown or there is a lot of ambiguity about when they ruled.

Fifteenth Dynasty (c. 1650–1544 BCE)

The fifteenth dynasty was founded by Salitas and covered a large part of the Nile region.

Salitas	c. 1650 BCE
Semqen	1649 BCE to unknown
'Aper-'Anat	unknown
Sakir-Har	unknown
Seuserenre (Khyan)	c. 30 to 35 years
Nebkhepeshre (Apepi)	1590 BCE?
Nakhtyre (Khamudi)	1555–1544 BCE

Sixteenth Dynasty (c. 1650–1580 BCE)

Rulers in the sixteenth dynasty were based at Thebes, the capital of this dynasty. The name and date of rule of the first pharaoh is unknown.

Sekhemresementawy (Djehuti)	3 years
Sekhemresemeusertawy (Sobekhotep VIII)	16 years
Sekhemresankhtawy (Neferhotep III)	1 year
Seankhenre (Mentuhotepi)	less than a year
Sewadjenre (Nebiryraw)	26 years
Neferkare (?) (Nebiryraw II)	c. 1600 BCE
Semenre	c. 1600 BCE
Seuserenre (Bebiankh)	12 years
Djedhotepre (Dedumose I)	c. 1588–1582 BCE

Djedneferre (Dedumose II)	c. 1588–1582 BCE
Djedankhre (Montensaf)	c. 1590 BCE
Merankhre (Mentuhotep VI)	c. 1585 BCE
Seneferibre (Senusret IV)	unknown
Sekhemre (Shedwast)	unknown

Seventeenth Dynasty (c. 1650–1550 BCE)

Rulers in the seventeenth dynasty ruled Upper Egypt.

Sekhemrewahkhaw (Rahotep)	c. 1620 BCE
Sekhemre Wadjkhaw (Sobekemsaf I)	c. 7 years
Sekhemre Shedtawy (Sobekemsaf II)	unknown to c. 1573 BCE
Sekhemre-Wepmaat (Intef V)	c. 1573–1571 BCE
Nubkheperre (Intef VI)	c. 1571–1565 BCE
Sekhemre-Heruhirmaat (Intef VII)	late 1560s BCE
Senakhtenre (Ahmose)	c. 1558 BCE
Seqenenre (Tao I)	1558–1554 BCE
Wadkheperre (Kamose)	1554–1549 BCE

NEW KINGDOM (c. 1550–1077 BCE)

Eighteenth Dynasty (c. 1550–1292 BCE)

The first dynasty of Egypt's New Kingdom marked the beginning of Ancient Egypt's highest power and expansion.

Nebpehtire (Ahmose I)	c. 1550–1525 BCE
Djeserkare (Amenhotep I)	1541–1520 BCE
Aakheperkare (Thutmose I)	1520–1492 BCE

Aakheperenre (Thutmose II)	1492–1479 BCE
Maatkare (Hatshepsut)	1479–1458 BCE
Menkheperre (Thutmose III)	1458–1425 BCE
Aakheperrure (Amenhotep II)	1425–1400 BCE
Menkheperure (Thutmose IV)	1400–1390 BCE
Nebmaatre 'the Magnificent' (Amehotep III)	1390–1352 BCE
Neferkheperure Waenre (Amenhotep IV)	1352–1336 BCE
Ankhkheperure (Smenkhkare)	1335–1334 BCE
Ankhkheperure mery Neferkheperure (Neferneferuaten III)	1334–1332 BCE
Nebkheperure (Tutankhamun)	1332–1324 BCE
Kheperkheperure (Aya II)	1324–1320 BCE
Djeserkheperure Setpenre (Haremheb)	1320–1292 BCE

Nineteenth Dynasty (c. 1550–1292 BCE)

The nineteenth dynasty is also known as the Ramessid dynasty as it includes Ramesses II, one of the most famous and influential Egyptian pharaohs.

Menpehtire (Ramesses I)	1292–1290 BCE
Menmaatre (Seti I)	1290–1279 BCE
Usermaatre Setpenre 'the Great', 'Ozymandias' (Ramesses II)	1279–1213 BCE
Banenre (Merneptah)	1213–1203 BCE
Menmire Setpenre (Amenmesse)	1203–1200 BCE
Userkheperure (Seti II)	1203–1197 BCE
Sekhaenre (Merenptah Siptah)	1197–1191 BCE
Satre Merenamun (Tawosret)	1191–1190 BCE

Twentieth Dynasty (c. 1190–1077 BCE)

This, the third dynasty of the New Kingdom, is generally thought to mark the start of the decline of Ancient Egypt.

Userkhaure (Setnakht)	1190–1186 BCE
Usermaatre Meryamun (Ramesses III)	1186–1155 BCE
Heqamaatre Setpenamun (Ramesses IV)	1155–1149 BCE
Heqamaatre Setpenamun (Ramesses IV)	1155–1149 BCE
Usermaatre Sekheperenre (Ramesses V)	1149–1145 BCE
Nebmaatre Meryamun (Ramesses VI)	1145–1137 BCE
Usermaatre Setpenre Meryamun (Ramesses VII)	1137–1130 BCE
Usermaatre Akhenamun (Ramesses VIII)	1130–1129 BCE
Neferkare Setpenre (Ramesses IX)	1128–1111 BCE
Khepermaatre Setpenptah (Ramesses X)	1111–1107 BCE
Menmaatre Setpenptah (Ramesses XI)	1107–1077 BCE

Twenty-first Dynasty (c. 1077–943 BCE)

Rulers in the twenty-first dynasty were based at Tanis and mainly governed Lower Egypt.

Hedjkheperre-Setpenre (Nesbanadjed I)	1077–1051 BCE
Neferkare (Amenemnisu)	1051–1047 BCE
Aakkheperre (Pasebakhenniut I)	1047–1001 BCE
Usermaatre (Amenemope)	1001–992 BCE
Aakheperre Setepenre (Osorkon the Elder)	992–986 BCE
Netjerikheperre-Setpenamun (Siamun)	986–967 BCE
Titkheperure (Pasebakhenniut II)	967–943 BCE

Twenty-second Dynasty (c. 943–728 BCE)

Sometimes called the Bubastite dynasty. Its pharaohs came from Libya.

Hedjkheneperre Setpenre (Sheshonq I)	943–922 BCE
Sekhemkheperre Setepenre (Osorkon I)	922–887 BCE
Heqakheperre Setepenre (Sheshonq II)	887–885 BCE
Tutkheperre (Sheshonq Llb)	c. the 880s BCE
Hedjkheperre Setepenre (Takelot I Meriamun)	885–872 BCE
Usermaatre Setpenre (Sheshonq III)	837–798 BCE
Hedjkheperre Setepenre (Sheshonq IV)	798–785 BCE
Usermaatre Setpenre (Pami Meriamun)	785–778 BCE
Aakheperre (Sheshonq V)	778–740 BCE
Usermaatre (Osorkon IV)	740–720 BCE

Twenty-third and Twenty-fourth Dynasties (c. 837–720 BCE)

These dynasties were led mainly by Libyans and mainly ruled Upper Egypt.

Hedjkheperre Setpenre (Takelot II)	837–813 BCE
Usermaatre Setpenamun (Meriamun Pedubaste I)	826–801 BCE
Usermaatre Meryamun (Sheshonq VI)	801–795 BCE
Usermaatre Setpenamun (Osorkon III)	795–767 BCE
Usermaatre-Setpenamun (Takelot III)	773–765 BCE
Usermaatre-Setpenamun (Meriamun Rudamun)	765–762 BCE
Shepsesre (Tefnakhte)	732–725 BCE
Wahkare (Bakenrenef)	725–720 BCE

Twenty-fifth Dynasty (c. 744–656 BCE)

Also known as the Kushite period, the twenty-fifth dynasty follows the Nubian invasions.

Piankhy (Piye)	744–714 BCE
Djedkaure (Shebitkku)	714–705 BCE
Neferkare (Shabaka)	705–690 BCE
Khuinefertemre (Taharqa)	690–664 BCE

LATE PERIOD (c. 664–332 BCE)

Twenty-sixth Dynasty (c. 664 – 525 BCE)

Also known as the Saite period, the twenty-sixth dynasty was the last native period before the Persian invasion in 525 BCE.

Wahibre (Psamtik I)	664–610 BCE
Wehemibre (Necho II)	610–595 BCE
Neferibre (Psamtik II)	595–589 BCE
Haaibre (Apreis)	589–570 BCE
Khemibre (Amasis II)	570–526 BCE
Ankhkaenre (Psamtik III)	526–525 BCE

Twenty-seventh Dynasty (c. 525–404 BCE)

The twenty-seventh dynasty is also known as the First Egyptian Satrapy and was ruled by the Persian Achaemenids.

Mesutre (Cambyses II)	525–1 July 522 BCE
Seteture (Darius I)	522–November 486 BCE
Kheshayarusha (Xerxes I)	November 486–December 465 BCE
Artabanus of Persia	465–464 BCE
Arutakhshashas (Artaxerxes I)	464–424 BCE
Ochus (Darius II)	July 423–March 404 BCE

Twenty-eighth Dynasty (c. 404–398 BCE)
The twenty-eighth dynasty consisted of a single pharaoh.

Amunirdisu (Amyrtaeus)   404–398 BCE

Twenty-ninth Dynasty (c. 398–380 BCE)
The twenty-ninth dynasty was founded following the overthrow of Amyrtaeus.

Baenre Merynatjeru (Nepherites I)	398–393 BCE
Khnemmaatre Setepenkhnemu (Hakor)	c. 392–391 BCE
Userre Setepenptah (Psammuthis)	c. 391 BCE
Khnemmaatre Setepenkhnemu (Hakor)	c. 390–379 BCE
Nepherites II	c. 379 BCE

Thirtieth Dynasty (c.379–340 BCE)
The thirtieth dynasty is thought to be the final native dynasty of Ancient Egypt.

Kheperkare (Nectanebo I)	c. 379–361 BCE
Irimaatenre (Teos)	c. 361–359 BCE
Snedjemibre Setepenanhur (Nectanebo II)	c. 359–340 BCE

Thirty-first Dynasty (c. 340–332 BCE)
The thirty-first dynasty is also known as the Second Egyptian Satrapy and was ruled by the Persian Achaemenids.

Ochus (Artaxerxes III)	c. 340–338 BCE
Arses (Artaxerxes IV)	338–336 BCE
Darius III	336–332 BCE

MACEDONIAN/ARGEAD DYNASTY (c. 332–309 BCE)

Alexander the Great conquered Persia and Egypt in 332 BCE.

Setpenre Meryamun (Alexander III of Macedon 'the Great')	332–323 BCE
Setpenre Meryamun (Philip Arrhidaeus)	323–317 BCE
Khaibre Setepenamun (Alexander IV)	317–309 BCE

PTOLEMAIC DYNASTY (c. 305–30 BCE)

The Ptolemaic dynasty in Egypt was the last dynasty of Ancient Egypt before it became a province of Rome.

Ptolemy I Soter	305–282 BCE
Ptolemy II Philadelphos	284–246 BCE
Arsinoe II	c. 277–270 BCE
Ptolemy III Euergetes	246–222 BCE
Berenice II	244/243–222 BCE
Ptolemy IV Philopater	222–204 BCE
Arsinoe III	220–204 BCE
Ptolemy V Epiphanes	204–180 BCE
Cleopatra I	193–176 BCE
Ptolemy VI Philometor	180–164, 163–145 BCE
Cleopatra II	175–164 BCE, 163–127 BCE and 124–116 BCE
Ptolemy VIII Physcon	171–163 BCE, 144–131 BCE and 127–116 BCE
Ptolemy VII Neos Philopator	145–144 BCE

Cleopatra III	142–131 BCE, 127–107 BCE
Ptolemy Memphites	113 BCE
Ptolemy IX Soter	116–110 BCE
Cleopatra IV	116–115 BCE
Ptolemy X Alexander	110–109 BCE
Berenice III	81–80 BCE
Ptolemy XI Alexander	80 BCE
Ptolemy XII Auletes	80–58 BCE, 55–51 BCE
Cleopatra V Tryphaena	79–68 BCE
Cleopatra VI	58–57 BCE
Berenice IV	58–55 BCE
Cleopatra VII	52–30 BCE
Ptolemy XIII Theos Philopator	51–47 BCE
Arsinoe IV	48–47 BCE
Ptolemy XIV Philopator	47–44 BCE
Ptolemy XV Caesar	44–30 BCE

In 30 BCE, Egypt became a province of the Roman Empire.

ANCIENT GREEK MONARCHS

This list is not exhaustive and dates are approximate. Where dates of rule overlap, emperors either ruled jointly or ruled in opposition to one another. There may also be differences in name spellings between different sources.

Because of the fragmented nature of Greece prior to its unification by Philip II of Macedon, this list includes mythological and existing rulers of Thebes, Athens and Sparta as some of the leading ancient Greek city-states. These different city-states had some common belief in the mythological gods and goddesses of ancient Greece, although their accounts may differ.

KINGS OF THEBES (c. 753–509 BCE)

These rulers are mythological. There is much diversity over who the kings actually were, and the dates they ruled.

Calydnus (son of Uranus)
Ogyges (son of Poseidon, thought to be king of Boeotia or Attica)
Cadmus (Greek mythological hero known as the founder of Thebes, known as Cadmeia until the reign of Amphion and Zethus)
Pentheus (son of Echion, one of the mythological Spartoi, and Agave, daughter of Cadmus)

Polydorus (son of Cadmus and Harmonia, goddess of harmony)

Nycteus (like his brother Lycus, thought to be the son of a Spartoi and a nymph, or a son of Poseidon)

Lycus (brother of Nyceteus)

Labdacus (grandson of Cadmus)

Lycus (second reign as regent for Laius)

Amphion and Zethus (joint rulers and twin sons of Zeus, constructed the city walls of Thebes)

Laius (son of Labdacus, married to Jocasta)

Oedipus (son of Laius, killed his father and married his mother, Jocasta)

Creon (regent after the death of Laius)

Eteocles and Polynices (brothers/sons of Oedipus; killed each other in battle)

Creon (regent for Laodamas)

Laodamas (son of Eteocles)

Thersander (son of Polynices)

Peneleos (regent for Tisamenus)

Tisamenus (son of Thersander)

Autesion (son of Tisamenes)

Damasichthon (son of Peneleos)

Ptolemy (son of Damasichton, 12 century BCE)

Xanthos (son of Ptolemy)

KINGS OF ATHENS

Early legendary kings who ruled before the mythological flood caused by Zeus, which only Deucalion (son of Prometheus) and a few others survived (date unknown).

Periphas (king of Attica, turned into an eagle by Zeus)

Ogyges (son of Poseidon, thought to be king of either Boeotia or Attica)

Actaeus (king of Attica, father-in-law to Cecrops I)

Erechtheid Dynasty (1556–1127 BCE)

Cecrops I (founder and first king of Athens; half-man, half-serpent who married Actaeus' daughter)	1556–1506 BCE
Cranaus	1506–1497 BCE
Amphictyon (son of Deucalion)	1497–1487 BCE
Erichthonius (adopted by Athena)	1487–1437 BCE
Pandion I (son of Erichthonius)	1437–1397 BCE
Erechtheus (son of Pandion I)	1397–1347 BCE
Cecrops II (son of Erechtheus)	1347–1307 BCE
Pandion II (son of Cecrops II)	1307–1282 BCE
Aegeus (adopted by Pandion II, gave his name to the Aegean Sea)	1282–1234 BCE
Theseus (son of Aegeus, killed the minotaur)	1234–1205 BCE
Menestheus (made king by Castor and Pollux when Theseus was in the underworld)	1205–1183 BCE
Demophon (son of Theseus)	1183–1150 BCE
Oxyntes (son of Demophon)	1150–1136 BCE
Apheidas (son of Oxyntes)	1136–1135 BCE
Thymoetes (son of Oxyntes)	1135–1127 BCE

Melanthid Dynasty (1126–1068 BCE)

Melanthus (king of Messenia, fled to Athens when expelled)	1126–1089 BCE
Codrus (last of the semi-mythological Athenian kings)	1089–1068 BCE

LIFE ARCHONS OF ATHENS (1068–753 BCE)

These rulers held public office up until their deaths.

Medon	1068–1048 BCE	Pherecles	864–845 BCE
Acastus	1048–1012 BCE	Ariphon	845–825 BCE
Archippus	1012–993 BCE	Thespieus	824–797 BCE
Thersippus	993–952 BCE	Agamestor	796–778 BCE
Phorbas	952–922 BCE	Aeschylus	778–755 BCE
Megacles	922–892 BCE	Alcmaeon	755–753 BCE
Diognetus	892–864 BCE		

From this point, archons led for a period of ten years up to 683 BCE, then a period of one year up to 485 CE. Selected important leaders – including archons and tyrants – in this later period are as follows:

SELECTED LATER LEADERS OF ATHENS

Peisistratos 'the Tyrant of Athens'	561, 559–556, 546–527 BCE
Cleisthenes (archon)	525–524 BCE
Themistocles (archon)	493–492 BCE
Pericles	c. 461–429 BCE

KINGS OF SPARTA

These rulers are mythological and are thought to be descendants of the ancient tribe of Leleges. There is much diversity over who the kings actually were, and the dates they ruled.

Lelex (son of Poseidon or Helios, ruled Laconia)	c. 1600 BCE
Myles (son of Lelex, ruled Laconia)	c. 1575 BCE
Eurotas (son of Myles, father of Sparta)	c. 1550 BCE

From the Lelegids, rule passed to the Lacedaemonids when Lacedaemon married Sparta.

Lacedaemon (son of Zeus, husband of Sparta)

Amyklas (son of Lacedaemon)

Argalus (son of Amyklas)

Kynortas (son of Amyklas)

Perieres (son of Kynortas)

Oibalos (son of Kynortas)

Tyndareos (first reign; son of Oibalos, father of Helen of Troy)

Hippocoon (son of Oibalos)

Tyndareos (second reign; son of Oibaos, father of Helen of Troy)

From the Lacedaemons, rule passed to the Atreids when Menelaus married Helen of Troy.

Menelaus (son of Atreus, king of Mycenae, and husband of Helen)	c. 1250 BCE
Orestes (son of Agamemnon, Menelaus' brother)	c. 1150 BCE
Tisamenos (son of Orestes)	
Dion	c. 1100 BCE

From the Atreids, rule passed to the Heraclids following war.

Aristodemos (son of Aristomachus, great-great-grandson of Heracles)

Theras (served as regent for Aristodemes' sons, Eurysthenes and Procles)

Eurysthenes   c. 930 BCE

From the Heraclids, rule passed to the Agiads, founded by Agis I. Only major kings during this period are listed here.

Agis I (conceivably the first historical Spartan king)	c. 930–900 BCE
Alcamenes	c. 740–700 BCE, during First Messenian War
Cleomenes I (important leader in the Greek resistance against the Persians)	524 – 490 BCE
Leonidas I (died while leading the Greeks – the 300 Spartans – against the Persians in the Battle of Thermopylae, 480 BCE)	490–480 BCE
Cleomenes III (exiled following the Battle of Sellasia)	c. 235–222 BCE

KINGS OF MACEDON

Argead Dynasty (808–309 BCE)

Karanos	c. 808–778 BCE	Alcetas I	c. 576–547 BCE
Koinos	c. 778–750 BCE	Amyntas I	c. 547–498 BCE
Tyrimmas	c. 750–700 BCE	Alexander I	c. 498–454 BCE
Perdiccas I	c. 700–678 BCE	Alcetas II	c. 454–448 BCE
Argaeus I	c. 678–640 BCE	Perdiccas II	c. 448–413 BCE
Philip I	c. 640–602 BCE	Archelaus I	c. 413–339 BCE
Aeropus I	c. 602–576 BCE	Craterus	c. 399 BCE

Orestes	c. 399–396 BCE	Perdiccas III	c. 368–359 BCE
Aeropus II	c. 399–394/93 BCE	Amyntas IV	c. 359 BCE
Archelaus II	c. 394–393 BCE	Philip II	c. 359–336 BCE
Amyntas II	c. 393 BCE	Alexander III 'the Great'	
Pausanias	c. 393 BCE	(also King of Persia and	
Amyntas III	c. 393 BCE; first reign	Pharaoh of Egypt by end of reign)	c. 336–323 BCE
Argeus II	c. 393–392 BCE	Philip III	c. 323–317 BCE
Amyntas III	c. 392–370 BCE	Alexander IV	c. 323/ 317–309 BCE
Alexander II	c. 370–368 BCE		

Note: the Corinthian League or Hellenic League was created by Philip II and was the first time that the divided Greek city-states were unified under a single government.

Post-Argead Dynasty (309–168 BCE, 149–148 BCE)

Cassander	c. 305–297 BCE
Philip IV	c. 297 BCE
Antipater II	c. 297–294 BCE
Alexpander V	c. 297–294 BCE

Antigonid, Alkimachid and Aeacid Dynasties (294–281 BCE)

Demetrius	c. 294–288 BCE
Lysimachus	c. 288–281 BCE
Pyrrhus	c. 288–285 BCE; first reign

Ptolemaic Dynasty (281–279 BCE)

Ptolemy Ceraunus (son of Ptolemy I of Egypt)	c. 281–279 BCE
Meleager	279 BCE

Antipatrid, Antigonid, Aeacid Dynasties, Restored (279–167 BCE)

Antipater	c. 279 BCE
Sosthenes	c. 279–277 BCE
Antigonus II	c. 277–274 BCE; first reign
Pyrrhus	c. 274–272 BCE; second reign
Antigonus II	c. 272–239 BCE; second reign
Demetrius II	c. 239–229 BCE
Antigonus III	c. 229–221 BCE
Philip V	c. 221–179 BCE
Perseus (deposed by Romans)	c. 179–168 BCE
Revolt by Philip VI (Andriskos)	c. 149–148 BCE

SELEUCID DYNASTY (c. 320 BCE–63 CE)

Seleucus I Nicator	c. 320–315, 312–305, 305–281 BCE
Antiochus I Soter	c. 291, 281–261 BCE
Antiochus II Theos	c. 261–246 BCE
Seleucus II Callinicus	c. 246–225 BCE
Seleucus III Ceraunus	c. 225–223 BCE
Antiochus III 'the Great'	c. 223–187 BCE
Seleucus IV Philopator	c. 187–175 BCE
Antiochus (son of Seleucus IV)	c. 175–170 BCE
Antiochus IV Epiphanes	c. 175–163 BCE
Antiochus V Eupater	c. 163–161 BCE
Demetrius I Soter	c. 161–150 BCE
Alexander I Balas	c. 150–145 BCE
Demetrius II Nicator	c. 145–138 BCE; first reign
Antiochus VI Dionysus	c. 145–140 BCE

Diodotus Tryphon	c. 140–138 BCE
Antiochus VII Sidetes	c. 138–129 BCE
Demetrius II Nicator	c. 129–126 BCE; second reign
Alexander II Zabinas	c. 129–123 BCE
Cleopatra Thea	c. 126–121 BCE
Seleucus V Philometor	c. 126/125 BCE
Antiochus VIII Grypus	c. 125–96 BCE
Antiochus IX Cyzicenus	c. 114–96 BCE
Seleucus VI Epiphanes	c. 96–95 BCE
Antiochus X Eusebes	c. 95–92/83 BCE
Demetrius III Eucaerus	c. 95–87 BCE
Antiochus XI Epiphanes	c. 95–92 BCE
Philip I Philadelphus	c. 95–84/83 BCE
Antiochus XII Dionysus	c. 87–84 BCE
Seleucus VII	c. 83–69 BCE
Antiochus XIII Asiaticus	c. 69–64 BCE
Philip II Philoromaeus	c. 65–63 BCE

Ptolemaic Dynasty (305–30 BCE)

The Ptolemaic dynasty in Greece was the last dynasty of Ancient Egypt before it became a province of Rome.

Ptolemy I Soter	305–282 BCE
Ptolemy II Philadelphos	284–246 BCE
Arsinoe II	c. 277–270 BCE
Ptolemy III Euergetes	246–222 BCE
Berenice II	244/243–222 BCE
Ptolemy IV Philopater	222–204 BCE
Arsinoe III	220–204 BCE
Ptolemy V Epiphanes	204–180 BCE

Cleopatra I	193–176 BCE
Ptolemy VI Philometor	180–164, 163–145 BCE
Cleopatra II	175–164 BCE, 163–127 BCE and 124–116 BCE
Ptolemy VIII Physcon	171–163 BCE, 144–131 BCE and 127–116 BCE
Ptolemy VII Neos Philopator	145–144 BCE
Cleopatra III	142–131 BCE, 127–107 BCE
Ptolemy Memphites	113 BCE
Ptolemy IX Soter	116–110 BCE
Cleopatra IV	116–115 BCE
Ptolemy X Alexander	110–109 BCE
Berenice III	81–80 BCE
Ptolemy XI Alexander	80 BCE
Ptolemy XII Auletes	80–58 BCE, 55–51 BCE
Cleopatra V Tryphaena	79–68 BCE
Cleopatra VI	58–57 BCE
Berenice IV	58–55 BCE

In 27 BCE, Caesar Augustus annexed Greece and it became integrated into the Roman Empire.

ANCIENT ROMAN LEADERS

This list is not exhaustive and some dates are approximate. The legitimacy of some rulers is also open to interpretation. Where dates of rule overlap, emperors either ruled jointly or ruled in opposition to one another. There may also be differences in name spellings between different sources.

KINGS OF ROME (753–509 BCE)

Romulus (mythological founder and first ruler of Rome)	753–716 BCE
Numa Pompilius (mythological)	715–672 BCE
Tullus Hostilius (mythological)	672–640 BCE
Ancus Marcius (mythological)	640–616 BCE
Lucius Tarquinius Priscus (mythological)	616–578 BCE
Servius Tullius (mythological)	578–534 BCE
Lucius Tarquinius Superbus (Tarquin the Proud; mythological)	534–509 BCE

ROMAN REPUBLIC (509-27 BCE)

During this period, two consuls were elected to serve a joint one-year term. Therefore, only a selection of significant consuls are included here.

Lucius Junius Brutus (semi-mythological)	509 BCE
Marcus Porcius Cato (Cato the Elder)	195 BCE
Scipio Africanus	194 BCE
Cnaeus Pompeius Magnus (Pompey the Great)	70, 55 and 52 BCE
Marcus Linius Crassus	70 and 55 BCE
Marcus Tullius Cicero	63 BCE
Caius Julius Caesar	59 BCE
Marcus Aemilius Lepidus	46 and 42 BCE
Marcus Antonius (Mark Anthony)	44 and 34 BCE
Marcus Agrippa	37 and 28 BCE

PRINCIPATE (27 BCE-284 CE)

Julio-Claudian Dynasty (27 BCE-68 CE)

Augustus (Caius Octavius Thurinus, Caius Julius Caesar, Imperator Caesar Divi filius)	27 BCE-14 CE
Tiberius (Tiberius Julius Caesar Augustus)	14-37 CE
Caligula (Caius Caesar Augustus Germanicus)	37-41 CE
Claudius (Tiberius Claudius Caesar Augustus Germanicus)	41-54 CE
Nero (Nero Claudius Caesar Augustus Germanicus)	54-68 CE

Year of the Four Emperors (68–69 CE)

Galba (Servius Sulpicius Galba Caesar Augustus)   68–69 CE

Otho (Marcus Salvio Otho Caesar Augustus)   Jan–Apr 69 CE

Vitellius (Aulus Vitellius Germanicus Augustus)   Apr–Dec 69 CE

Note: the fourth emperor, Vespasian, is listed below.

Flavian Dynasty (66–96 CE)

Vespasian (Caesar Vespasianus Augustus)   69–79 CE

Titus (Titus Caesar Vespasianus Augustus)   79–81 CE

Domitian (Caesar Domitianus Augustus)   81–96 CE

Nerva-Antonine Dynasty (69–192 CE)

Nerva (Nerva Caesar Augustus)   96–98 CE

Trajan (Caesar Nerva Traianus Augustus)   98–117 CE

Hadrian (Caesar Traianus Hadrianus Augustus)   138–161 CE

Antonius Pius (Caesar Titus Aelius Hadrianus
Antoninus Augustus Pius)   138–161 CE

Marcus Aurelius (Caesar Marcus Aurelius
Antoninus Augustus)   161–180 CE

Lucius Verus (Lucius Aurelius Verus Augustus)   161–169 CE

Commodus (Caesar Marcus Aurelius Commodus
Antoninus Augustus)   180–192 CE

Year of the Five Emperors (193 CE)

Pertinax (Publius Helvius Pertinax)   Jan–Mar 193 CE

Didius Julianus (Marcus Didius Severus Julianus)   Mar–Jun 193 CE

Note: Pescennius Niger and Clodius Albinus are generally regarded as usurpers, while the fifth, Septimius Severus, is listed below

Severan Dynasty (193–235 CE)

Septimius Severus (Lucius Septimus Severus Pertinax)	193–211 CE
Caracalla (Marcus Aurelius Antonius)	211–217 CE
Geta (Publius Septimius Geta)	Feb–Dec 211 CE
Macrinus (Caesar Marcus Opellius Severus Macrinus Augustus)	217–218 CE
Diadumenian (Marcus Opellius Antonius Diadumenianus)	May–Jun 218 CE
Elagabalus (Caesar Marcus Aurelius Antoninus Augustus)	218–222 CE
Severus Alexander (Marcus Aurelius Severus Alexander)	222–235 CE

Crisis of the Third Century (235–285 CE)

Maximinus 'Thrax' (Caius Julius Verus Maximus)	235–238 CE
Gordian I (Marcus Antonius Gordianus Sempronianus Romanus)	Apr–May 238 CE
Gordian II (Marcus Antonius Gordianus Sempronianus Romanus)	Apr–May 238 CE
Pupienus Maximus (Marcus Clodius Pupienus Maximus)	May–Aug 238 CE
Balbinus (Decimus Caelius Calvinus Balbinus)	May–Aug 238 CE
Gordian III (Marcus Antonius Gordianus)	Aug 238–Feb 244 CE
Philip I 'the Arab' (Marcus Julius Philippus)	244–249 CE
Philip II 'the Younger' (Marcus Julius Severus Philippus)	247–249 CE
Decius (Caius Messius Quintus Traianus Decius)	249–251 CE
Herennius Etruscus (Quintus Herennius Etruscus Messius Decius)	May/Jun 251 CE

Trebonianus Gallus (Caius Vibius Trebonianus Gallus) 251–253 CE

Hostilian (Caius Valens Hostilianus Messius
  Quintus)   Jun–Jul 251 CE

Volusianus (Caius Vibius Afinius Gallus
  Veldumnianus Volusianus)   251–253 CE

Aemilian (Marcus Aemilius Aemilianus)   Jul–Sep 253 CE

Silbannacus (Marcus Silbannacus)   Sep/Oct 253 CE

Valerian (Publius Licinius Valerianus)   253–260 CE

Gallienus (Publius Licinius Egnatius Gallienus)   253–268 CE

Saloninus (Publius Licinius Cornelius
  Saloninus Valerianus)   Autumn 260 CE

Claudius II Gothicus (Marcus Aurelius Claudius)   268–270 CE

Quintilus (Marcus Aurelius Claudias
  Quintillus)   Apr–May/Jun 270 CE

Aurelian (Luciua Domitius Aurelianus)   270–275 CE

Tacitus (Marcus Claudius Tacitus)   275–276 CE

Florianus (Marcus Annius Florianus)   276–282 CE

Probus (Marcus Aurelius Probus Romanus;
  in opposition to Florianus)   276–282 CE

Carus (Marcus Aurelias Carus)   282–283 CE

Carinus (Marcus Aurelius Carinus)   283–285 CE

Numerian (Marcus Aurelius Numerianus)   283–284 CE

DOMINATE (284–610)

Tetrarchy (284–324)

Diocletian 'Iovius' (Caius Aurelius Valerius Diocletianus) 284–305

Maximian 'Herculius' (Marcus Aurelius Valerius
  Maximianus; ruled the western provinces) 286–305/late 306–308

Galerius (Caius Galerius Valerius Maximianus; ruled the eastern provinces)	305–311
Constantius I 'Chlorus' (Marcus Flavius Valerius Constantius; ruled the western provinces)	305–306
Severus II (Flavius Valerius Severus; ruled the western provinces)	306–307
Maxentius (Marcus Aurelius Valerius Maxentius)	306–312
Licinius (Valerius Licinanus Licinius; ruled the western, then the eastern provinces)	308–324
Maximinus II 'Daza' (Aurelius Valerius Valens; ruled the western provinces)	316–317
Martinian (Marcus Martinianus; ruled the western provinces)	Jul–Sep 324

Constantinian Dynasty (306–363)

Constantine I 'the Great' (Flavius Valerius Constantinus; ruled the western provinces then whole)	306–337
Constantine II (Flavius Claudius Constantinus)	337–340
Constans I (Flavius Julius Constans)	337–350
Constantius II (Flavius Julius Constantius)	337–361
Magnentius (Magnus Magnentius)	360–353
Nepotianus (Julius Nepotianus)	Jun 350
Vetranio	Mar–Dec 350
Julian 'the Apostate' (Flavius Claudius Julianus)	361–363
Jovian (Jovianus)	363–364

Valentinianic Dynasty (364–392)

Valentinian I 'the Great' (Valentinianus)	364–375
Valens (ruled the eastern provinces)	364–378

Procopius (revolted against Valens)	365–366
Gratian (Flavius Gratianus Augustus; ruled the western provinces then whole)	375–383
Magnus Maximus	383–388
Valentinian II (Flavius Valentinianus)	388–392
Eugenius	392–394

Theodosian Dynasty (379–457)

Theodosius I 'the Great' (Flavius Theodosius)	Jan 395
Arcadius	383–408
Honorius (Flavius Honorius)	395–432
Constantine III	407–411
Theodosius II	408–450
Priscus Attalus; usurper	409–410
Constantius III	Feb–Sep 421
Johannes	423–425
Valentinian III	425–455
Marcian	450–457

Last Emperors in the West (455–476)

Petronius Maximus	Mar–May 455
Avitus	455–456
Majorian	457–461
Libius Severus (Severus III)	461–465
Anthemius	467–472
Olybrius	Apr–Nov 472
Glycerius	473–474
Julius Nepos	474–475
Romulus Augustulus (Flavius Momyllus Romulus Augustulus)	475–476

Leonid Dynasty (East, 457–518)

Leo I (Leo Thrax Magnus)	457–474
Leo II	Jan–Nov 474
Zeno	474–475
Basiliscus	475–476
Zeno (second reign)	476–491
Anastasius I 'Dicorus'	491–518

Justinian Dynasty (East, 518–602)

Justin I	518–527
Justinian I 'the Great' (Flavius Justinianus, Petrus Sabbatius)	527–565
Justin II	565–578
Tiberius II Constantine	578–582
Maurice (Mauricius Flavius Tiberius)	582–602
Phocas	602–610

LATER EASTERN EMPERORS (610–1059)

Heraclian Dynasty (610–695)

Heraclius	610–641
Heraclius Constantine (Constantine III)	Feb–May 641
Heraclonas	Feb–Nov 641
Constans II Pogonatus ('the Bearded')	641–668
Constantine IV	668–685
Justinian II	685–695

Twenty Years' Anarchy (695–717)

Leontius	695–698
Tiberius III	698–705

Justinian II 'Rhinometus' (second reign)	705–711
Philippicus	711–713
Anastasius II	713–715
Theodosius III	715–717

Isaurian Dynasty (717–803)

Leo III 'the Isaurian'	717–741
Constantine V	741–775
Artabasdos	741/2–743
Leo V 'the Khazar'	775–780
Constantine VI	780–797
Irene	797–802

Nikephorian Dynasty (802–813)

Nikephoros I 'the Logothete'	802–811
Staurakios	July–Oct 811
Michael I Rangabé	813–820

Amorian Dynasty (820–867)

Michael II 'the Amorian'	820–829
Theophilos	829–842
Theodora	842–856
Michael III 'the Drunkard'	842–867

Macedonian Dynasty (867–1056)

Basil I 'the Macedonian'	867–886
Leo VI 'the Wise'	886–912
Alexander	912–913
Constantine VII Porphyrogenitus	913–959
Romanos I Lecapenus	920–944

Romanos II	959–963
Nikephoros II Phocas	963–969
John I Tzimiskes	969–976
Basil II 'the Bulgar-Slayer'	976–1025
Constantine VIII	1025–1028
Romanus III Argyros	1028–1034
Michael IV 'the Paphlagonian'	1034–1041
Michael V Kalaphates	1041–1042
Zoë Porphyrogenita	Apr–Jun 1042
Theodora Porphyrogenita	Apr–Jun 1042
Constantine IX Monomachos	1042–1055
Theodora Porphyrogenita (second reign)	1055–1056
Michael VI Bringas 'Stratioticus'	1056–1057
Isaab I Komnenos	1057–1059